Regional Imbalances and Regional Development Policies :
Turkey Experience Volume I

Haktan Sevinç (ed.)

Regional Imbalances and Regional Development Policies : Turkey Experience Volume I

Bibliographic Information published by the Deutsche Nationalbibliothek
The Deutsche Nationalbibliothek lists this publication in the Deutsche Nationalbibliografie; detailed bibliographic data is available online at http://dnb.d-nb.de.

Library of Congress Cataloging-in-Publication Data
A CIP catalog record for this book has been applied for at the Library of Congress.

Printed by CPI books GmbH, Leck

ISBN 978-3-631-81368-3 (Print)
E-ISBN 978-3-631-82199-2 (E-PDF)
E-ISBN 978-3-631-82200-5 (EPUB)
E-ISBN 978-3-631-82201-2 (MOBI)
DOI 10.3726/b16971

© Peter Lang GmbH
Internationaler Verlag der Wissenschaften
Berlin 2020
All rights reserved.

Peter Lang – Berlin · Bern · Bruxelles · New York · Oxford · Warszawa · Wien

All parts of this publication are protected by copyright. Any utilisation outside the strict limits of the copyright law, without the permission of the publisher, is forbidden and liable to prosecution. This applies in particular to reproductions, translations, microfilming, and storage and processing in electronic retrieval systems.

This publication has been peer reviewed.

www.peterlang.com

Preface

This book refers many regional disparities and regional development issues of developed, emerging or underdeveloped countries. Regional imbalances that arises because of economic, geographical, historical or sociocultural reasons, can turn into an important development problem when required preventions are not taken. Therefore, Turkey tries to solve its regional development problems by using regional development policy tools applied seen in many places of the World. For these purposes, each chapter of the book contains the effects and consequences of regional development policies carried out by specific characteristics of regions of Turkey. Therefore, I would like to express my gratitude to the authors who wrote these chapters.

Contents

Haktan Sevinç
Introduction Region, Regional Imbalance and Regional Development
              Policies 9

Sabri Azgün, Berna Ak Bingül and Demet Eroğlu Sevinç
Chapter 1   Regional Income Inequality and Its Measurement 19

Sertaç Hopoğlu and Demet Eroğlu Sevinç
Chapter 2   Regions and Sustainable Development 31

Nazım Çatalbaş
Chapter 3   The Relationship Between Regional Development and
            Regional Development Agencies 53

Emine Demet Ekinci Hamamcı
Chapter 4   The Innovation Systems from National to Regional
            Level: The Role of RIS in the Regional Development 71

İdil Gülnihal Yazici
Chapter 5   The Process of Regional Development in Turkey and the
            Interaction of Non-governmental Organizations 93

Esra Doğan
Chapter 6   The Impact of the Change in the Investment Incentive
            System Application in Turkey on Regional Income
            Convergence 119

Necmettin Çelik
Chapter 7   The Division and Specialization Proposals to Regions in
            Line with the Spatial and Sectoral Concentration Patterns
            of Turkey 137

Murat Çiftçi
Chapter 8   Regional Clustering in Social Service Workers: An
            Application with Three Star Analysis (2008–2017) 159

Haktan Sevinç[1]

Introduction
Region, Regional Imbalance and Regional Development Policies

In this book, in which the discussions on the regional imbalances and regional development policies are made, firstly the regional imbalance problems that are the reason for implementing the regional development policies are discussed and the factors causing the regional imbalances are investigated. Then, in the next step, the fundamental points in Turkey's policies in struggling with the regional imbalance are presented and the analyses are made on the efficiencies of Turkey's regional development policies.

The concepts of economic growth and development are the points that developed, developing, and underdeveloped countries put significant emphasis on and are among the most important objectives of economic policies that they develop through various politic instruments. On the other hand, the differences between regions in terms of economic or sociocultural development result in developmental differences both between countries and between regions. The interregional development differences may pose difficulties in increasing the level of welfare, as well as the economic development of the countries. From this aspect, the regional development policies conducted in the way involving all the country or specific regions are the policy complements that must be in harmony with the general economic policies because the regional development policies designed in order to eliminate various problems arising from the interregional imbalances constitute a sub-group of general economic policies. Thus, the factors causing regional imbalances should be examined and the policy measures should be in harmony with the general economic policies in order to resolve the problem of interregional imbalances. From this aspect, the concepts, definitions, instruments, and policies related with region, development, and imbalance were discussed in parallel with local or regional development in this chapter.

The concept of region: This term is used in defining the regions exhibiting a unity or similarity in terms of natural, sociocultural, humane, or economic

---

1   Assoc. Prof., Iğdır University, Faculty of Economics and Administrative Sciences, Department of Economics, 76000, Iğdır/TURKEY

characteristics. Although the names, types, authorities, functions, etc. of the units defined as region are different, they have unity within themselves. In this parallel, according to many researchers, the concept of "region" refers to a stationary structure, which means a part of land, whereas come others express that, besides the fact that the stationarity still applies to the land-related definitions, the term "region" also refers to a non-exact variability. From this aspect, the term "region" generally means a non-static (i.e., a dynamic) structure.

The dynamic condition emphasized in the concept of region is mainly because the definition referring to the "region" according to a variable may be excluded from this concept according to another variable or in the following process. For this reason, the definitions of region generally reflect a dynamic condition. For instance; a region may differ in the course of time in terms of climate or flora, whereas the regions may shrink or expand based on their administrative, politic, cultural, or population characteristic or they may fall outside of the definition by falling short or making progress from economic, industrial, agricultural, or commercial aspects (Kvicalova et al., 2014: 244). Thus, the definitions that are based on the concept of region may change. The important point is to involve the "homogeneity" in the definitions.

The definition of "region", which originates from the Latin word "regio", is used for defining the group, social, or administrative structures such as direction, side, part, area, basin, field, neighborhood, province, and district. Moreover, it may also be defined as all the units or a part of land constituting a whole from the aspect of physical characteristics. Again, it is a definition that is widely used for defining the units constituting a whole in terms of historical or cultural values or heritages. Besides that, some of the researchers define the region from geographic, sociocultural, politic, and medical aspects (Dejan et al., 2015: 69).

In the light of these explanations, the region can be defined as a spatial unit, borders of which have been drawn and determined using specific descriptive instruments (land, climate, flora, economic conditions, socio-culture, politics, population, etc.), which forms a whole from administrative or managerial aspects identified through specific, and which is between the state and local governments (Wannop, 1995). Moreover, the fundamentals of the concept of region can be listed as follows (Tekeli, 2008: 174; UN, 2001: 24);

- The concept of region involves the idea of continuity.
- The concept of region involves the idea of discrimination.
- The concept of region involves the idea of similarity or integrity.
- The concept of region involves the generalization in itself.

The concept of development: In general, it refers to the progression of economic growth and sharing the benefits of economic growth by everyone. From this aspect, one of the most widely used terms of the last century is development. As expressed, the term "development" that refers to progressing the economic growth also involves the meanings of "civilization" and "modernization" and it is generally used as the synonym of "progression", "modernization", and "becoming contemporary" (Başkaya, 2000: 16–23; Siggel, 2005: 1). The economic advancement is defined as the change of individuals' educational and medical conditions, world views, production and consumption habits, values, and politic and sociocultural behaviors and the consequent progression and transformation in both social and institutional structures (Kılıç, 2012: 204).

Moreover, although the term "development" is generally considered as an economic concept, it can be clearly seen in the definitions that it covers a large field beyond the solely economic one. From this aspect, in addition to increasing the production and revenue, the development aims to change the sociocultural, politic, institutional, and administrative structure. Thus, the process of economic development includes restructuring or reorganizing various social and economic structures, variables, and/or institutions, as well as increasing the level of national production and income (Tıraş, 2012: 59).

On the other hand, the term "development", which is generally confused with economic growth, refers to a much wider concept as can be seen in the definition. Hence, the economic growth of countries or regions may not bring development but economic development is a result of economic growth. Moreover, while economic growth refers to a net increase in the level of national production and the income per capita, economic development refers to the changes in, in addition to the economic growth, the income distribution and general condition of economy. The economic growth is the quantitative change in the economic structure, whereas economic development refers to the whole of qualitative and quantitative improvements in economy. For this reason, economic growth noes not necessarily include economic development, but economic development always incorporates economic growth. Hence, economic growth is a narrower concept, whereas development is a wider process that takes longer time.

Types of region: For which purposes the criteria used for defining the types or borders of the regions have been set is very important. From this aspect, it is clearly specified while making definitions of region that the fundamental point here is the homogeneity. Thus, many economy-oriented definitions or theories identify the types of region, and the necessity of distinguishing the regions in terms of homogeneity is emphasized. The regions are determined using similar or same criteria and the preliminary condition of identifying the regions is met.

Hence, in order to analyze the regions from economic aspect, it is necessary to distinguish and identify the types of region. There are various types of regions arising from the social, cultural, and political decisions (polarized, cross-border, administrative, autonomous, independent, plan, underdeveloped, developed, homogeneous), and the types of regions will be discussed here from economic aspect. For this reason, the economic classification of the regions is divided into two classes as regions by the economic structure and regions by the level of economic development.

Types of region by economic structure: In classifying the regions based on the economic structure, the classification is made by using the conditions at a specific time or space. Hence, the concepts of time and space add stability and stationarity to the concept of region by the economic structure. Accordingly, the economic regions are discussed under three classes as homogeneous regions, polarized regions, and plan regions.

Homogeneous regions: It is used for defining the regions showing parallelism of forming a unity or formed by the coexistence of possible criteria or those determined by the administrative or managerial authorities at the same or similar levels. Thus, the homogeneous regions refer to the areas having similar or same characteristics. Some of these characteristics are geographic structure, level or structure of income, type of economic activity, structure of employment, population characteristics, and structure of goods and services. Moreover, the physical or homogeneous dependences between central- or sub-regions are among the most important characteristics of the homogeneous regions (Kaştan, 2004: 35).

Polarized regions: The polarized regions identified as polarized, core or nodal regions refer to a type of region forming a concentration because of specific characteristics, which distinguish the region from the other regions. Hence, the areas where the regions are in an intense relationship with each other become polarized regions. The decrease of intensity from center to periphery because of the concentration and clustering of specific distinguishing economic characteristics such as goods, services, and labor force around a specific center and the strengthening relationship between center and periphery refer to this type of region (Brown and Holmes, 1971: 387). The relationships between the center and periphery arise from the decreasing outwards relationship from the center and it makes the center gradually further develop the periphery. Moreover, the polarized regions making the peripheral regions dependent through the network of relationships will become a center of attraction and the polarization will naturally end (Zivanoviç, 2017: 70).

Plan regions: It refers to the regions established by the managerial or administrative authorities in accordance with specific objectives and maintained in parallel with the targets. Moreover, the term "plan regions" is also used for identifying types of region established or designed in order to put specific strategies or plans into practice. The plan regions are identified by the administrative authorities in order to implement the wholes of specific sociocultural, political, economic, etc. policies or making it easier to implement them, as well as increasing the level of their effect. Hence, the plan regions mainly refer to the regions, which have been determined or targeted by the specified authorities, which aim to achieve specific economic targets and where the regional development policies are implemented.

The regions by level of economic development: The level of economic development necessitates certain classifications between the regions. Thus, the criteria used while classifying the countries by their level of development are also used for classifying the regions. Accordingly, the regions are classified according to their development level as developed regions, underdeveloped regions, and developing regions

Developed regions: These are the regions that are at a higher level when compared to the average of country in terms of regional income level, rate of income growth, rate of savings, level of investment, and the variables such as sociocultural, infrastructural, educational, health, etc. These regions are generally the regions, which aim to govern and where the economic and diplomatic policies of the country are made.

Underdeveloped regions: On the contrary with developed regions, the underdeveloped regions refer to the regions that are below the average level of country in terms of income level and other sociocultural variables and have no advantage because of the loss of development potential. Since the level of income and the growth rate of income are low in the underdeveloped regions, there are significant imbalances and inequities in terms of income per capita. On the other hand, the underdeveloped regions are divided into two classes as developing underdeveloped regions and underdeveloped regions by the potential. The developing underdeveloped regions are the regions that could not increase to the next level of development because they couldn't exactly explore or realize their existing potential. The underdeveloped regions by the potential are the regions that are not very different from the average of country in terms of income level but have lost their development potential. The rate of income growth is low in these regions.

Developing regions: These are the regions having a near-average rate of income growth (although not higher than the average of country) and having a high potential to develop. Moreover, if the growth inclination of the developing regions continues growing, then they may turn this mild process into a sustainable growth potential and they may achieve the level of developed regions. On the other hand, the regions that cannot execute the process in a sustainable way may also decrease to the level of underdeveloped regions.

As well as causing various difficulties in determining the borders of a region, this defining or grouping difficulty related with the concept of region plays an important role in the absence of a consensus on the factors causing regional imbalances. From this aspect, the growth or development problem arising from the "region definition" in any area might not be accepted as the same regional imbalance in another region. Furthermore, the basic development policies implemented for regional development in some regions might not yield growth and development in other regions. Hence, it is very difficult to treat the regional imbalances and implement the regional development policies as a single receipt or method that applies to every region. However, despite these difficulties, it is known that even though the historical backgrounds, economic conditions, and political approaches of countries may cause differences between them; there are many similar and even common characteristics in practice.

Interregional imbalance: It is a problem that is seen in almost any country at any time, in any form, and under any condition. Many historical, natural, geographic, politic, sociocultural, or economic problems may cause the problem of interregional imbalance. From this aspect, the unbalanced economic growth of the different regions negatively affects their demographic structure and causes intense migration of labor force from the underdeveloped regions to the developed regions, which have strong industrial capacity. As a result of this labor force migration, the sending region loses its qualified labor force and the arising interregional imbalance further deepens the factors playing role in the disadvantaged position of underdeveloped regions. On the other hand, although the migration of qualified labor force to the developed regions further increases the level of development in these regions, it might also have negative effect on the level of wages. Moreover, the migration to these regions also causes unplanned housing and unplanned and excessive growth of cities. It may bring external costs for the policy-makers. Thus, the interregional imbalance may turn into much more complicated problem.

Regional development: It is the whole of efforts aiming to increase the region's level of welfare through improving the human resources, constituted by the region's interaction with neighbor regions and the entire country, and based on the principles of sustainability and participation (DPT, 2003: 250). The approach of regional development is based on eliminating or removing the imbalances between the regions arising from socio-economic differences. In order to achieve this objective, many instruments including incentives, promotions, investment referrals, bureaucratic regulations, development agencies, and regional development zones (RDZs, which consist of organized industrial zones or technocities that are based on clustering) have been developed and are being utilized. On the other hand, regional development is considered to be both outcome and process of economic development. The regional development, which is seen as an outcome of economic development, refers to the increase in region's employment opportunities, welfare level, investment capacity, life standards, and professional standards. As a process, it is considered as supporting the industry, improving the infrastructure, and developing the labor markets (Stimson et al., 2006: 4). Moreover, in order to overcome the imbalance arising from the accumulation of industries in specific regions, in addition to ensuring a fair income distribution in the country, it is also aimed to enable the underdeveloped regions to achieve the level of industrialized regions. Similarly, it also proposes an increase in the level of investments in targeted areas and sectors in order to achieve the economic development in those areas (Arslan, 2005: 291; Kaya, 2009: 24).

Besides all these instruments and objectives aiming the regional development, especially the approach of growth with internal dynamics by mobilizing the local potential has been widely implemented through the regional development agencies in the recent period. This idea originates from the fact that the regional development policies, which are considered as a part of general economic policies, are prepared not in parallel with the necessities of shareholders in the region but in accordance with the requests of bureaucrats. In other words, the regional policies are prepared not from the society (bottom) to the top but from the bureaucrats (top) to the bottom. As an inevitable result of this, the development policies fall short in offering a development strategy that is specific to the potential and characteristics of the regions. Hence, rather than the policies and fund transfers that are directly performed by the central authority, the policies that are based on the local dynamics and inner potential yielded a more organized and rational form of regional development. As a result of these changes, determining the inner development dynamics of regions and which one of these dynamics will offer a faster movement capacity and play active role in the regional development have been left to the initiative of local decision-makers. On the other hand, as a result of the local actors'/units' determinant roles becoming more prominent, it was also observed that the local authorities gained more importance in determining these policies. Hence, the principle of regional development by decentralized intervention was adopted and the chance of success in local development was increased. Thus, accurately determining the problems and priorities of the local and taking the locality and participation as base, which are among the most important conditions of success, have become an integral part of regional development policies. This is very important for both participatory democracy and locally determining the necessities.

In conclusion, it is known that regional development problems cannot be resolved by making use of conventional policies. Thus, the policies to be implemented should be designed by carefully analyzing both region's inner potentials and country's potential and in the way ensuring development at both regional-local and national level together with a complete governance system because the local actors and the institutions that will be structured in their parallel will be the units that are more aware of the region's necessities and make more effort for the solution. Thus, these units will be capable of directly reaching the local society and directly planning the determinants of local development. The regional development that is planned and achieved with the pioneering role of these units will allow improvement of economic and social indicators, especially the income and employment. Thus, the interregional and intraregional development differences would be minimized and it would contribute to spreading the positive effects of regional development on the entire country.

After this short discussion about regional development, here are the resting chapters of this book. The next chapters are listed below:

First chapter; titled "Regional Income Inequality and Its Measurement" written by Prof. Dr. Sabri Azgün from Atatürk University, Dr. Berna Ak Bingül from Kırklareli University, and Dr. Demet Eroğlu Sevinç from Iğdır University. This chapter focuses on the concept of income inequality in general and investigates the methods for measuring the regional income inequalities in specific.

Second chapter; titled "Regions and Sustainable Development" written by Dr. Sertaç Hopoğlu from İskenderun Technical University and Dr. Demet Eroğlu Sevinç from Iğdır University. The authors discuss the importance of sustainable development of regions by analyzing the problem of growth and development from another perspective.

Third chapter; titled "The Relationship Between Regional Development and Regional Development Agencies" written by Assoc. Prof. Nazım Çatalbaş from Anadolu University. In this chapter, the problem of regional development was analyzed by making use of the theoretical approaches and the role of development agencies, which are considered to be one of the most important instruments of regional development, in regional development is discussed.

Fourth chapter; titled "The Innovation Systems from National to Regional Level: The Role of RIS in the Regional Development" written by Dr. Emine Demet Ekinci Hamamcı from Erzurum Technical University. In this chapter, the importance of innovation systems in regional development is emphasized. The author expresses the importance of regional innovation systems for the establishment and success of national innovation systems. Moreover, it is also emphasized that the regional innovation systems should be used as a regional development strategy.

Fifth chapter; titled "The Impact of the Change in the Investment Incentive System Application in Turkey on Regional Income Convergence" written by Dr. Esra Doğan from Eskişehir Osmangazi University. In this chapter, the effects of investment incentives, which are one of the most important promotion and incentive mechanisms for the regional development, on the regional income convergence in Turkish economy are discussed. The analyses are deepened by comparing the effectiveness of previous and current investment incentive systems.

Sixth chapter; titled "The Process of Regional Development in Turkey and the Interaction of Non-Governmental Organizations" written by Dr. İdil Gülnihal Yazıcı from İstanbul University. In this chapter, the regional development policies implemented in Turkey are presented but the historical backgrounds of regional development policies implemented in the European Union are explained first. Then, it is discussed to what extent the non-governmental organizations contribute to the regional development policies implemented in Turkey and what should be done to increase the effectiveness of NGOs in regional development.

Seventh chapter; titled "Regional Clustering in Social Service Workers: An Application with Three Star Analysis" written by Assoc. Prof. Dr. Murat Çiftçi from Trakya University. In this chapter, the importance of the clustering strategy, which is an important instrument in establishing special development areas for regional development, is emphasized and an analysis is made on the social services of regions in Turkey. According to the analyses, the effects of regions' social services on the regional growth and development, the conclusions are made at both provincial and regional levels.

Eighth chapter; titled "The Division and Specialization Proposals to Regions in Line with the Spatial and Sectoral Concentration Patterns of Turkey" written by Dr. Necmettin Çelik from İzmir Katip Çelebi University. The author emphasizes for which regions of Turkey the sectoral specialization, which is considered to be important for regional development, is important, and to what extent it would affect the competitiveness of the regions.

References

Arslan, K. (2005). Bölgesel Kalkınma Farklılıklarının Giderilmesinde Etkin Bir Araç: Bölgesel Planlama ve Bölgesel Kalkınma Ajansları, İstanbul Ticaret Üniversitesi Sosyal Bilimler Dergisi, 4(7), 275–294.

Başkaya, F. (2000). Kalkınma İktisadının Yükselişi ve Düşüşü, İmge Kitapevi.

Brown, L. A. and Holmes, J. (1971). The Delimitation of Functional Regions, Nodal Regions, and Hierarchies by Functionaldistance Approaches, Ekistics, 32(192, From Theory to Policy: Economic Development and Urban Planning), 387–391.

Dejan, R., Renate, P., Sofija, R. and Darko, V. (2015). Region as a Basic Territorial Unit of Regional Development (Concepts and Types), Economic Analysis, 48(3–4), 69–80.

DPT (2003). "Ön Ulusal Kalkınma Planı (2004–2006)", T.C. Başbakanlık Devlet Planlama Teşkilatı Müsteşarlığı, Bölgesel Gelişme ve Yapısal Uyum Genel Müdürlüğü, Ankara.

Kaştan, Y. (2004). Sosyo-Ekonomik Gelişmede Devlet Yatırımı ve Bölge Kavramlarının Tarihi Gelişimi, Akademik Araştırmalar Dergisi, 21, 29–40.

Kaya, A. (2009). "Türkiye'de Bölgesel Net Mali Yansıma", T.C. Maliye Bakanlığı Strateji Geliştirme Başkanlığı Yayın No: 2009/395.

Kılıç, S. (2012). Sürdürülebilir Kalkınma Anlayışının Ekonomik Boyutuna Ekolojik Bir Yaklaşım, İ.Ü. Siyasal Bilgiler Fakültesi Dergisi, 47, 201–226.

Kvicalova, J., Mazalova, V. and Siroky, J. (2014). Identification of the Differences between the Regions of the Czech Republic based on the Economic Characteristics, Procedia Economics and Finance, 12(2014), 343–352.

Siggel, E. (2005). Development Economics: A Policy Analysis Approach, Ashgate Publishing Company, USA.

Stımson, R. J., Stough, R. and Roberts, B. H. (2006). Regional Economic Development: Analysis and Planning Strategy, Second Edition, Springer, Germany.

Tekeli, İ. (2008). Türkiye'de Bölgesel Eşitsizlik ve Bölge Planlama Yazıları, Tarih Vakfı Yurt Yayınları, İstanbul.

Tıraş, H. H. (2012). Sürdürülebilir Kalkınma ve Çevre: Teorik Bir İnceleme, Kahramanmaraş Sütçü İmam Üniversitesi İktisadi ve İdari Bilimler Fakültesi Dergisi, 2(2), 57–73.

United Nations (2001). Reducing Disparities: Balanced Development of Urban and Rural Areas and Regions Within the Countries of Asia and The Pacific", Economic and Social Commission for Asia and The Pacıfıc, ST/ESCAP/2110.

Wannop, A. U. (1995), The Regional Imperative. Regional Governance in Britain, Europe and the United States, London.

Zivanoviç, V. (2017). The Role of Nodal Centers in Achieving Balanced Regional Development, Journal of the Geographical Institute "Jovan Cvijić", 67(1), 69–84.

Sabri Azgün[1] Berna Ak Bingül[2] Demet Eroğlu Sevinç[3]
Chapter 1 Regional Income Inequality and Its Measurement

Introduction

The most discussed concepts in economic science to date are income, income distribution, division, equality concepts. In economic literature the concepts are sometimes used differently and sometimes in the same sense. Therefore, it is necessary to take into consideration the concept of confusion that emerges and to make an appropriate description of the content of the study.

In the sense of the dictionary, income is defined as money provided by various means to an economic unit. In short, the definition of income in economic terms is the share of factors involved in production from the increase in value in production. If this increase is made by money, monetary income (nominal income) becomes real income name in the form of goods and services. The main characteristic that separates income from wealth or capital is that it is a current. Whereas wealth or capital expresses accumulated stock that is, state of wealth at a certain point in time. The reward of income from the value added created in a particular period is the purchase power. It takes place as a current within a certain period of time.

Along with being different density from country to country, regional income disparities are one of the main economic problems that both developed and developing countries face. Distribution at different intensity on the country location of economic factors that have a dynamic structure and guide development process cause regional income inequalities. There are more or less income disparities in almost every country today. Economic opportunity inequality refers to the fact that people in different regions cannot have the opportunity to get equal pay for both work and equal work. Social inequality is the inability of

---

1 Prof. Dr. Atatürk University, Faculty of Economics and Administrative Sciences, Department of Economics, 25000, Erzurum/TURKEY
2 Ph.D., Kırklareli University, Faculty of Economics and Administrative Sciences, Department of Economics, 39000, Kırklareli/TURKEY
3 Ph.D., Iğdır University, Faculty of Economics and Administrative Sciences, Department of Economics, 76000, Iğdır/TURKEY

individuals who live in different regions to benefit from health services, educational services, artistic activities at the same level, even in the choice of spouses.

Regional inequality is not unique to underdeveloped countries. Regional development disparities are a problem of varying weight at every stage of development. Thus, according to Rostow, in the maturation phase, all regions of a country and/or all sectors of an economy do not provide the same level of development by fully applying modern technology.

In the study, we examined mainly methods of measuring regional income inequality and income inequality. The study is a literature search for researchers working on regional income inequality. The study consists of five sections. The first section is the entrance to the work. In the second section, we have explained the distribution of income, its causes and consequences at the conceptual level. In the third and fourth sections, respectively we examined statistic and dynamic measures of income inequality in detail. The fifth section constitutes the evaluation and conclusion part of the study.

Conceptual Framework of Income Inequality

National income is the sum of the shares of the factors that are involved in the production process in an economy and is calculated by means of factor prices. The elements that generate national income are labor, nature, capital and entrepreneurs and their revenues are wages, rents, interest and income respectively. Moreover, the sum of factor income gives the national income. In economic literature, the concepts of distribution, distributional relations and income distribution are sometimes used in the same and sometimes different meanings. In this case, a terminology problem arises. In literature, the concepts of distribution and income distribution are generally used in the same sense. In addition, from the concepts functional and personal income distribution is understood. Income distribution is basically an economic concept that shows the share of production factors in the national income. In other words, income distribution is both a monetary magnitude that shows how national income is shared and a concrete economic scale. Division is a concept that is an abstract and socio-economic dimension that includes the form of distribution of the shared out income between segments of society, production factors and/or regions. Dividing is a concept that is the abstract and socio-economic dimension that includes the distribution of income, the distribution form between the social segments, factors and regions. However, income distribution and division are used many times in the same sense. Also, Divisional relationships is the whole of social relations that determine the form of division and the sharing between individuals, social classes, factors and/or regions of the national income. It has a broader meaning, including income distribution. In other words, income distribution is the monetary sharing of national production as a result of the divisional relationships. As a result of the explanations, the definition of divisional relationships and income distribution can be made as follows. Social relations, which determine the way in which national income is shared among persons or social groups, are called as divisional relationships. As a result of the divisional relationships, the share of social classes and/or regions in a specific period of production determines the distribution of income. Thus, income distribution is the sharing between individuals, social groups, regions or production factors of the income obtained in a particular period in an economy. As understood from the income distribution definition, there are four main types of income distribution. These are regional, sectoral, functional and personal income distributions.

Income distribution or Primary distribution refers to the distribution of income (personal, regional, functional, sectoral) resulting from the processing of the market process. Three primary factors determine the primary income distribution: i) globalization, ii) structural factors and iii) social norm and structure. Governments try to influence primary income distribution through factor prices, wealth and education policy. Therefore, the state intervenes primarily in the distribution of primary income by affecting the structural factors.

Secondary income distribution or income redistribution refers to the income distribution of occurring as a result of the interventions made by the state through the public incomes and expenditures on the operation of the market. The most effective way to make radical changes in income distribution is to change the basic divisional relationships. That is, the primary distribution in the stage of income formation is to intervene. However, governments intervene through fiscal policy at the stage of more redistribution of revenues (secondary income distribution) to income inequality due to the relatively low level of reaction and more conventional. In this context, fiscal policy instruments that governments use to reduce income inequality are public revenues (taxes), public expenditures and borrowing.

The excessive deterioration of income distribution in a society, leads to a decrease in economic activity in the long run. The increase in personal and regional income disparity, on the one hand, while causing the population of the country to accumulate in certain regions, on the other hand, leads to the accumulation of income and wealth in the hands of certain segments of society. Personal and regional income inequality also leads to deterioration in sectoral income distribution. In developing countries, income inequality increases migration from rural areas to urban areas and raises the social cost of living in rural areas. This leads to a loss of production in the agricultural sector. And despite increased incentives, agricultural production does not increase. Ultimately, the economy is increasingly dependent on the outside for agricultural products.

On the other hand, Accumulation in specific society segments of income and wealth and concentration in specific regions of the population as a result of the deterioration of income distribution has a negative impact on economic growth and prosperity by the shortage of demand in the long run. While the rate of savings in popular segments with high-income levels is extremely high, community segments with low-income levels do not have enough income to meet their compulsory needs. Wealth holders due to high incomes make their investments more to the developed country and/or regional economies in which the law and economic systems function properly. Disruption of regional and personal income distribution causes social and political unrest by increasing the crime rates in the region and community segments where income distribution is impaired. In this case, as in Turkey, while leading to an increase in terrorist incidents in the east and southeast of the country, of mafia-style formation in the community segments with low-income levels in metropolitan areas in the western part of the country leads to an increase. The spread of drug addiction previously not occupying too much space between crime rates in the poor society segments and the falling down of the age of drug abuse using in Turkey is the result of increasing income inequality.

Neoliberal policies that affected the world after the 1980s also led to an increase in regional and personal income inequalities. Neoliberal economic policies cause to lose the role of the state in the economy. The diminishing the role of the state in the economy, on the one hand, while leads to the gathering in certain segments of society and certain regions of the capital on the other hand, it has caused the union to lose its importance. In fact, it complicates the organization of public employees, the execution by service purchase method of the state's public services. In other words, the construction of public services by subcontractors leads to a decrease in the labor force wages. It causes human migration to developed regions by leading to accumulation and concentration economies the increased economic activities in specific regions of the country. The collection of population and income in certain regions is a result of permanent income inequality.

In parallel with the obstacle of income inequality to economic development, income distribution measurement approaches also have developed. Because, the first step of the struggle with income inequality is to determine the dimensions of income inequality. Regional income inequality is determined by two basic approaches: i) static approach ii) dynamic approach.

Static Approach to the Measurement of Regional Income Inequality

Static regional income distribution methods has emerged as a result of use to determine income distribution of statistical methods developed for various purposes. The methods that measures the dimension of income inequality at a certain point in time are static approach to the measurement of regional income inequality. Here, we describe Elteto-Frigyes income inequality criterion, relative mean deviation, coefficient of variation, Theil index and Gini coefficient from static income inequality measurement methods.

A. Elteto-Frigyes measure of income inequality

Elteto and Frigyes (1968) developed the Elteto-Frigyes index to measure inequality in income distribution. The index is defined by three variables. $(\bar{Y})$ indicates the average of regional incomes. (Y_L) indicates the average of regional revenues below of average regional income. And (Y_U) indicates the average of regional incomes over average regional incomes. The index established on three variables are as follows:

$$U = \frac{\bar{Y}}{Y_L}, \quad V \frac{Y_U}{Y_L} \quad \text{and} \quad W = \frac{Y_U}{Y}$$

Where U is the lower part of the regional distribution. V is all of regional distribution is the upper part of the distribution. And W is the upper part of the distribution. The indexes provide clear information While U show how many times the regions that earn income below the regional income averages, earn less than the average regional income, V indicates how many times the regions that earn income above the regional income averages, earn more than the average regional income.

B. Relative Mean Deviation

Kakwani (1980, 1990), Williamson (1965), Shankar and Shah (2003) describe the relative mean deviation as follows.

$$R_w = \frac{\sum_i |y_i - \bar{y}| \frac{p_i}{p}}{\bar{y}}$$

Here, y_i represents the real gross domestic product per capita of the region i. $\bar{y}$ indices the average of the national per capita income. p_i devotes the population of the region i. And p represnts the total country population. The relative average deviation is a criterion obtained by weighting the population rates of the regions. The Value of relative mean deviation R_w varies from 0 to 2. Convergence of the relative mean deviation to zero indicates that the income is evenly distributed among the regions. The convergence of the relative average deviation index to two means the increase in income inequality.

C. Coefficient of Variation

The coefficient of variation (*CV*) is one of the most commonly used criteria for the measurement of regional income inequality. The coefficient of variation is a measure of the propagation around the mean. The variation coefficient is calculated in several ways due to the propagation. The coefficient can be used to make comparisons between regions by time. The coefficient of variation can be calculated in two ways. First. It is the simple coefficient of variation, which gives weightless measurement as follows.

$$CV_u = \frac{\sqrt{\sum_i \frac{(y_i - \bar{y}_u)}{N}}}{\bar{y}_u} \quad (1)$$

Here, (y_i) refers to the per capita income of the region i, N refers the number of regions and $\bar{y}_u$ indices the per capita income of unweighted people. Average income per person without weight, $\bar{y}_u$ is calculated as follows without considering the population of the regions.

$$\bar{y}_u = \frac{1}{N} \sum_i y_i$$

The coefficient of variation varies between 0 and $\sqrt{N-1}$. The coefficient is sensitive to the number of regions. In case of equal distribution of income between regions, while the coefficient of variation converges to zero, In the case of absolute inequality, where all income is obtained by a single region, the coefficient equals $\sqrt{N-1}$

Secondly, weighted coefficient of variation is calculated by weighting the region's population with the country's total population. In this way, the sensitivity of the inequality value to the number of regions can be eliminated. Weighted coefficient of variation (CV_W) is as follows.

$$CV_w = \frac{\sqrt{\sum_i (y_i - \bar{y})^2 \frac{p_i}{p}}}{\bar{y}} \quad (2)$$

Here, (y_i) refers to the per capita income of the region i. ($\bar{y}$) refers the per capita national income average. p is the national population and p_i is the population of the region i. The weighted coefficient of variation varies between 0 and $\sqrt{(p_i - p)/p}$. The convergence of the coefficient value to zero means that the income is distributed evenly between regions.

D. Theil Index

Theil (1967) has developed the measurement method. The Theil index measures the loss of information that occurs during the transfer of information between economic actors. The index is used in various areas, especially in income inequality. The formula used to measure income inequality is as follows.

$$T = \sum_i x_i \log\left(\frac{x_i}{q_i}\right) \tag{3}$$

Here, T denotes the value of the index. x_i denotes the share that i receives from the national income of the region i. q_i denotes the share in total population of the region i. Zero index value means that each region has an equal share of both population and income. In other words, the convergence of the index value to zero means that regional income inequality is reduced.

E. Gini Coefficient

Gini coefficient is one of the most widely used measures in income inequality literature. Gini coefficient is defined in two ways: unweighted and weighted coefficients. Unweighted Gini coefficient is as follows.

$$G_u = \left(\frac{1}{2\bar{y}_u}\right) \frac{1}{n(n-1)} \sum_i^n \sum_j^n |y_i - y_j|$$

Here, y_i and y_j shows the gross added value per capita of the i and j regions, respectively. n refers the number of zones. $\bar{y}_u$ refers to the weightless average of regional gross value added per capita. Unweighted Gini coefficient, G_w ranges from 0 to 1. While the convergence of the coefficient to zero expresses the equal distribution of income between regions, convergence to 1 refers to income inequality. The weighted Gini coefficient calculated by considering the population rates of the regions is as follows.

$$G_w = \left(\frac{1}{2\bar{y}}\right) \sum_i^n \sum_j^n |y_i - y_j| \frac{p_i p_j}{p^2}$$

Here $\bar{y}$ shows national income per capita. p_i and p_j represents the populations of the i and j regions, respectively. p refers to the total population. The weighted Gini coefficient, G_w varies between 0 and $1 - (p_i/p)$. While the convergence of the weighted Gini coefficient to zero represents the equal distribution of income between regions, the convergence of the $1 - (p_i/p)$ refers to income inequality. Although the population of region i has a small share in the total population, if the region i is producing almost all of the country's output, the $1 - (p_i/p)$ value will converge to one.

Dynamic Approach to Measurement of Regional Income Inequality: Convergence Analysis

The dynamic measurement of income inequality is performed within the framework of convergence analysis. In fact, convergence analysis is a dynamic analysis of the fact that the income levels of countries and/or regions are converging or diverging with each other. Sala-i-Martin (1990), Baro (1991), Sala-i-Martin and Barro (1991), Barro and Sala-i-Martin (1992) conducted studies on the convergence of income levels between countries and/or regions. The neoclassical model predicts that the relative poorer countries or regions will grow faster than the rich countries or regions, and that these two groups will converge to each other in terms of the per capita income levels of the economy. There are two basic concepts in the classical literature about whether the income levels of countries or regions converge to each other; β-convergence and α-convergence. β-convergence is based on the investigation of the relationship between the growth rates of the per capita incomes of the economies and initial per capita income levels. β-convergence is the fact that poor economies grow faster than rich economies. Growth is expressed in terms of real income per capita. A certain number of economies (countries, regions or provinces) is defined as a model by taking the gross value added. Assume that the region i shows any economies that have been analyzed. If $1/T \log \left(\frac{Y_{it+T}}{Y_{it}} \right) = \log y_{it}$ shows the annual average between t and t + T periods, β-The convergence equation 4 is as follows.

$$\log y_{it} = \alpha - \beta \log (y_{it}) + \varepsilon_t \qquad (4)$$

If there is $\beta < 0$, there is convergence between the analysis-based variables. In the literature, β-convergence is defined in two ways: unconditional (absolute) convergence and conditional convergence. In the unconditional convergence, economies are assumed to be homogenous in terms of structural factors such as technology, capital. In the conditional convergence, It is used shadow variables for structural differences such as technology and capital structure between economies.

α-convergence is based on the examination of the spread of per capita incomes of economies. α-convergence is defined as follows. If a group of the economies has α-convergence, the standard deviation and variance of the level values of the per capita gross value added values of the economies should decrease in time. If there is α-convergence, the standard deviations are as follows.

$$\sigma_{t+T} \langle \sigma_t \qquad (5)$$

As in Equation 2, the decrease in the standard deviation as of the analysis period means that the income levels of the economies will converge. The β-convergence and α-convergence are naturally interrelated. If the sample variance of log (y_{it}) in Equation 1 is taken, the relationship between σ_t and σ_{t+T} depending on β is obtained. If the poor regions grow faster than the rich regions, the Gross Value Added values of the regions will converge in time. As an alternative to α-convergence, the coefficient of variation is used. The coefficient of variation is obtained by dividing the standard deviation by mean. Decrease in the coefficient of variation as of the analysis period, shows convergence (Karaca, 2004).

Conclusion

Increasing globalization and a macroeconomically unstable World leads to distortions in income distribution. In the event that the income generated in an economy is unfairly distributed, a sociocultural conflict in the society is inevitable. It is not possible for an economy to achieve sustainable growth and development in the long run without a balanced distribution of the country's production between the regions, sectors and society segments of the economy. The objective of the restoration of income distribution is to achieve a certain level of socio-economic prosperity and to preserve social peace in the country. Increased deterioration of income distribution in a society leads to a decrease in economic efficiency in the long term. Personal and regional income inequality leads to the accumulation of the population in certain regions on the one hand, and on the other hand leads to the collection of the income and wealth in certain society segments.

Personal and regional income inequality also cause deterioration in sectoral income distribution. Income inequality increases migration from rural to urban areas in developing countries and increases the cost of living in rural areas. This situation causes loss of production in the agricultural sector. Agricultural production does not increase despite increasing incentives. Ultimately, the economy becomes dependent on foreign goods for agricultural products. On the other hand, as a result of the deterioration of the income distribution, the collection of the population in certain regions and of income and wealth in certain social segments leads to a shortage of demand in the long term, adversely affecting economic growth and prosperity. Although the rate of savings in high-income community segments is high, the low-income community segments do not have enough income to meet their compulsory needs. The high-income and wealth segments of the society makes their investments in developed countries/regional economies where law and economic systems work more soundly. Disruption of regional and personal income distribution leads to social and political unrest by increasing the crime rates in the region and community segments where income distribution is deteriorated.

In this study, the income inequality problem that affects almost all world economies more or less is examined from a theoretical point of view. Income inequality and the consequences of income distribution are explained theoretically. In addition, income inequality measurement methods are explained. While dynamic income distribution measurement method describes changes in income distribution over a period of time, Static income inequality measurement methods are statistical methods that provide information about income distribution in a given period.

References

Barro, R. J. and Sala-i-Martin, X. (1992). Convergence, Journal of Political Economy, 100(21), 223–251.

Barro, R. J. (1991). Economic Growth in a Cross Section of Countries, Quarterly of Journal Economics, 106(2), 407–443.

Elteto, O. and Frigyes, E. (1968) New Income Inequality Measures As Efficient Tools for Causal Analyses and Planning, Econometrica, 36(2), 383–396.

Kakwani, N. C. (1980). Inequality and Poverty – Methods of Estimation and Policy Applications, The World Bank Research Publication/Oxford University Press, Washington, DC.

Kakwani, N. C. (1990) Large Sample Distribution of Several Inequality Measures-With Application To C'ote D'lvore, The World Bank, Washington DC.

Karaca, O. (2004). Türkiye'de Bölgeler Arası Gelir Farklılıkları: Yakınsama Var mı?, Türkiye Ekonomi Kurumu, Tartışma Metni, 2004/7, Nisan, http://www.tek.org.tr.

Sala-i-Martin, X. (1990). On Growth and State, PhD Dissertation, Harward Üniversity.

Shankar, R. and Shah, A. (2003). Bridging the Ekonomic Divide Within Countries: A Scorecard on the Performance of Regional Policies in Reducing Regional Income Disparities, World Development, 31(8), 1421–1441.

Theil, H. (1967) Economics and Information Theory, North Holland Publishing.

Williamson, J. G. (1965). Regional Inequality and Process of National Development: A Description of the Patterns, Economic Development and Cultural Change, 13(4), 1–84.

Sertaç Hopoğlu[1] Demet Eroğlu Sevinç[2]

Chapter 2 Regions and Sustainable Development

Introduction

There has been mounting evidence that our ecosystem's capability of supporting a decent human life in the future is at risk due to increasing damage by an increasing human population and harmful human activities. Advances made in health sciences and medical technologies during the Twentieth and the Twenty first Centuries have minimized the possibilities of death from certain common diseases, causing human population to increase rapidly. Increasing economic activity of a growing population is now putting a significant and restrain on the earth's resources. Such an unsustainable load puts the livelihood of future generations at risk. Since all systems, social and economic, are subsystems of the ecological system (Feldhoff, 2002), sustainability of the global ecosystem is also important for the continuity of human civilization.

Not only the well-being of the future generations are but also the well-being of many communities which are disadvantaged in terms of access to natural, economic, human and technological resources or which are just situated in disadvantaged regions is in jeopardy if human economic activity continues at its current pace. Such an uneven access to resources often creates migration waves that put more pressure on the ecosystems of the regions receiving migrants as well as their economies. Thus, sustaining the balance of an ecosystem is not only important for the future but also important for the well-being of the present generation.

At the very heart of the problem lies, thrive of human beings for more well-being. Human beings consume raw resources or transform raw resources or mix it with other resources to create new materials (tangible or intangible, goods or services) in order to be better off. Ever increasing needs of a growing human population means more consumption and more production. As human needs

---

1 Ph.D., Asst. Prof., Iskenderun Technical University (ISTE), Faculty of Management and Administrative Sciences, Department of International Management and Trade, Merkez Kampus, 31200, Iskenderun, Hatay/TURKEY, sertac.hopoglu@iste.edu.tr
2 Ph.D., Iğdır University, Faculty of Economics and Administrative Sciences, Department of Economics, 76000, Iğdır/TURKEY

increase, we require more resources, more space and more economic activity to be able to deliver more well-being to a growing population. The major constraint is the limited regenerative capacity of our natural environment. As we become better off, we wish to be more comfortable than before and the means of earth to supply everyone what they need is limited. Thus, as our activity to satisfy our needs becomes intensified, we are left off with fewer resources to continue to do so. The case of more people getting better off in terms of per capita goods and services they consume is called economic development. The interesting thing is that science of economics measures economic growth and development by means of consumption; consumption of more goods and more services is a measure of how much welfare human beings have. However, economic development does not, and should not, necessarily mean an improvement in the quality of life through an increase in consumption and a consequent utilization of resources to produce for consumption (Costanza, Daly, and Bartholomew, 1992: 7). The important question is, then, how can we develop by balancing our needs and the available means presented by our ecosystem.

In parallel to the evidence of weakening of our ecosystem, there has also been an increasing awareness on taking reparative action to reduce earth's load down to a more acceptable level in order to bring the ecosystem back to a more advantageous position to support both the present and the future human activity. The idea of sustainable development reflects the concerns of all mankind for "development that meets the needs of the present without compromising the ability of future generations to meet their own needs" (World Commission on Environment and Development [WCED] – The Brundtland Report, 1987). Thus, balancing and adjusting of human economic activity with the given natural environment has become an important policy aim at the global and national levels. However, in practice, achieving sustainable development becomes a complicated task since it requires harmonization of the interests of economic, social and political circles and the requirements of the ecology for supporting the whole system (Rees, 1989).

Since human economic activity is causing the problem, it is logical to look for economic solutions at relevant economic levels. The regulation of global economic activity, with such global agreements as the Paris Agreement on climate change, for the continuity of our planetary system is carried at the metaeconomic level. At the macroeconomic level, states ratify global agreements and regulate domestic markets for an ecologically sensitive economy. Mesoeconomic level, i.e. regional and/or local level, requires different approaches to sustainable economic development since regional development policies must comply with the objectives of national macroeconomic planning while trying to satisfy the needs of regional communities and firms at the same time. In fact, the regional level may reflect the complicated nature of sustainable development better. The complex relationship between the regional and environmental economic phenomena, which includes many interactions between the region, society, environment and economics, can be best observed at the regional level since the space (the region) acts as the geographical medium through which the effects of environmental externalities are reflected on the economy and since the scarcity of space as a good has far-reaching consequences for both the present and the future generations (Nijkamp, 1997).

This chapter tries to explain the concept of regional sustainable development and contends that the regional level is significant for achieving sustainable development objectives. Whether the regional level is the most appropriate level for achieving sustainability is discussed in the following section of the study. The third section deals with the general problem of specifying a clear definition for the concept of sustainable development and, thus, regional sustainable development. Some important points in planning for regional sustainable development are discussed in the fourth section. The fifth section concludes.

Importance of the Regional Level as a Space for Sustainable Development

"Think globally, act locally" has been a well-known slogan of environmentalists. The slogan also reflects the importance of regional/local level in achieving sustainable development at the global scale as well as the bottom-up approach to sustainable development. From an ecological point of view, sustainable development includes the redefinition of the relationship between human beings and the natural environment they are living in. As in every other spatial level, social, productive and cultural processes of a region are determined by its environmental characteristics yet these processes may also be harmful on the environment itself. Achieving sustainable development then requires spatial organization of all processes in a way that maximizes their benefits to the human beings and minimizing their harm to the environment. The region may be the ideal spatial level for sustainability since it contains both macroeconomic and microeconomic elements, is a limited geographical area, which makes planning, coordination and monitoring easier, and hosts a community, which shares certain social and cultural values.

The importance of the region as an economic entity has been rising since the last quarter of the twentieth century. There is a number of interacting factors behind the recognition of the regional, level as an important economic policy level (Çakmak, 2006). The failure of state-led development policies based on import-substitute industrialization, which became apparent after the oil crisis of 1970s, made decision-makers and researchers to look for more bottom-up, outward-oriented policies. In contrast to assigning production roles to regions, policy-makers started to formulate development policies based on endogenous capabilities and comparative advantages of the regions. Planning for regional development became more bottom-up as regional communities and business people are involved in the formulation of regional development plans through various mechanisms. Such decentralized decision-making can be seen in different countries at different levels. In fact, such an involvement of regional actors and the sense of a region that has a say in its own destiny may also be a result of the weakened ability of the state in financing large-scale, centrally-tailored development programs. Instead of centrally allocating resources for regional development schemes which are not owned by the region and which may not be fully-compatible with the endogenous economic dynamics of the region, delegation of decision making to the region enabled state to allocate resources more efficiently and democratically. By decentralization of decision making in the sphere of development, the state also avoided the risk of being the only responsible in case of failure of the development path selected by the regional level.

Another reason for the rise of the regions is the reorganization of the economy due to the changes brought about by globalization. Improvements in transportation and communication technologies, accompanied by the liberalization of the global trade, rapidly increased flows of goods, services, finances and people. The global trade is currently conducted with fewer barriers and faster compared to the twentieth century. While policy changes adopted as a result of General Agreements on Tariffs and Trade (GATT) are further liberalizing the global trade, regional integrations such as the European Union increased the volume of trade within geographically and politically close countries. On the other hand, changing nature of consumption and production contributed to the acceleration of the global trade as access to market information became less costly and easier for both consumers and producers due to technological development. Consumer tastes change rapidly since consumers can now see and demand products or services on anywhere around the world. Producers can also see and respond to consumer demand from all around the world. Thus, consumers demand slightly differentiated goods and services and if this demand is not met rapidly this may result in loss of profits. Production must be flexible to cope with changing consumer demand. In this respect small-and-middle sized enterprises at the regional and local level can respond to changing consumer demand better than larger organizations. Innovation, which is the key for a dynamic economy, mostly occurs in spatially concentrated clusters of small-and-middle-sized enterprises in this new economy as well (Porter, 2000). Agglomeration of economic activity around clusters also creates highly innovative and competitive regions with high growth rates.

Large organizations also adapt to changing conditions of the global economy by carrying different stages of the production to different regions around the world. Since capital moves faster and more freely, big companies are able to move parts of production to different regions around the world that can give them cost effectiveness by providing cheaper inputs or proximity to target markets. In addition to competing for national resources, regions also compete for attracting international capital today for growth and development. Moreover, while some regions gained importance as global economic nodes in this new economy, economic importance of some other regions is declined. As a result, regions which can bring up solid development plans based on endogenous capabilities, which can establish proper institutional infrastructures, and which have an innovative, export-oriented economic base with dynamic SMEs become successful in the new economy.

Increasing importance of the regions and elevated regional economic activity create new problems for sustainability at the regional level. First of all, although regions are becoming more important economic units, the differences in terms development between regions still continue to exist. Regions who try to catch-up with relatively more developed regions still depend on regional natural resources despite programs to diversify regional economic bases and adopt more knowledge-intensive production methods (Sevinç, 2011). Thus, the pressure of being successful by relying on endogenous resources may cause an overutilization of regional resources and may endanger the sustainability of regional socio-economic systems. This situation also endangers sustainable development in the relatively more developed regions. In case where extractive industries, such as mining and metallurgy, are the engines of the regional economy, effects of intensified economic activity on the regional ecology would be more serious. Horlings and Padt (2013) argue that the competition between regions for attracting globally mobile capital and labor for economic development, which reflects a very narrow approach to regional development, also creates "winners" and "losers" in terms of sustainability: those regions that are wealthier and attach a certain value to natural resource utilization and local assets are perceived as "winners" while other regions who rely heavily on utilization of natural resources and lack endogenous assets are seen as "losers".

Population flows between regions in the form of migration from relatively disadvantaged regions to developed regions may also hinder efforts for sustainability. As labor in lagging regions migrates to more developed regions for better opportunities, the increase in population not only causes social and economic problems but also put a stress on natural resources of the receiving regions. The influx of people into certain developed areas reduce the carrying capacity of the natural environment, change the composition of local workforce and reduce the effect of sustainability measures (La Torre, Liuzzi, and Marsiglio, 2019). Rapid regional growth through clustering may also have similar affects. Agglomeration of economic activity around specialized regional clusters draws more people, machines and equipment to the region and this increases the load on the regional environment.

Large volume of trade also creates problems for regional sustainability. Changing nature of human life necessitates fast production and effective delivery of goods and services. Production, in its basic sense, is a process of transforming resources to a new entity. Due to rapidly changing consumer behavior and technological developments, this transformation has been taking place more rapidly especially after the 1980s. Increasing demand for raw materials, energy, transportation, etc. also contribute to overutilization of regional resources and degradation of regional environment. The increased tourist flows due to increasing welfare around the world in general also put a strain on the resources of regions whose economy are based on tourism. Not only increased flow of goods, services and people but also an increased flow of waste can contribute to sustainability problems. While some regions that export waste may be viewed as clean and sustainable regions, regions that import waste and energy-intensive goods and intermediate goods (Thierstein and Walser, 1997: 167). Moreover, transnational flow of capital may result in more waste and change of regional ecologies.

Nijkamp et al. (1991) argues that this fluvial characteristic of the regional systems, which are more open today, can be an alternative approach to regional sustainable development. In this respect, regional sustainable development becomes a matter of balancing all physical, social and economic flows in a region in accordance with the global sustainable development principles. If sustainable development can be achieved at the regional level, then sustainability at the global level can be achieved easily (Nijkamp et al., 1991: 3). Thus, in addition to being an important economic scale, the regional level is also the proper scale for achieving sustainable development and materializing what is meant by the motto "think globally, act locally". Mishenin et al. (2018) also argue that the lack of a clear and general definition of guidelines for global implementation of sustainable development makes the regional level an important policy level for generating modern models of sustainable development

On the other hand, following Thierstein and Walser (1997) who cite Fürst (1993), the regional level also has advantages as well as disadvantages in terms of implementation of sustainable development policies. These advantages are as follows:

1) The region provides a space for people to identify themselves with. It would be easier to generate widespread ownership of regional sustainable development plans and programs with people who identify themselves with a specific region. Moreover, community awareness and involvement in sustainable development would also make it easier to establish cooperative partnerships and governance structures to promote sustainability. Such a background would strengthen the institutionalization of sustainable development principles within the regional community and would decrease transaction (political, communication, preparation and implementation) costs for future regional sustainable development plans.
2) In addition to being a space of ingoing and outgoing flows, the region is also a relational space. There may be many regional actors with different points of view and interests. High levels of communication between actors would strengthen relational networks between these actors and formulation of a regional sustainable development that benefit all actors from public, private and civil sectors through negotiations would generate trust which would facilitate further development. The importance of social capital, formed by constructive communication and trust within communities, for regional development is well-documented (*inter alia*, Putnam et al., 1993; Boschma, 2005; Malecki, 2012). Well-functioning regional social networks can be effective in regional sustainable development through by creating channels for sharing specialized knowledge and expertise and by facilitating efficient allocation of resources (Devine-Wright, Fleming, and Chadwick, 2001). Rydin and Holman (2004) also argue that regional social capital can solve problems in regional mobilization, cooperation, definition of sustainable development objectives and lack of resources and capacity.
3) The political value of the region is also rising. Economic policy favors regional sectoral policies and the bottom-up approach to regional planning makes the region a more proper and transparent level for solid sustainable planning.
4) The regional level is the spatial level in which we can observe the interaction of many types (Boisier, 2001) of endogenous capital. However, with the advance of globalization and technology the nature of involvement and the effects of traditional resources are changing and endogenous resources and softer resources (social capital, institutional capital, etc.) are gaining importance.

While the advantages of the region to be the proper level for sustainable development are all endogenous, disadvantages are a mix of exogenous and endogenous factors. First of all, recognizing the degree of openness of all countries and regions in our time, it would be erroneous to think the region is sterile from the influences of what is going on in the international and national domains and in its neighboring regions. Regions exist in the space together and their actions affect each other. From the point of view of "the region as a space of flows" approach, each region may be the recipient of an outgoing flow from another region. In this respect, any choice of development path (favoring the industry or favoring the sustainability) or wealth-affecting event (such as crises, disasters, wars, etc.) may be effective on the sustainability of another region elsewhere. Moreover, the boundaries between countries still exist as well as the superiority of state in making the choice for the national development policy. This makes it harder for regions, as well as for nations, to cooperate for and coordinate sustainable development efforts.

As great philosopher Ibn Khaldoun once said "Geography is destiny". The geography in which we live in is effective in shaping our economic activities, social organization and culture and institutions. Thus, it might be said that every region has its own unique endowment of resources and its development path is shaped by the availability and the rate of utilization of these resources. The level of development of a region may also influence the utilization rate of natural resources and attitudes of the regional community towards sustainability. Moreover, it may be hard to establish networks or effective governance structure due to lack of social and human capital. These shortcomings are the endogenous disadvantages in achieving sustainable development at the regional level.

As a result, it can be said that sustainable development is a multifaceted, if not a complex, process. The achievement of sustainable development depends on understanding and implementation of its principles at the local level. The regional level possesses advantages for sustainable development since it is home to economic, social and physical transactions within and from outside the region. Because of its position as a middle level between macro and micro environments, the regional level also represents advantages for effective management of sustainable development. However, achieving sustainable development at the regional level necessitates a custom approach that maximizes the effects of above-mentioned advantages over disadvantages and creates the best possible balance between the industry, society and environment. Thus, transformation of the regional economy and community to a continuous state that does not exceed the supportive boundaries of the regional environment can be referred to as "regional sustainable development". However, due to the large coverage area of the concept of sustainable development, the understanding of sustainability and definitions originated thereof vary between disciplines and policy areas.

Problems of Definition

When we think of sustainable development, we naturally tend to view the whole process from an ecological point of view and often overlook the implications of the concept in other spheres of human life. Yet, when the focus is on regional development or development in general, we tend to overlook environmental issues and expect the development policy to achieve sustainability automatically. In both cases, the resulting policies or approaches satisfy neither the developmental needs nor the requirements for sustainability.

A possible reason for this may be the perception of sustainable development as a "soft" issue by both the policy-makers and the industry. Economy seems to be prevailing over sustainability every time and sustainability becomes reduced to a few topics in development plans which represent expressions of goodwill rather than solid measures for action. However, the most important reason for this, as discussed in the literature, is the elusiveness of the concept of sustainable development. In fact, everybody have an idea of what sustainable development should be but nobody can give a general definition. There is also confusion how regional sustainable development is defined. A Google search on the subject gives studies that reflect ecologically sensitive approach to development as well as studies that are concerned with sustaining a certain level of welfare in a region. Therefore, it would be better to have an understanding of the concept of sustainable development first and then define regional sustainable development.

The concept of sustainable development has drawn interest from all science disciplines and from all levels of policy-making. Thus, definitions of sustainable development may vary according to the field of study or practice, and, in addition to traditional economic and environmental concepts, they include such concepts as ethics, solidarity, governance, equity, progress, culture, civilization and so on (Scleicher-Tappeser et al., 1999). Thierstein and Walser (1999) also argue that the concept of sustainable development has become a melting pot for many different approaches; however, it is as well a useful concept politically since it can be used flexibly to address many issues and change the public opinion.

The most popular definition given by the Brundtland Report (1987) emphasizes two important dimensions in defining sustainable development:

i. *A development that meets the needs of the present without compromising the ability of future generations to meet their own needs, and*

ii. *A process in which the exploitation of resources, the direction of investments, the orientation of technological development, and institutional change are all in harmony and enhance both current and future potential to meet human needs and aspirations.*

The definition implies a systemic approach in which economy, technology and governance work together to ensure that resources are utilized without disturbing their rates of reproduction. This approach also implies a continuous balancing of the economy, technology and governance in cases of any changes to sustain a certain level of welfare for all generations.

Rees (1989) argues that the concept of sustainable development encompasses not only the economic activities but also processes that regulate and facilitate the implementation of these activities. His definition of sustainable development represents a more holistic view of sustainable development:

"Sustainable development is positive socioeconomic change that does not undermine the ecological and social systems upon which communities and society are dependent. Its successful implementation requires integrated policy, planning and social learning processes; its political viability depends on the full support of the people it affects through their governments, their social institutions, and their private activities"

According to Rees (1989: 3), this definition of sustainable development highlights some additional points that reflect the holistic nature of the concept:

i. Sustainable development is oriented towards the achievement of well-defined and explicit ecological, social and economic objectives,
ii. Sustainable development aims at human and community development while trying to keep human consumption within the limits of the ecological system,
iii. Sustainable development is a process that is initiated by government intervention but cannot be advanced without the inclusion, leadership and cooperation of the private sector,
iv. Sustainable development is a process which is based on scientific, conscious and democratic practices in all areas of public domain,
v. Sustainable development cannot be achieved if policy integration and coordination are not achieved at all spatial scales and among relevant jurisdictions.

Lonergan (1993) also advocates that space should be taken as an integral element in any analysis of sustainable development since development is constructed historically and spatially. According to Lonergan (1993) sustainable development is about attaining a more equitable human society internationally, nationally and intergenerational. Such a challenge requires narrowing the gap between the developed and developing nations, ensuring future generations to have at least the same living standards we have been enjoying and ensuring a better distribution of resources both within and among countries.

From an economic point of view Daly (1992: 185–186) distinguishes three specific areas of action for achieving sustainability. The first area is "allocation" and it refers to the efficient use of resources for delivering for the needs of the human beings. Allocation includes apportioning scarce resources for the production of goods and services preferred by the people; it is "the relative division of the resource flow among alternative products". In brief, allocation means equitable distribution of the resources among alternative usage areas. The second area is also concerned with distribution. However, the focus of this area is to distribute goods and services equitably among people and among future generations. The third area, which is called as "scale", is concerned with the transformation of resources and the waste produced as a result of the transformation process. "Scale" refers to the capacity of the ecosystem to absorb waste and regenerate resources over time. Our finite ecosystem draws the limits of the scale for all subsystems (economic, social, etc.) it hosts, and if economy's scale extends beyond the limits of the ecosystem, then the regenerative and absorptive capacity of the ecosystem is altered. In other words, the value of the future carrying capacity of the ecology is diminished if the scale of the economic activity grows larger than that of the ecosystems. Such an approach implies that a sustainable scale should be a limited geography within which the rate of utilization of natural resources is smaller than or equal to the rate of regeneration of the environment and the scale of economy is manageable for achieving such balance. In this respect, the regional or local level may be the ideal scale for sustainable development.

Thus, regional sustainable development means "the integration of sustainable development principles into regional development practice" (Clement, Hansen and Bradley, 2003) in very simple terms. Incorporation of sustainability principles to regional development is important since mankind need to find new ways to further improve the quality of life on the planet for all through a reassessment of today's economy in the face of multiple crises experienced in the delivery of basic human needs (food, water, etc.) and in the delivery of the needs of the economy (finances, energy, raw materials, etc.) (The UN Regional Commissions, 2012). Regional sustainable development is "a development which ensures that the regional population can attain an acceptable level of welfare – both at present and in the future – and that this regional development is compatible with ecological circumstances in the long run while at the same time it tries a globally sustainable development" (Nijkamp et al., 1991: 3). In this respect, regional sustainable development is the promotion of sustainable development within the boundaries of the regional economy and it reflects the important role of the region as an intermediate level between the national and local levels. In addition to ecology and economy, the term also implies improved coordination and cooperation at the regional level and a modification of human behavior at the individual level for sustaining a certain level of welfare.

There may also be differences related to use and understanding of the terms "regional sustainable development" and "sustainable regional development", which are generally used interchangeably. While regional sustainable development refers to all policies that primarily aim to achieve ecological sustainability by sustaining all living and nonliving and natural and man-made assets while making economic and social progress, sustainable regional development refers to a process by which a region achieves a certain level of development that enables self-financing further development efforts. Thus, while the former term reflects an understanding that prioritizes ecology as a starting point, the latter term reflects an approach that prioritizes the economy over other domains (Mengi and Algan, 2003: 86–87).

Although there is an agreement on that regional sustainable development incorporates global sustainability principles into regional practice, the importance and understanding of these principles may vary among regions. Lonergan (1993) argues that the general definition of sustainable development does not indicate a specific spatial level; however, its definition may change from region to region. Moreover, holistic definition of the concept of sustainability may also lead to vague definitions of sustainable development at the regional level (Campbell, 1996) and regional plans based on such definitions may be inoperable or may produce immeasurable outcomes. Since regions differ in terms of levels of development, resource endowments, economic and environmental capacity, social and cultural characteristics, the definition of regional sustainable development becomes somewhat contextual. Therefore, it may be better to look at policies and plans for sustainable development at the regional level. Yet, we may use the discussion on the global definition of sustainable development and draw a framework for regional sustainable development as follows:

- *Incorporation:* Regional sustainable development involves incorporation of global sustainable development principles to regional development efforts. It is a process of increasing regional welfare without disturbing the capacity of regional environment.
- *Spatiality:* Regional sustainable development involves the efforts to achieve sustainability within a limited geographical area. It reflects a spatially

bottom-up approach. If sustainability is achieved at the regional level, it can be achieved at national and global levels.
- *Good Governance:* Regional sustainable development involves political and institutional development and more respect for democracy at the regional level since equity is the central idea in sustainability. It reflects a politically bottom-up approach. Regional sustainable development cannot be achieved without efficient governance based on cooperation and trust.
- *Informed Community:* Regional sustainable development involves human development as well as community development. More educated and more cooperating societies will perform better towards more sustainability.
- *Mobilization:* Regional sustainable development requires cooperation and coordination of all individuals, public, private and civil sectors to be achieved. It is easier to communicate and cooperate at the regional level than at the national level.

Regional sustainable development policy should reflect these features at the minimum. However, there may be many factors affecting the weight of these factors in regional sustainable development plans as well as their practical implementation.

Planning for Regional Sustainable Development

The scope of regional development has been evolved from a narrow focus on economic issues to a more holistic view which considers social, institutional, cultural and environmental aspects (Pike, Rodriguez-Pose, and Tomaney, 2007) as important indicators of as well as important objectives of the development process. Such a transformation is followed by a more process-focused approach in planning (Berke, 2002). The multidimensional nature of sustainable development fits in well with the holistic approach to regional development. Planning for regional development thus has to consider many processes and various balances within the regional system. It should not take the ecology or the economy as its only focus but represent an ecological sensitivity while trying to preserve economic and social integrity of a region (Carroll and Stanfield, 2001).

The starting point for regional sustainable development planning is incorporation of sustainable development principles to regional development planning. However, merely incorporating sustainable development principles into regional economic development policies, programs and plans is not sufficient condition for achieving sustainable development. Such incorporation must clearly reflect the inter- and intra-generational equity principles of sustainable development thinking (Gibbs, 1998) and must be accepted and applicable by all regional stakeholders. A regional development policy with incorporated sustainable values would most probably entail a reorganization of the regional economy and governance towards sustainability goals. That means creation of new equilibriums between the ecology, the economy, the community and the polity.

However, creating a long-term equilibrium seems not always to be the objective of sustainability planning. Reyer et al. (2012) argue that sustainability plans often focus on effects of unexpected events, rather than focusing on long-term effects of such important phenomena as the climate change, and they are based on the idea of adaptation to abrupt changes brought about by these unexpected events, rather than adaptation to the changes brought about by long-term and more important phenomena. Reyer et al. (2012) stress the need for viewing the region as a system which is composed of many subsystems and emphasize that a careful and systemic approach to planning is necessary in order to sustain regional systems in the long term. Such an approach includes looking for new and more ecologically sensitive forms of economic organization that minimizes effects of negative externalities of development, promoting forms of social organization that will minimize the excessive use of natural resources and finding the most efficient combination of sectoral and spatial elements to ensure environmentally responsible and balanced planning for regional development (Roberts, 1994).

Sustainable development covers a multilevel spectrum that involves relations between nations at the global level and social, economic and political circles at the local level (Hardy and Lloyd, 1994). The involvement of multiple levels of planning requires building a balance between all these levels. Nijkamp and Rietveld (1987) mentions four important levels for regional planning: individual level, at which where conflicts between the preferences of people may arise, intraregional level, where tensions between regional actors may occur, multiregional level, where preferences of a region creates externalities to other regions, and supranational level, where tensions between the central government and regional decision making may occur. The latter level is significantly important since regional sustainable development policies and plans should also create a balance between the objectives of the overall (national) development policy and regional development needs. Differences in understanding and interpretation of sustainable development may result in tensions between the various levels of planning and inapplicable plans (Haughton and Counsell, 2004). Thus, successful planning for regional sustainable development should include measures for achieving vertical consistency between actions at local, national, and international levels and horizontal coordination between all planning levels while providing for sustainability (McDonald, 1996).

Other possible tensions may include the harmonization of sustainability plans with neighboring regions. It should not be forgotten that regions are heterogeneous in nature and this heterogeneity may require implementation of different regional sustainable development policies which may have different consequences at different spatial levels over time (Nijkamp, 1997). While, Jonas and Gibbs (2010) points out to the fact that regional sustainable development policies may not produce intended outcomes as long as imbalances between regions continue. Since there are differences between the regions in terms of level of development, there are also differences in the geographical distribution of environmental degradation as in distribution of wealth. This variance in environmental quality may be stemming from the industrial base of a region, population, capacity of the local environment and perceptions of the regional community towards environment (Lakshmanan and Bolton, 1987). Indeed, the latest waste problem between the Philippines and Canada is a good example of more developed countries and regions seeking different countries and regions for "treatment" of waste materials away from the original country or region. Moreover, relatively more developed regions are generally more conscious towards environmental problems and look for solutions while less developed regions continue to engage in environmentally damaging production practices simply because these practices are only means through which to generate income for the region as a whole. However, as While et al. (2010) argue, this is not a direct problem of the policy side; the problem is purely microeconomic and stems from the profit seeking behavior of regional firms. The national or the regional administration then compulsorily intervenes in the economy in order to minimize the social cost of regional environmental degradation. In this respect, implementation of a regional sustainable development policy creates a new equilibrium for all stakeholders within a region as well as those stakeholders outside the region.

Creating awareness about sustainable development and sustaining this over generations cannot be possible without the common efforts and full cooperation of the regional communities. Common action for sustainability occurs more easily in regions which have a common culture of cooperation, and it may not be easily formed in societies which have low levels of social capital. Social capital and institutional capital are not easily constructible, however, regional sustainable development plans, as general guiding documents, may establish guidelines and platforms to facilitate creation of cooperation and formation of governance structures. Vision statements, coalition building activities, institutional development activities, national and regional incentive frameworks for collective action, campaigns for public involvement, and creation of environments for social learning (Wheeler, 2000) may be helpful tools in rooting social capital within communities.

All in all, regional sustainable development requires a careful planning. It involves many variables from micro and macro environments, including human beings (as producers and consumers), firms, local institutions, neighboring regions, national governments and so on. To have a reasonable regional sustainable development plan in the face of such complexity, following points can be considered as a simplified framework for planning:

i. The definition of regional sustainable development should be made clearly since and should be cleared out from the ambiguity of general definitions. A definition recognizing the immediate problems of the region and its relations with the other regions would best serve the interests of regional sustainability.
ii. Planning should recognize the complex relations between regional actors keeping equity principle in mind and should include applicable measures for attaining sustainability as defined in the plan.
iii. Effectiveness of regional sustainable development plans significantly depends on a long-term approach with measurable indicators. However, changes in regional equilibria, as intended in the regional sustainable development plan, may be a cause for new unsustainable practices within the region or may have negative externalities in neighboring regions. Thus, regional sustainability plans should be designed flexible, consider effects of changes in equilibria between regional processes and provide contingency plans or reparative measures.
iv. Regional sustainable development plan should also be consistent with national sustainability policies and should be in harmony with sustainability plans at other levels, especially with those of the neighboring regions.
v. Since regional sustainable development plan aims to change today's behavior for the benefit of the future's society, some tensions among the present stakeholders are highly likely to occur. Regional sustainable development plan should therefore ensure political support and community approval through democratic processes.
vi. Community involvement and stakeholder cooperation should be emphasized, through official channels if necessary, in order to establish the governance structure for regional sustainable development.

Conclusion

Rising human populations and increasing economic activity constitutes a significant risk for our social order. In order to continue our civilization, we must find ways to minimize our harm to the ecosystem while maintaining the utility we get from the ecosystem at an acceptable level. The concept of sustainable development reflects such concerns and it highlights the most important problem of the mankind.

Sustainable development is concerned with the continuity of the earth's ecosystem and is generally defined by ecological terms. Since all social and economic systems are subsystems of the ecology, the concept has a larger and deeper meaning. In addition to keeping the economic value of the environment fixed for future generations by redefining and reorganizing the relationship of production with the environment, the concept also implies redefinition of the relationships among individuals, societies and governments and between these and the environment and the ecology. Thus, due to the large coverage area of sustainable development and due to confusing taxonomy, there is no commonly agreed definition for the concept. Definitions based solely on ecology and equity between the generations are criticized in terms that they represent vague explanations of the concept of sustainable development. In this case, it also becomes hard to define regional sustainable development, which is also used interchangeably with "sustainable regional development", another term explaining a different concept.

However, the inclusion of the term "regional" somewhat removes the ambiguity on the meaning of "regional sustainable development". If it is regional, then it has to be related with creating an environmentally sensitive economy within a geographical area where we may find a community that shares similar values as well as a shared environment. In this respect, we may define regional sustainable development as development of the regional economy and improvement in quality of life of the regional community through adopting environmentally and socially responsible production methods.

Regional sustainable development is important since the region presents the ideal spatial level for sustainable development. Sustainable development at the global level may be complicated due to differences in state policies. Harmonization of different sustainability policies at the state level reflecting different expectations, economic considerations and political backgrounds may slow down, if not totally hamper, efforts for global sustainable development. On the other hand, the region offers a more limited political space for coordinating efforts in a limited geographical area as well as in terms of coordination within other regions and the central government.

From an economic point of view, the rising importance of the regions as a node of economic activity also makes the region important for sustainable development. Since most of the problems associated with sustainability are related to the economic activity it is logical to aim at sustainability from the regional level. Increasing regional economic activity in terms of flows of goods, people and capital and agglomeration of economic activity have negative consequences for the regional sustainability. It is more likely to change individual and production attitudes at the local level since regional communities can experience the negative externalities of increased economic activity firsthand. The region offers a relational space at a limited geography as well, which makes it easier to generate stakeholder support and popular ownership of sustainable development policies and plans. Moreover, as a middle level between macro and micro environments, the regional level also represents advantages for effective management of sustainable development. All these advantages make the region the appropriate spatial level for sustainable development.

Yet, differences between regions still exist and regions still have to comply with policies at the supraregional level. In this case there is also no uniform definition of sustainability and common regional sustainable development plan for each region. It is better to have a region-specific definition of sustainable development and move on from there to formulate policies. The planning for regional sustainable development requires consideration of many subsystems and processes within the regional system and their interaction. Definition of regional sustainable development according to advantages and disadvantages of the region, identifying measurable measures and making informed estimations of their effects, establishing operational governance structures and mobilizing community for sustainable development are critical points for regional sustainable development planning.

A solid regional sustainable development plan must also demonstrate flexibility to respond to changes in regional, national and global conditions. It is most likely that the technological developments to come in the future within the frame work of Industry 4.0 would change our approach to sustainability as well as to other social and economic processes. The use of more automation, especially artificial intelligence at different extents, will have effects on all economy as well as on the way we conceive sustainability. While technological development would ecologically optimize our utilization of the space by optimizing use of natural resources, better management of waste material and optimizing land use, it is still unclear how equal and decent income will be generated for those whose skills became obsolete with technological advance. Such issues will present new opportunities as well as new challenges for regional sustainable development in the future.

References

Berke, P. R. (2002). Does Sustainable Development Offer a New Direction for Planning? Challenges for the Twenty-First Century. *Journal of Planning Literature*, 17:1 21–36.

Boisier, S. (2001). Territorial Development and the Construction of Synergetic Capital: A Contribution to the Discussion on the Intangibility of Development. In A. Kumssa & T. McGee (Eds.). *New Regional Development Paradigms* (17–32). London: Greenwood Press.

Boschma, R. A. (2005). Social Capital and Regional Development: An empirical Analysis of the Third Italy. In R. A. Boschma and Robert C. Kloosterman (Eds.). *Learning from Clusters A Critical Assessment from an Economic-Geographical Perspective* (139–168). Dordrecht: Springer.

Campbell, S. (1996). Green Cities, Growing Cities, Just Cities?: Urban Planning and the Contradictions of Sustainable Development, *Journal of the American Planning Association*, 62:3, 296–312, DOI: 10.1080/01944369608975696.

Carroll, M. C. and Stanfield, J. R. (2001). Sustainable Regional Economic Development, *Journal of Economic Issues*, 35:2, 469–476

Clement, K., Hansen, M. and Bradley, K. (2003). *Sustainable Regional Development: Learning From Nordic Experience.* Nordregio Report 2003: 1. Stockholm: Nordregio.

Costanza, R., Daly, H. E. and Bartholomew, J.A. (1992). Goals, Agenda and Policy Recommendations for Ecological Economics. In R. Costanza (Ed.). *Ecological Economics: The Science and Management of Sustainability.* New York: Columbia University Press.

Çakmak, E. (2006). *Local Economy and Regional Development Agencies* (in Turkish). Ankara: İmaj Publication.

Daly, H. E., (1992). Allocation, Distribution, and Scale: Towards an Economics That Is Efficient, Just, and Sustainable, *Ecological Economics*, 6, 185–193.

Devine-Wright, P., Fleming, P. D. and Chadwick, H. (2001). Role of Social Capital in Advancing Regional Sustainable Development, *Impact Assessment and Project Appraisal*, 19:2, 161 167, DOI: 10.3152/147154601781767096.

Feldhoff, T. (2002, July). Japan's Construction Lobby Activities-Systemic Stability and Sustainable Regional Development, *ASIEN*, 84, 34–42.

Fürst, D. (1993). Raum-die politikwissenschaftliche Sicht, *Staatswissmsdaften und Staatspraxis*, 2, 293–315.

Gibbs, D. (1998). Regional Development Agencies and Sustainable Development, *Regional Studies*, 32:4, 365–368, DOI: 10.1080/00343409850117825.

Hardy, S. and Lloyd, G. (1994). An Impossible Dream? Sustainable Regional Economic and Environmental Development, *Regional Studies*, 28:8, 773–780.

Haughton, G. and Counsell, D. (2004). *Regions, Spatial Strategies and Sustainable Development.* London: Routledge.

Horlings, I. and Padt, F. (2013). Leadership for Sustainable Regional Development in Rural Areas: Bridging Personal and Institutional Aspects, *Sustainable Development*, 21, 413–424, DOI: 10.1002/sd.526.

Lakshmanan, T. R. and Bolton, R. (1987). Regional Energy and Environmental Analysis. In P. Nijkamp (Ed.). *Handbook of Regional and Urban Economics. Volume I: Regional Economics* (581–628). Amsterdam: North-Holland.

La Torre, D., Liuzzi, D. and Marsiglio, S. (2019). Population and Geography Do Matter for Sustainable Development. *Environment and Development Economics*, 24:2, 201–223, DOI: 10.1017/S1355770X18000475.

Lonergan, S. (1993). Sustainable Regional Development, *Canadian Journal of Regional Science/Revue canadienne des sciences régionales*, XVI:3, 335–339.

Malecki, E. J. (2012). Regional Social Capital: Why it Matters, *Regional Studies*, 46:8, 1023–1039.

McDonald, G. T. (1996). Planning as Sustainable Development. *Journal of Planning Education and Research*, 15:3, 225–236.

Mengi, A. and Algan, N. (2003). *Regional Sustainable Development in the Age of Globalization and Localization: Cases of the EU and Turkey* (in Turkish). Ankara: Siyasal Kitabevi.

Mishenin, Y., Koblianska, I, Medved, V. and Maistrenko, Y. (2018). Sustainable Regional Development Policy Formation: Role of Industrial Ecology and Logistics, *Entrepreneurship and Sustainability Issues*, 6:1, 329–341. DOI: 10.9770/jesi.2018.6.1(20)

Nijkamp, P. (1997). *Environmental and Regional Economics*, Research Memorandum 1997–27, Amsterdam: Vrije Universitet.

Nijkamp, P., Lasschuit, P. and Soeteman, F. (1991). *Sustainable development in a regional system. Research Memorandum 1991–93*, Amsterdam: Vrije Universitet.

Nijkamp, P. and Rietveld, P. (1987). Multiple Objective Decision Analysis in regional Economics. In P. Nijkamp (Ed.). *Handbook of Regional and Urban Economics. Volume I: Regional Economics* (493–541). Amsterdam: North-Holland.

Pike, A., Rodríguez-Pose, A. and Tomaney, J. (2007). What Kind of Local and Regional Development and for Whom?, *Regional Studies*, 41:9, 1253–1269, DOI: 10.1080/00343400701543355

Porter M. E. (2000). Location, Competition, and Economic Development: Local Clusters in a Global Economy, *Economic Development Quarterly*, 14, 15–34.

Putnam, R. D., Leonardi, R., and Nonetti, R. Y. (1993). *Making Democracy Work: Civic Traditions in Modern Italy*. New Jersey: Princeton University Press.

Rees, W. (1989, May). Defining "Sustainable Development", CHS Research Bulletin, Vancouver: BC Centre for Human Settlements, University of British Columbia.

Reyer, C., Bachinger, J., Bloch, R., Hattermann, F. F., Ibisch, R. L., Kreft, S., Lasch, P., Lucht, W., Nowicki, C., Spathelf, P., Stock, M. and Welp, M. (2012). Climate Change Adaptation and Sustainable Regional Development: A Case Study for the Federal State of Brandenburg, Germany, *Regional Environmental Change*, 12:3, 523–542, DOI: 10.1007/s10113-011-0269-y.

Roberts, P. (1994). Sustainable Regional Planning, *Regional Studies*, 28:8, 781–787.

Rydin, Y. and Holman, N. (2004). Re-evaluating the Contribution of Social Capital in Achieving Sustainable Development, *Local Environment*, 9:2, 117–133, DOI: 10.1080/1354983042000199561.

Schleischer-Tappeser, R., Lukesch, R., Strati, F., Sweeney, G.P., and Thierstein, A. (1999). *The INSURED (Instruments for Sustainable Regional Development) Project Final Report*. Freiburg: EURES.

Sevinç, H. (2011). Bölgesel Kalkınma Sorunsalı: Türkiye'de Uygulanan Bölgesel Kalkınma Politikaları. *Girişimcilik ve Kalkınma Dergisi*, 6:2, 35–54.

The UN Regional Commissions (2012, June). *Green Growth and Sustainable Development: Regional Perspectives*. New York: United Nations.

Thierstein, A. and Walser, M. (1997). Sustainable Regional Development the Squaring of the Circle or A Gimmick? *Entrepreneurship & Regional Development*, 9:2, 159–174, DOI: 10.1080/08985629700000008.

Thierstein, A. and Walser, M. (1999). *Sustainable Regional Development: Interplay of Topdown and Bottom-up Approaches*. ERSA Conference Papers, 1999. European Regional Science Association, St. Gallen, Switzerland.

Wheeler, S. M. (2000). Planning for Metropolitan Sustainability, *Journal of Planning Education and Research*, 20:2, 133–145.

While, A., Jonas, A. E. G. and Gibbs, D. (2010). From Sustainable Development to Carbon Control: Eco-state Restructuring and the Politics of Urban and Regional Development, *Transactions of the Institute of British Geographers*, NS 35, 76–93.

World Commission on Environment and Development (WCED) (1987). *Our common future (The Brundtland Report)*. Accessible at: https://www.are.admin.ch/are/en/home/sustainable-development/international-cooperation/2030agenda/un-_-milestones-in-sustainable-development/1987--brundtland-report.html.

Nazım Çatalbaş[1]

Chapter 3 The Relationship Between Regional Development and Regional Development Agencies

Introduction

With the effect of the Classical Economy School, the countries entering into an economic development period together with the industrialization process left the distribution of the production capacity between the regions to the market forces. It was observed that this distribution couldn't be effectively made under the effects of economic and social problems that have been experienced and, as a result of this, it was also revealed that the inequality/disequilibrium between the regions started to increase.

As well as causing differences between the countries, the Industrial Revolution is also the reason for the emergence of interregional differences (Dinler, 2008: 99). The other factors causing the interregional development differences are the geographic conditions, natural sources, demographic structure, innovativeness of the local society, demand to the products produced in the region, quality of infrastructure, skills of the entrepreneurs, etc. The reason for the growth inequality between the regions is that the investments concentrate generally on the locations, where they may achieve the profit maximization.

The Great Depression in 1929 drew the attention on the disequilibrium between the regions, besides the differences between the countries (Vatansever Deviren and Yıldız, 2014). Especially in the period after World War II, the policies aiming to decrease the interregional differences were given importance. In the late 1950s, the subject "region" has started to be discussed in the USA and the platforms have been established in the universities for this purpose. In Europe, especially in the European Economic Community, the policies aiming to ensure the development of regions and to reduce the developmental differences between the regions were given priority (Elmas, 2001: 49; Ildırar, 2004: 13; Vatansever Deviren and Yıldız, 2014).

---

[1] Assoc. Prof., Anadolu University, Faculty of Economics and Administrative Sciences, Department of Economics, 25000, Eskişehir/TURKEY

It was determined that, in order to minimize the developmental differences between the regions, it is necessary not to leave the distribution of economic activities between the regions to the market forces but to make investments through the partial intervention of the state (government). The governments have prepared development plans and emphasized the importance of reducing the developmental differences between the regions. The advancements in the economic theory caused an increase in state intervention. While the country-wide development plans are the subject of macroeconomics, the policies aiming to decrease the interregional developmental differences increased the importance of microeconomics and regional economics in the development at national and regional levels. In the present study, the regional development, regional developmental differences, and regional development theory and policies are discussed in summary, and the relationship between regional development and regional development agencies is emphasized in the explanations related with theory and policy. From this aspect, the regional development and regional growth subjects were discussed in order to reveal the interregional inequalities. Then, the fundamental theories on regional development are presented in general. And, in the final step, the study is completed by discussing the role of regional development agencies in eliminating the regional inequalities.

Regional Development

Before defining regional development, it is necessary to define the development first. For an economy, the development refers to the growth bringing transformation in the social and corporate structure including the changes in values, worldview, and consumption behavior patterns of the society (TDK, 2011: 247). The term development incorporates economic, social, political, cultural, and other structural changes and transformations besides the economic growth. The term economic development covers a wider area than the economic growth does.

From a narrower perspective, regional development refers to the economic policies that the public authorities adopt in order to eliminate the economic development differences between the geographic regions (TDK, 2011; 64). Together with the globalization process, the meaning assigned to the regional development changes in the course of time. The determinative role in the responsibility and decision-making process, which has been attributed only to the central government before, is now delegated to the local actors.

The regional development covers the elimination of the developmental differences between the regions, increasing the global-scale competitive power of the regions, mobilizing the local dynamics, making use of the regional potential, and thus develop the countries as a whole (Akın, 2006: 29). The regional development can also be defined as the whole of studies aiming to increase a region's level of welfare by mobilizing the economic and social potential of the human sources. In another definition, it is stated that the "regional development" refers to the whole of studies based on the principle of participation and sustainability, adopting the vision of region comprising of the mutual interaction between regions, neighboring regions, and the whole world, and aiming to improve the human sources and to increase the region's level of welfare by mobilizing economic and social potentials. From the definitional aspect of the term "regional development", it can be seen that the meaning attributed to this term may vary significantly depending on the definition of region (Arslan, 2005: 278) and the policies and policy practitioners.

Regional Development Theories

The studies on the development of a specific region or area date back to von Thünen, who is accepted to the founder of areal economics. A. Weber, T. Palander, and A. Lösch and W. Christaller have carried out pioneering studies on where the production and establishment locations should be.

According to the Central Place Theory developed by Walter Christaller, a German geographer, the areas are divided into 7 groups by their functions. In this classification, the economic relationships between the areas have been considered. The model has been criticized because it incorporates over-simplifying assumptions such as homogeneous and ideal space. In order to make the model more realistic, Christaller added the transportation networks and administrative organization into the model. Although the economists such as Isard, Böventer, and Parr contributed to the model after Christaller, the Theory of Central Places remained as a static theory and fell short in terms of explaining the regional development (Ildırar, 2004: 73). The Theory of Central Places explains only the geographic distribution and local concentration of the economic activities.

After Christaller, A. Isard expanded the Theory of Central Places and became one of the researchers investigating the regional economy. The other researchers, who have investigated the Theory of Places (Regions) and the propagation of economic development throughout an area, were V. Böventer, F. Perroux, and J. R. Boudeville (Dinler, 2008; 37–38).

It can be seen that the studies on regional development emerged in the late 1950s. The theories on regional development are based on the studies in the discipline combining the macroeconomic growth and development after World War II and the place theory of von Thünen (Ildırar, 2004: 45). In general, it can be seen that the first theories developed on regional development couldn't sufficiently address the problems and, thus, the development of new theories and approaches was needed.

It can be seen that, until the late 1980s, the theoretical studies on determining the main arguments of the regional development concentrated in two groups based on the difference between growth and development. In the early 1990s, the new approaches arose in regional development in parallel with the literature on growth.

In the present study beginning with the Keynesian regional development theories, the regional development theories influenced by the neoclassical and endogenous growth theories are discussed, as well as the new regionalist approach. The studies on regional growth have largely been affected by the theory of growth (Ildırar, 2004: 46).

Keynesian Regional Development Models

The Keynesian development economists discussed the importance of the state's active role from the perspective of regional development, as well as the general economic development. In parallel with the initiative of nation-state based on the paradigm of the Keynesian state of welfare, the regional development policies have been conducted in a balanced manner.

In the Keynesian regional growth model, the marginal propensity to consume is an important variable. In this model, the size, industrial structure, and location of the region determine the regional factor by influencing the marginal propensity to consume the local products. In the Keynesian regional growth model, the marginal propensity to consume is of significant importance in increasing the amplitude of factor.

The determining variables of the Harrod-Domar growth model, which is another Keynesian growth model, are the savings and investments. In this model, economic growth depends on the investments in determining the national income, and the amount of investments is dependent on the level of saving. In conclusion, the growth depends on the savings.

Since the Keynesian regional growth models are the demand-side ones, they focus on the marginal propensity to consume and the savings. This model has never directly interested in the supply. On the other hand, the main limitations of the model are that it overlooked the interregional feedback, that is focused on a single sector, and that it overlooked the factor market. These limitations have directly influenced the failure of Keynesian policies in terms of regional development.

In the Keynesian model, a high level of load on the state for the development increased the pressures on the public budget. Besides that, the crises that have occurred in the global economy in the 1970s weakened the budgets and the fact that sufficient funds couldn't be allocated to the investments has led the Keynesian regional development policies to the failure.

Neoclassical Regional Growth Model

When compared to the Keynesian model, the neoclassical regional growth model is a supply-side model. According to this model, the activity and determining the role of the state in the economy should be reduced and the market should be left to its own endogenous dynamics. Thus, the decisions of rationally-behaving economic units would make the market efficient. In this model, the analyses are made via the production functions. Besides the labor and capital, also the technological advancement was added into the analyses in this model.

In the neoclassical growth model developed by R. M. Solow (1956), the increase in short-term income per capita depends on capital accumulation and technological advancement. Since the return rate of capital is a decreasing value, the long-term growth can be achieved only through technological advancement. In the model of Solow, the technological advancements arise from foreign countries and, thus, this model cannot explain the long-term increase in the income per capita.

In the neoclassical regional growth model, it is assumed that the production factors have full mobility between the regions. Moreover, the model also includes the convergence hypothesis. Accordingly, it has been asserted that the difference between the underdeveloped countries (regions) and developed regions will be closed. However, no consensus could be achieved on this subject (Berber, 2017: 202). In practice, it was observed that the factor migration from the disadvantaged region so the advantaged one negatively affected the regional growth (Ildırar, 2004: 55).

The weakness of the neoclassical approach was that the local economies that were not ready for the global competition were led to failure. The local regions, which have become independent from the space and remained far away from global markets in terms of production and distribution and they gradually became marginal since they couldn't bear with the global competition (Vatansever Deviren and Yıldız, 2014). And this situation further increased the growth differences between the regions. According to the model, the differences between labor and capital stock and technological advancements played an important role in the emergence of interregional differences.

Endogenous Regional Growth Theories

The endogenous growth models consider the results and weakness of the neoclassical growth models. In years (1980s), when the neoclassical and Keynesian regional policies entered into crisis, the local and regional economic development efforts based on the endogenous growth theories gained currency (Eceral, 2005: 97). The regional development approaches focusing on the local and regional, emphasizing the local dynamics, and stressing the endogenous potential gained importance.

Some of the assumptions of endogenous regional growth theory are the incremental revenue of capital, the presence of incomplete competition markets, the acceptance of externalities, spillover, and technological advancement as endogenous variables, emphasizing the importance of human capital, and accepting the social infrastructure as an important factor in the growth process. The technology, which has been considered as an external phenomenon although it has been the determinant of long-term growth in neoclassical growth theory, has been internalized in the endogenous growth models and related to the factors within the economy (Türker, 2009: 93).

In the endogenous growth theory, the convergence hypotheses asserted by the neoclassical scholars is rejected. On the contrary, the endogenous growth theory states that, if the underdeveloped countries (regions) do not take required measures, then the income differences from the developed countries (regions) will gradually increase (Berber, 2017: 203). This argument is based on the fact that the creation and distribution of the information show differences between the regions (Ildırar, 2004: 75).

The endogenous regional development theory aims to reveal the mechanisms creating the welfare by using the own sources of region, to have the regions dominate the process, and to enable them to be the subject of this process (Çakmak and Erden, 2004: 82). On the contrary with the neoclassical model, the endogenous regional development theories aimed to explain the economic development by using the variables within the system (know-how, human capital, R&D, technological advancements, financial innovation, new role of state, market structure, etc.) (Türker, 2009: 88).

According to the endogenous growth theory, the state's encouraging and guiding policies on the innovative fields may influence the growth in the long term. On the contrary with the neoclassical theory, the responsibilities of the state have increased in the endogenous growth theory in the way of creating a competitive and balanced economic environment. The state may promote the R&D activities by directly contributing to the companies performing R&D

activities, making necessary legal regulations for the market, and protecting the intellectual property rights (Türker, 2009: 93). The proper functioning of endogenous regional development model requires the promotion of R&D activities, as well as the social infrastructure, and investments in education, health, and other infrastructural domains.

New Economic Geography Approach

The economic geography approach seeks the answer for the questions such as why the economic activities concentrate on specific regions and organize there. According to the economic geography model, the reasons for economic activities' accumulation to the limited number of locations are the centralist (accumulation) and centrifugal (distribution) forces. The centralist forces are the labor stock, forward and backward connections between the companies, and the technological externalities (Ekinci and Ersungur, 2013: 207). According to the new economic geography approach, the accumulation of economic activities to a specific region is shaped by the interaction between firm and supplier and between the firm and consumer, as well as the increasing returns to scale and the transportation costs (Schmutzler, 1999: 356).

Krugman (1991) developing the center-surrounding model within the scope of the new geography approach considered the companies producing the differentiated products with incrementing revenue under the monopolist competition conditions of Dixit-Stiglitz, and he explained the commerce, accumulation, and specialization in this production structure (Ekinci and Ersungur, 2013: 222). Krugman assumed that the externalities causing the emergence of the center-surrounding model were the monetarist externalities related with supply or demand, rather than pure technological externalities.

According to Krugman, the emergence of the center-surrounding model was based on the transportation costs, scale economies, and the share of production in the national income (Krugman, 1991: 483). When some of the indicators taking the transportation costs, scale economies, and share of non-agricultural products in the expenses as basis passes beyond a critical threshold, then the population starts to concentrate and the regions emerge. This process would continue by feeding its own (Krugman, 1991: 487). The center-surrounding model provides a frame determining the fundamentals of new economic geography.

Krugman (1991) has discussed the center-surrounding model by excessively simplifying it and has not discussed anything but the location of specific industries. Krugman (1991) showed that, under the conditions of incrementing scale economies, the production accumulates at specific locations as a result of the interaction between the free movement of labor and commercial activities. Venables (1996), however, showed that the accumulation may occur even when the labor is immobile (Venables, 1996: 356).

The main contribution of the new economic geography can be summarized as using the knowledge such as accumulation, specialization, urbanization, formation of center and surrounding, and cumulative strengthening of specific models obtained from the spatial economic development analysis tradition, as well as developing the models passing through this process by making use of micro bases in a stable frame (Vatansever Deviren and Yıldız, 2014).

Although the "new economic geography model" has used mainly the orthodox economic terms, it also stretched the terms "perfect competition" and "constant returns to scale". The new economic geography approach added the "increasing returns to scale" and "imperfect competition" to its models. Finally, it provided a wider perspective on the events when compared to the neoclassical approach did.

New Regionalism Approach

The new regionalism approach provides solutions based on the mobilization of local sources (Amin, 1999: 375). At this point, it landed the state with new responsibilities. The state supports the market forces and private sector through various incentives and subventions and contributes to the local/regional development. The entrepreneur city developments, learning regions, R&D, innovation, and network-based governance are among the supports and incentives prioritized by the new regionalism approach.

The problems caused by the globalization since the 1990s have a significant share in the role assigned to the state in the new regionalism approach. The presence of the state is a necessity for the elimination of these problems and the functioning and protection of the market system. According to the new regionalism approach, it would not be enough to leave the articulation of the regions into international market to solely the market forces. For this reason, the role of state in supporting the regional economic development should be re-analyzed.

According to the new regionalism approach, rather than a development model completely independent from the state or a development model driven by the state, a mixed development understanding taking the local and regional initiatives into account is a necessity. The role of the state, in this case, differs from the regional development approaches in 1950s and 1960s. In this approach, the role of state is to exhibit a behavior pattern different from the Keynesian state of welfare and to gain a quality meeting the needs of the global economy.

In the regional development and in the process of regions integration with the global economy, the responsibility assigned to the state is a regulatory and (to a certain extent) supportive role. In the new period, the complementary relationship comes to the forefront rather than the substitution relationship between the governments and markets within the context of the market-friendly state. The governments became responsible for regulating the corporate infrastructure that is necessary for the development of the markets. Nowadays, the state aims to increase technological advancement and innovation capacity through administrative mechanisms addressing economic efficiency. The regional development agencies constitute one of the most important steps taken for this purpose.

Regional Development Policies

In general, there are developmental differences between the regions in all countries throughout the world. In order to reduce the interregional development differences, the countries adopted policies in parallel with the advancements in economic theory especially related with growth and development). Since the Great Depression in 1929 until the 1970s, the central governments played a significant role in the regional policies. In the traditional regional policies in this period, the central government has played the leading role in the decision-making processes. After 1970, it can be seen that the weight of central government in the regional development policies has decreased and the role of local administrations has increased under the effects of social and political progressions. After the 1990s, the regional development drifted apart from the central government's intervention and started to progress through the participation of regional, national, and international actors.

Objectives of Regional Development Policy

The main objective is to reveal and utilize the potentials of regions, increase the interaction between the region and the other regions and world, and consequently contribute to the economic and social development. The most important success of the regional development is to ensure the effective and efficient use of local sources and to strengthen the governance mechanism (Korkmaz and Taşlıyan, 2012: 366).

The most important objective of the regional development policy is to eliminate the interregional developmental differences arising from various reasons. For an economy aiming to develop, the elimination of the developmental differences between a peak and neighboring areas is a very important problem to solve because a structure in form of "a pole and neighboring areas" arises because of the interregional developmental differences and these unbalanced structures start hindering the development once the growth reaches a certain level. In order to solve this problem, it is necessary to change the structural factors causing the developmental difference (Ildırar, 2004; 21).

By eliminating the reasons for unbalanced growth between the regions, it is necessary to develop effective and efficient practices that might distribute the investments to the regions. The regional development policy would contribute to the economic development by decreasing the developmental differences between the regions, as well as contributing to the economic growth and stability of the region.

Instruments of Regional Development Policy

The instruments of regional development policies may vary depending on the development level of countries and the conditions of the region. Given these differences, the instruments of development policy can be listed as follows: region planning, realizing the public investments, adapting the administration organization to the regional development problems, financial and tax-related incentive measures, supporting the entrepreneurship, and other instruments (Ildırar, 2004: 20–21).

The regional development instruments having corporate character are development agencies, investment support offices, regional development plans, operational programs, and SWOT analysis. The regional development instruments having economic character are organized industrial zone (OIZ)/industrial parks, regional support practices, venture funds, and joint regional development practices. Moreover, the regional development instruments having social network character are regional innovation system, regional innovation strategy, business/innovation/technology centers, innovation transfer center, business/professional groups/associations, public-private sector partnerships, catalyzer institutions, commercial unions, intraregional sectoral industrial networks, technoparks/technocities, and business/company incubators (DPT, 2008: 18–42).

Given the practices throughout the world, it can be stated that the fundamental instruments supporting the regional development significantly vary. These numerous instruments with different characteristics and functions further increase their importance (Akın, 2006: 297). Among these instruments, the regional development agencies have an important place because of the practices in the USA and Europe. The development agencies may operate in the way covering a large portion of these instruments.

Regional Development Agencies

According to the World Bank, the regional development agencies are the structures establishing, operating, and supporting the endogenous networks, main objective of which is to create employment opportunities, support and enhance the SMEs in different fields of production, and improve the general conditions and opportunities of the region and which are capable of catalyzing the development (Çakmak, 2006: 64). According to the European Association of Development Agencies (EURADA), the regional development agencies (RDA) are the institutions investigating the collective or general interests of a region, fulfilling the task of economic development, and which are significantly linked with the local, metropolitan or regional authorities from the aspect of management, funding or operations (http://www.eurada.org/about/, 12 September 2019).

The RDAs operate in a specific geographic region and they play an important role in revealing and improving the endogenous potential of the region because the RDAs prepare the strategic plan of local economic development with the participation of all the actors in order to achieve the social development. In order to put this plan into practice, RDAs ensures the coordination among the local actors and, for this purpose, mobilize the local sources and draw the off-region sources to the region.

RDAs are partially or completely dependent on the central or local administrations from the financial aspect, but they have a certain level of administrative autonomy varying depending on the situation (Çakmak, 2006: 65). The administrative bodies of RDAs and the local and central administrations and the representatives of the private sector (NGOs) make the decisions together. The regional development agencies are a point of meeting determined by the local actors.

History of Regional Development Agencies

The first example of RDAs, which is the Tennessee Valley Agency (TVA) has been established in the USA in year 1931. The regional development agencies emerged in western European countries in the second half of twentieth century. As a result of the destructive effects of World War II and the rapid technological advancements, the interregional differences became more prominent. It also caused the establishment of regional development policies and mechanism (Ildırar, 2004: 117–118). The first RDAs established after World War II have been founded for the purposes of restructuring and to make spatial planning. The main duty of these agencies has been limited to drawing the direct foreign investments and managing the industrial parks. And then, the RDAs started to suggest solutions for other economic and social problems. In the following period, the RDAs were given more responsibilities and authorities in order to implement the regional development strategy. RDAs undertook various duties such as providing the local or regional companies with non-financial services by themselves or in partnership with other and improving the specialized social infrastructure such as business centers, business incubators, and science parks (Çakmak, 2006: 69; Toktaş et al., 2013: 670–671).

The popularization of RDAs overlaps with the emergence of regional development approach (Çakmak, 2006: 66). The economic and social changes experienced in the metropolitans during the 1960s and 1970s caused a rapid increase in the number of regional/local development agencies in these countries. The regional development practice of Western Europe led the other economies to RDA-like organizations (Çakmak, 2006: 67–68). The new practices have emerged in regional development because of the failure of traditional (classical) regional development approach that relies especially on the Keynesian policies. In this new period, in which the competition between the regions rapidly increases in parallel with the globalization, the endogenous economic growth theories and policies with the development of regions gained importance.

Are the Regional Development Agencies Solely Enough for Regional Development?

The rapid increase in the globalization propensity and the prominence of competition-oriented development strategies caused the development of the strategies to ensure the development of regions' own, create fund separately from the central government, developing cooperation, and make use of knowledge and technology. This led the central governments to delegate some of their authorities related with public services to the local administrations, to allocate more source to regional development and innovation, and to further support the local dynamics and civil initiatives (Akın, 2006: 296–297). The development agencies are generally considered as an instrument designed in order to ensure the development of the region within the scope of a new regional development paradigm (Sevinç, 2011: 46).

An important point to consider in regional development is that the RDAs cannot solely bridge all the gaps in the corporate structure. The efficiency of regional development agencies would be limited if they are structured without support of other local/regional institutions and without determining the division of labor with central institutions. For this reason, it is very important to make it possible to act in cooperation with the local actor, as well as improving and supporting the cooperation between these actors, to educate the labor force needed for the regional development, and providing government support for organizing the physical and social infrastructure (Arslan, 2005: 286–287).

Relationship Between Regional Development Policies and Regional Development Agencies Within the Scope of Regional Development Theories

High level of interregional development difference is one of the most important problems, which the developing economies face with. Contrary to the approaches advocating the public intervention in order to reduce the excessive developmental difference between the regions, there also are approaches opposing to the state intervention. There also is another regional development approach suggesting the involvement of local actors to the solution process in addition to the proportional intervention by the state.

Regarding the causes and solution suggestions for the interregional developmental difference, the economists, social scientists, as well as the politicians, exhibited different approaches. The conditions of these countries and the meaning assigned to the regional development play an important role in these differences. In the Keynesian regional development policies, the regional development has been carried out somehow in parallel with the initiative of the nation-state; however, the high level of responsibility assigned to the state increased the pressure on the budget. With the effects of crises in the global economy in 1970s, the Keynesian regional development policies have failed. Although they have limited responsibilities, RDAs played significant roles in the period, in which the Keynesian policies have been implemented.

In the neoclassical regional development model, it was recommended to reduce the activities and determining role of the state in the economy and to leave these fields to the endogenous dynamics of the market. Even though the neoclassical approach claimed that the interregional differences would be reduced using the theory of convergence, the results suggested the opposite. And it further increased the need for RDAs.

The endogenous regional development models are relied on the local/region for the regional development, emphasize the local dynamics for the competitive advantage, and stress the importance of inner potential. At this point, besides the economic infrastructure, the proper functioning of the endogenous regional development model requires the social infrastructure, incentives on R&D expenses, and the educational, medical, and other infrastructures. Moreover, the convergence assumption of the neoclassical model was rejected. In the period, in which the endogenous regional growth (development from a wider perspective) has been implemented, the number and functions of RDAs have increased especially in European Union countries.

The new regionalist approach suggested solutions for mobilizing the local sources. At this point, the state has been assigned with new responsibilities as in the endogenous regional growth model. The presence of the state as a regulatory body is a necessity for eliminating the inequalities brought by the globalization, ensuring the proper functioning of market, and protecting it. Accordingly, it is not suitable to leave the integration of regions into the international markets only to the market forces. For this reason, the role of state in supporting the regional economic development should be reconsidered.

The responsibility assigned to the State in the regional development and the integration of regions into the global economy is to act as a regulatory and (to a certain extent) supportive body. The governments organize the corporate infrastructure required for the development of markets, as well as contributing to the regional development by increasing the technologic advancements and innovative capacity through the administrative mechanisms addressing the economic efficiency. The regional development agencies constitute one of the important steps taken for this purpose. RDAs play an important role in revealing and improving the endogenous potential of the region.

Conclusion

In the period after the Industrial Revolution, the imbalances and development differences between the regions have increased after the concentration of economic activities at specific locations. All the countries experience this problem. Since the first theories on the regional development couldn't answer the problems, it became necessary to develop new theories and approaches. Especially in the endogenous regional growth, new economic geography approach, and new regionalist approach, the local/regional actors came to the forefront in the regional development.

Although the developmental differences between the regions have drawn the attention of scientists and policy-makers in the 1930s, the remarkable policies addressing these problems gained more importance after World War II (especially after 1960s). The establishment and popularization of the RDAs, which have achieved significant success in regional development especially in the developed countries, date back to those days.

During the period between the Great Depression in 1929 and 1970s, the central governments had significant dominance on the regional policies. In this period, the traditional (classical) regional development approach based on the Keynesian policies was prevailing. In the traditional regional policies, the central government plays a leading role in the decision-making process. In this development process, the state has undertaken too much load and it increased the pressures on the budget. Thus, a sufficient amount of fund couldn't be allocated to the regional development in the course of time, and the Keynesian policies couldn't yield the desired outcomes.

It can be seen that, under the effects of economic, social, and political developments since 1970, the role of the central government in the regional development policies decreased and the local administrations came to the forefront. In the new period, in which the competition between the regions increased in parallel with the globalization, the endogenous economic growth theories and policies gained importance in regional development. Since 1990s, the regional development fell away from the interventionist approach of central government and started to progress with the participation of local, regional, national, and international actors. The success that the Tennessee Valley Authority, which is the first RDA founded in the USA in 1930s, and the RDAs, which have been established in European Economic Community since 1960s, increased the importance of RDAs in regional development since 1990s. In parallel with the regional approach of development, the RDAs became more widespread. Although the first RDAs have been established for reconstruction and spatial planning purposes, they started to suggest solutions for the other economic and social problems of the region. Then, the RDAs became an important instrument of regional development policy.

References

Akın, N. (2006). Bölgesel Kalkınma Araçları ile Kalkınma Ajanslarının Uyum, İşbirliği ve Koordinasyonu, TEPAV, *Bölgesel Kalkınma ve Yönetişim Sempozyumu Kitabı*, pp. 295–304.

Amin A. (1999). An Institutional Perspective on Regional Economic Development. *International Journal of Urban and Regional Research*, 23(2), pp. 365–378.

Arslan, K. (2005). Bölgesel Kalkınma Farklılıklarının Giderilmesinde Etkin Bir Araç: Bölgesel Planlama Ve Bölgesel Kalkınma Ajansları. *İstanbul Ticaret Üniversitesi Sosyal Bilimler Dergisi*, 4(7), pp. 275–294.

Berber, M. (2017). İktisadi Büyüme ve Kalkınma. 6. Baskı. Trabzon: Celepler Matbaacılık Yayın ve Dağıtım.

Çakmak, E. (2006). Yerel Ekonomi ve Bölgesel Kalkınma Ajansları. Ankara: İmaj Yayınevi.

Çakmak, H. K. & L. Erden (2004). Yeni Bölgesel Kalkınma Yaklaşımları ve Kamu Destekleme Politikaları: Türkiye'den Bölgesel Panel Veri Setiyle Ampirik Bir Analiz. *Gazi Üniversitesi İktisadi ve İdari Bilimler Fakültesi Dergisi*, 6(3), pp. 77–96.

Dinler, Z. (2012). Bölgesel İktisat. Dokuzuncu Basım. Bursa: Ekin Yayınevi.

Dinler, Z. (2008). Bölgesel İktisat. Sekizinci Basım. Bursa: Ekin Kitabevi.

DPT (2008). Dokuzuncu Kalkınma Planı 2007–2013 Bölgesel Gelişme Özel İhtisas Komisyonu Raporu. Ankara: DPT Yayını.

Eceral, T. Ö. (2005). Bölgesel/Yerel Ekonomik Kalkınma Kuramlarının Tarihsel Süreç İçerisindeki Gelişimleri. *Ekonomik Yaklaşım*, 16(55), pp. 89–106.

Ekinci, E. D. & Ş. M. Ersungur (2013). Yeni Ekonomik Coğrafya ve Teorik Modelleri. *Atatürk Üniversitesi Sosyal Bilimler Enstitüsü Dergisi*, 17(3), pp. 205–224.

Elmas, G. (2001). Küreselleşme Sürecinde Bölgesel Dengesizlikler. Ankara: Nobel Yayın Dağıtım.

Ildırar, M. (2004). Bölgesel Kalkınma ve Gelişme Stratejileri. Ankara: Nobel Yayın Dağıtım.

Krugman, P. (1991). Increasing Returns and Economic Geography. *Journal of Political Economy*, 99(31), 483–499.

Romer, P. M. (1990). Endogenous Technological Change. *Journal of Political Economy*, 98(5), pp. 71–102.

Schmutzler, A. (1999). The New Economic Geography. *Journal of Economic Surveys*, 13(4), pp. 355–379.

Sevinç, H. (2011). Bölgesel Kalkınma Sorunsalı: Türkiye'de Uygulanan Bölgesel Kalkınma Politikaları. *Girişimcilik ve Kalkınma Dergisi*, 6(2), pp. 35–54.

Sungur, O. & H. Keskin (2009). Coğrafi Yakınlık Hala Önemli Mi? Yerel İnovasyon Modellerinden Çokyerelli Bilgi Dinamiklerine Dönüşüm. *Alanya İşletme Fakültesi Dergisi*, 1(2), pp. 107–131.

Taşcı, K., R. Akpınar, & M. E. Özsan (2011). Teoride ve Uygulamada Bölgesel Kalkınma Politikaları. 1. Baskı. Bursa: Ekin Yayınevi.

Taşlıyan, M. & H. Korkmaz (2012). Kalkınma Ajanslarının Bölgesel Sorunların Çözümünde ve Kalkınmadaki Önemi ve Katkıları: Doğaka, İka ve Zeka Örneği. II. Bölgesel Sorunlar ve Türkiye Sempozyumu Bildiriler Kitabı, pp. 365–373.

TDK (2011). İktisat Terimleri Sözlüğü. Ankara: TDK Yayınları.

Toktaş, Y., Sevinç, H., & E. Bozkurt (2013). The Evolution of Regional Development Agencies: Turkey Case, *Annales Universitatis Apulensis Series Oeconomica*, 15(2), pp. 670–681.

Türker, M. T. (2009). İçsel Büyüme Teorilerinde İçsel Büyümenin Kaynağı ve Uluslararası Ticaret Olgusuyla İlişkisi, *Dumlupınar Üniversitesi Sosyal Bilimler Dergisi*, 25, pp. 87-94.

Vatansever Deviren, N. & O. Yıldız (2014). Bölgesel Kalkınma Teorileri ve Yeni Bölgeselcilik Yaklaşımının Türkiye'deki Bölgesel Kalkınma Politikalarına Etkileri. *Akademik Bakış Dergisi*, 44, pp. 1-36.

Venables, J. (1996). Equilibrium Locations of Vertically Linked Industries. *International Economic Review*, 37(2), pp. 341-359. http://www.eurada.org/about/ (12.09.2019).

Emine Demet Ekinci Hamamcı[1]

Chapter 4 The Innovation Systems from National to Regional Level: The Role of RIS in the Regional Development

Introduction

As of the last quarter of the twentieth century, the distances across the countries began to shrink and the borders got blurred as a result of the globalization and developments in information technologies. It pushed the countries, regions, cities, and firms towards a fierce competition, by interconnecting them.

To survive this harshly competitive environment of the new age, all the economic units have to know their capacity and potential, and should make investments in order to improve their unique potential. Accordingly, it is of vital important for all the actors, especially the economic actors, to remain open to innovations standing as the most salient indicators of technological advancement and to develop strategies that can match with the shifting conditions. Yet, an innovative perspective should not be a one-time experience but rather be systematized as a sustainable and repeatable structure. In parallel with this system approach, the concept of innovation systems has emerged at the national or regional level.

National Innovation System (NIS) is a system constituted by the market or non-market institutions that are capable of influencing the speed and direction of innovation and technologic diffusion in a country. "The system is characterized based on the distinctive attributes as the specific patterns of scientific, technological and industrial specialization, specific organization of institutions, and policy priorities" (OECD, 1998: 61). The main actors in NIS are the firms, research organizations, and government. These actors enable the creation and implementation of science and technology through the networks established among them. Thus, in the competitive environment, the country could survive against her rivals maintaining own innovative capacity.

---

1 Assist. Prof., Faculty of Economics and Administrative Sciences, Department of Economics, Erzurum Technical University, Erzurum Turkey, emine.hamamci@erzurum.edu.tr

While NIS emphasizes the overall economic development of the country, its roots are based on regional dynamics. For this reason, dealing with the institutions constituting the system and the networks among these institutions at the regional scale, rather than the national level, increase the potential success of the system. The success achieved at the local level is eventually reflected on the entire country and, thus, can lead to an empowered NIS. In that way, it is stated that regional innovation system (RIS) is a sub-branch of NIS. However, the RIS strengthens the national development with its attained success on one hand, and it also determines the position of region in the global world on the other hand.

Today, RIS has become a model for all the regions aiming to achieve a more competitive, sustainable and stable development. The system bases the development potential of the regions on the creation and commercialization of technological innovation. Nonetheless, the success of the system relies not only on the universities generating knowledge or companies utilizing this knowledge. Through a holistic development process, the RIS focuses on all institutional and cultural elements creating a region and aims to transform these factors into structures that adopt innovation. Hence it is essential to be aware of the main components of the system and underlying regional features of these factors. Otherwise, the RIS could become a source that increases interregional inequalities around the world. In this direction, the research aims to address the RIS, the role of the system on regional development, and the issues required for a successful RIS.

The remaining part of this study is designed as two sections. In the first section, the NIS and RIS and the relations among them are discussed. In the second section, the role of the system in regional development and the issues required for a successful RIS are addressed.

Innovation System from National to Regional

The concept of NIS has been discussed in the literature since the 1980s (Lundvall, 2007) and rapidly put into practice by the developed countries that have adopted this concept. Nonetheless, the roots of the concept could be linked with Frederich List, a German intellectual. In his work titled "The National System of Political Economy", List (1841) stated that the way for Germany to catch up and pass Britain, which was the leading country of the time, was to create a strong innovation strategy (Freeman, 1995). According to List, the innovation strategy relies on the mental capital shaped by means of a successful education system; science and technology created by this capital and industry sector, in which the created technology can find a field of application. Suggestions proposed by List not only laid the basis for Germany's catch-up strategy (Johnson et al., 2003) but also created the foundation of today's concept of NIS (Freeman and Soete, 2003).

In the formation of NIS in the form we know today, the pioneer works are those carried out by Christopher Freeman (1982, 1987) and Bengt-Ake Lundvall (1985, 1992). Besides that, this concept keeps improving through the contributions of many researchers.

In his work titled "Technological Infrastructure and International Competitiveness", Freeman (1982) mentioned the significance of state's role in supporting the technological infrastructure and under which conditions the free trade would be in favor of the country. According to Freeman, NIS is interaction network between public and private sector organizations that create, import, modify, and spread new technologies.

Lundvall improved the concept and treated it as "theory of innovation and interactive learning" with the work of "Product Innovation and User-Producer Interaction-1985" and "National Systems of Innovation: Towards a Theory of Innovation and Interactive Learning-1992". As explained by Lundvall (1992), NIS is a system created by the factors and relations interconnected in the process of creating, spreading and using the new and economically useful knowledge in a country. Analyzing NIS from a wider perspective, Lundvall has taken all the economic structure and institutional formations stimulating the innovativeness into the system.

Richard Nelson is another scholar, who immensely contributed to NIS. In the work titled "National Innovation Systems: A Competitive Analysis-1993", Nelson has analyzed how the implementation of NIS in different countries has been affected by different institutional structures. The institutional structures include the higher education system, industrial R&D activities, communication and transportation infrastructure, monetary policy, financial system, etc. Accordingly, Nelson (1993) defined NIS as a set of organizations determining the performance of innovation and the interaction among these organizations.

To place NIS on a wider framework, Charles Edquist, (Systems of Innovation: Technologies, Institutions and Organizations-1997), has defined it as a system that not only entailed the economic factors, but also the social and political factors as well.

As can be understood from the above explanations, there has not yet been a consensus on the definition of NIS. One of the main underlying reasons is that this concept keeps on evolving from various aspects such as firm, sector (Breschi and Malerba, 1997; Cooke et al., 1997), region (Braczyk et al., 1998), etc. Another salient reason is that could be differed the fundamentals of NIS, functioning process and encountered problems in the context of developed or developing countries. In the pioneering studies on NIS, the focus has primarily been set upon developed economies. However, as this concept started to be implemented in the entire world, studies have shifted towards developing economies as well. The studies above illustrated the difference with respect to the development level of countries in the functioning of NIS (Kitanovic, 2007). A final reason may be linked with explaining NIS from a narrow or wide perspective. From a narrow perspective, NIS focuses on R&D systems producing advanced technology and science-based innovations. From a wide perspective, NIS is defined as unifying different types of knowledge and methods that are all complementary (İmamoğlu and Açıkgöz, 2012). Accordingly, from a narrow perspective, NIS entails institutes that are relevant with research and development whilst in a wide perspective it refers to the entire economic structure.

Knowledge is the main pillar of NIS. In the system, the process follows the stages of generating, spreading, and commercializing the knowledge. Main actors here are the universities that generate knowledge and educate scientists, as well as the companies investing in and executing new technologies in this process. The government is a supportive structure that provides an innovative medium required for coordinating all the actors participating in this system. Besides that, NIS can be functional only by gathering the support of a wider base. These institutes constituting the system can be classified into six groups (cited by Saatçioğlu, 2005);

- Firms engaged in technological innovation activities,
- Research institutes (public or private nonprofit research institutes, laboratories, patent office, etc.),
- Education system (Universities),
- Supporting and bridge organizations,
- Financial institutes,
- Policy-makers.

System can attain success once different actors above effectively access the knowledge on innovation and this access is the symbol of knowledge's potential for spreading (OECD, 1998). Nonetheless, in order to access this potential for spreading, it is essential for different institutional structures to have a strong interactive network.

Taking the national borders into account, NIS examines both the institutions and the network structure among them. However, analyzing NIS on a national scale could cause various problems and a perspective based on national scale could be ineffective in construing technological change. Because, most of the innovative interactions in the system primarily take place at a regional level rather than the national level (Cooke et al., 1997). This is related with the fact that the spatial distances could diminish the degree of interpersonal interaction and these interactions could be best observed at the regional level. Moreover, the innovative activities in a country mostly demonstrate an unbalanced distribution across and mainly focus on the specific regions. In addition to the economic reasons, the underlying causes for the interregional difference are historical process, geographical conditions, demographic structure, sociocultural features, and many other factors. Therefore, it seems to be an accurate approach to analyze the innovation system at a regional level (cited by Lenger, 2006).

RIS is an institutional infrastructure supporting the innovation within the production structure of a region (Asheim and Coenen, 2005). In other words, it is the compilation of contributions of the firm, university and government to the innovation process on a regional scale.

Cooke et al. (1997) defined RIS as a collective order based on microconstitutional regulation. The collective order bases on the characters of general associational, cooperative, and trust-dependent These characters make learning process valuable within the boundaries of a region. Cooke (2005: 3) then has updated this definition, where regional boundaries stand out, as "interacting knowledge generation and exploitation subsystems linked to global, national and other regional systems".

RIS having a normative and descriptive approach underlines the economic and technological organizations of a region and examines how technological development takes place within this region. Thus, RIS has been widely adopted in order to highlight the policies that increase the innovative capacity of regions (Doloreux and Parto, 2005).

Since the early 1990s, RIS has begun to play a central role in the regional policy and the focus on NISs has then been directed at a regional level. There are a range of factors underlying shift of the focus. Firstly, the increased attention on innovation has affected local level in addition to national level; therefore, regions have aimed to be more innovative. Secondly, as previously mentioned, it has been explored that local dynamics better explained the innovation process; and hence, it was thought that the creation of a unique innovation system to each region would accelerate the success. Lastly, as of 1970s, traditional regional development policies lost their effectiveness, and this has led to seek new approaches. These new approaches have directed the regions towards policies aiming to increase their innovative capacity. At the end of all these changes, regions have started to construct their own RISs in order to be a member of global world, gain competitive advantage and catch the evolving technology.

For the last 30 years, RIS has been recognized as one of the most salient strategies of regional economic development. However, RIS has a very long theoretical background. The roots of the system are supported by many theories ranging from Marshall's industrial region concept, economic geography, and innovative environment approach to NIS (Asheim et al., 2011). In this regard, RIS is considered as a sub-branch of the NIS and also bolsters whole national system while developing its own region.

Similar to NIS, the main actors are also the universities organizing scientific research and the companies commercializing the knowledge on RIS. Government plays role as a regulatory structure facilitating and supporting the proper functioning of the system. It is also possible to classify these actors into supply and demand sides, as well as the intermediaries (TÜSİAD, 2003: 150):

- Supply side: research institutions creating knowledge, which mainly belong to the public sector.
- Demand side: firms or market utilizing scientific and technological output. The firms usually attain technology through the means of experts, consultants, intercompany research, and several other ways.
- Intermediaries: innovation support organizations, regulatory agencies, financial institutions, etc. that act as a bridge between supply and demand sides.

The development of RIS depends on integrating the innovation skills of supply or demand side with the interactive learning (Lundvall, 1988). In this system, the relations serve for spreading the knowledge, whereas the interactions serve for generating and learning new sets of knowledge. To ensure that interactive innovation process takes place in the RIS, it is important for knowledge to be tacit or codified. The success or effectiveness of the system could differ depending on the means of attaining tacit knowledge. Tacit or codified knowledge is obtained from gained experience with production, marketing and distribution processes, and covers settled and improved behavior patterns over time (Kumral and Değer, 2005).

The functioning of the system is based on the cooperation and the chain-linked formed by the local actors. The "chain-linked", introduced by Kline and Rosenberg (1986), is a model analyzing both supply push and demand pull in relation with the scientific knowledge. Chain-linked model enables the agents to learn through interaction, and to create and share the new knowledge among them. Therefore, the innovation system exhibits a complex structure (Sternberg, 2007). This chain-linked structure not only encompasses the unique environment of the region but also entails the environment on a larger macroeconomic

The Innovation Systems from National to Regional Level 77

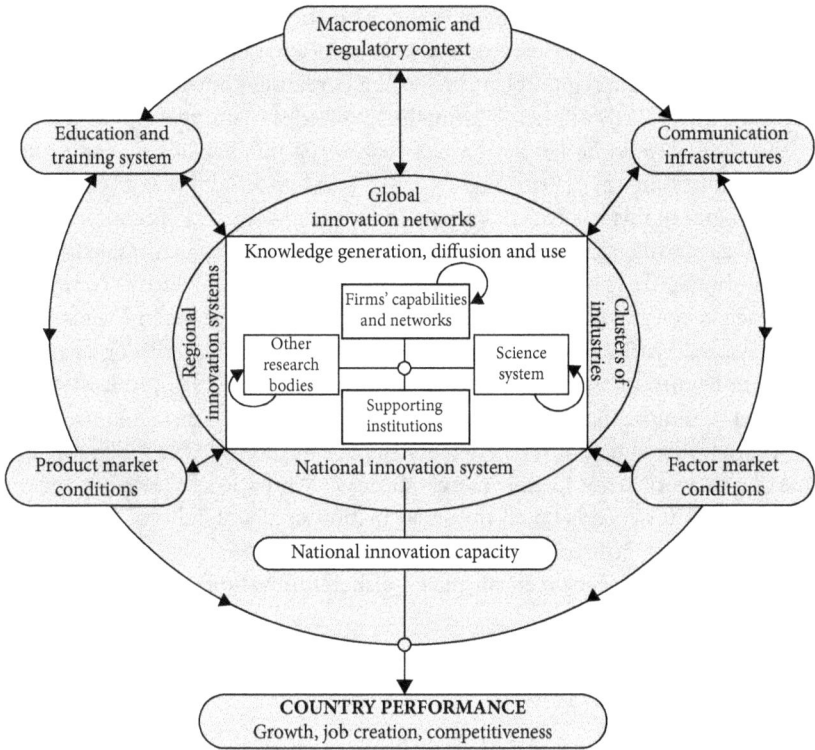

Fig. 1: Actors and Linkages in the Innovation Systems
Source: OECD, 1999: 23

structure and various infrastructures in this environment. Therefore, with its complex structure, RIS is expected to operate as an open system. In this sense, the local actors of RIS (TÜSİAD, 2003: 150):

- Interact with similar agents outside the system (International agreements between university and research centers, international relations among firms, interregional/international knowledge exchange among technology centers, exchange programs among educational institutes, etc.).
- Cooperate with different actors outside the system (Contractual researches that firms sign with external research centers, foreign researcher exchange programs between firms and education institutes, activities that expand outside the regional system of technology transfer institutes, etc.).

To ensure the success of RIS, the existence of institutions laying the foundation of system in the region is vital. Primarily, quantity and quality of universities and research centers in a region plays vital role in creating knowledge (Fritsch and Slavtchev, 2007). Yet, commercializing the knowledge is as important as creating it. The system could be fed by the fact that a vast number of firms and other sectors supporting these firms with forward and backward linkages are located in the region. In this regard RIS supports sectoral agglomeration economies and regional clustering. Via spatial proximity, these clusters offer a favorable foundation for interactive learning (Andersson and Karlsson, 2006). Firms, competing with each other, but cooperating, could share knowledge and allow the knowledge to spread with clustering. Hence, in regional cluster, a range of externalities from labor pool to knowledge pool emerge, and the RIS becomes stronger. However, the most significant issue in the RIS is that relations between system actors are in the nature of the network structure (TÜSİAD, 2003). Creating this type of a network is not feasible merely through economic structure of a region. Furthermore, it depends on all the socio-institutional and cultural characteristics of the region. For such reasons, the regions need to achieve total economic development in order to create an accomplished innovation system.

Regional Innovation System as a Strategy in Regional Development

The regional development, which is a consequence of the industrial society, is discussed as three periods. The first period corresponds to the period between World War II and 1970s, in which the traditional approach played role. In the traditional regional development policies, there was a system, which was directed by a central institution referring to top-down decision-making process. In this system, it was aimed to eliminate the developmental differences between the regions by focusing on the underdeveloped regions and, thus, a balanced development approach was put in practice. However, "those policies fell short in adapting to the new conditions brought by the globalization and large economic supports fairly allocated by the government to many regions couldn't yield the desired results... Thus, the long-term benefits of the state aids started to be questioned" (Kumral, 2008: 5–6).

Because of the economic crises experienced in the 1970s, the state aids started to be questioned more severely and it caused the space to enter into a restructuring process. Thus, a new period, not the regions relying on the state aid but those putting their own potential into practice gain the success, has started. It was a transition period and the foundations of today's regional development policies have been laid in that period. In 1990s, the new regional development approach created by the information society, which has lasted until today, has been initiated.

In the new period, it could be clearly seen that the importance of the concept "region" has significantly increased in both theory and policy implementations. In this organization, an understanding that is exactly opposite to the traditional approach is in practice and, rather than the top-down decisions, a system functioning from bottom-up and utilizing the limited sources more efficiently is constructed. Thus, considering the regions' own potentials – necessities, weaknesses, and strengths – are given priority and the fields, in which the region will specialize, is determined based on the comparative advantages. Moreover, by placing the "competition" perception at the core of system, the competition of the region with both other regions within the country and those in other countries is stimulated and it is aimed to achieve the instruments needed for this purpose. At this point, "the concepts of new era such as information, capacity of creating knowledge, and innovative capacity come to the forefront and they are accepted as the fundamental components making a region more attractive within the global competition" (Özer, 2008: 393). In the new system, another important point is the success of local actors. These actors are the provincial organization of the central authority, municipalities, NGOs, universities, chambers of commerce and industry, development agencies, firms, etc. The corporate infrastructure of local actors and the cooperation between these actors have positive effects on the competitive capacity.

In sum, it can be stated that the regional policies brought by the new world order are based on an understanding having characteristics specific to the space and yielding the region's competitive advantage by prioritizing the local actors. The key factor yielding the competitive advantage is the innovation. For this reason, both the academic society and the policy-makers develop and implement new models/ideas explaining the relationship between innovation and regional development. Some of these models are new industrial districts, innovative environment, learning regions, and RISs.

These models have different names but the same objective, which is to grow the regions with their own sources and capacities and to make them strategic actors in the world. Moreover, emphasizing a system consisting of the interaction between different actors, these models aimed to have the dynamics of industry and technology to be better understood (Lenger, 2006).

Among these models highlighting the system, the RIS aims to mobilize the region-specific sources and to maintain the process in cooperation with the local actors.

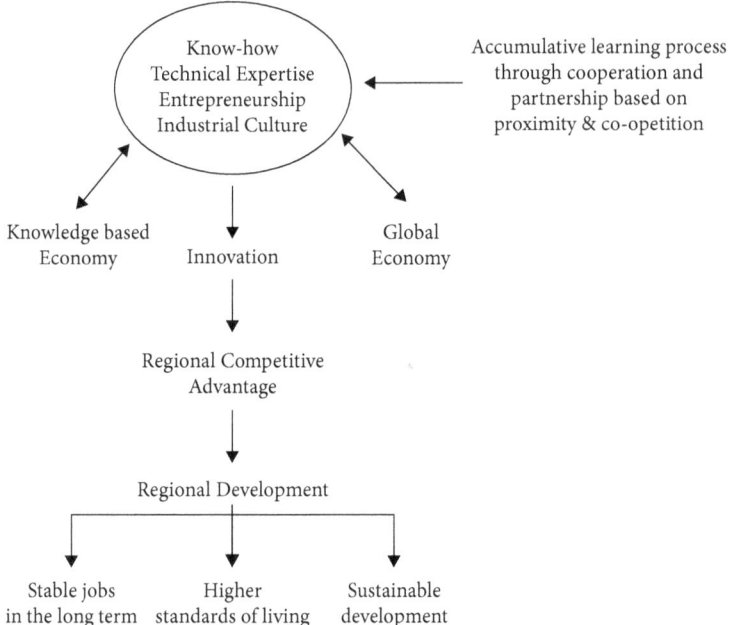

Fig. 2: Role of Regional Innovation System in the Regional Development
Source: Landabaso and Reid, 2005: 26

As stated before, RIS has been introduced in the 1990s for the first time. In the course of time, it became one of the main development strategies of the regions aiming to achieve regional competitive advantage, ensure corporate development, make use of technologic advancement by improving the innovation capacity, and intensify the regional cooperation. In Fig. 2, the role of RIS in the regional development is illustrated.

According to Fig. 2, the regions create innovation by integrating their technical capacities, entrepreneurial spirit, and industrial culture, and then the innovations yield regional competitive advantage. Thus, by ensuring the sustainable development of the region in the long–term, it would be possible to provide the residents with stable job opportunities and higher life standards.

Nowadays, the importance of RIS for the regional development is unquestionable. However, RIS that is very important for the regional development might also cause an increase in regional inequalities. If the regions have difficulties or delay in establishing their own innovation system, they would be defeated by their rivals

The Innovation Systems from National to Regional Level   81

in global competition. For this reason, it is very important to successfully understand the system, to meet the necessary conditions of the system because this system incorporates not only the economic components but also social, historical, corporate ones, etc. First of all, the innovation system established by a region is primarily specific to that region. For this reason, RIS has different characteristics. These characteristics might be listed as follows (Dökmen, 2009: 52–53)

- *RIS varies depending on the spatial components.* The geographical, historical, economic, and sociocultural factors play a role in this differentiation. For instance; from the economic aspect, the regions focus on different industries according to the comparative advantages. For this reason, the innovation systems established and needed by the regions differ. Even the regions having the same industry may have specific routines, norms, and traditions and, thus, the RISs may differ among the regions.
- *RIS considers the activities of innovative actors of the region in the network structure and this network lays the foundation of the system.* The network structure incorporates firms, research and technology institutions, innovation support units, venture capital companies, and local/central administrations. The institutional and cultural structure of the region determines the network structure.
- *The tacit knowledge is important for the emergence of the interactive innovation process in the RISs.* The faster and more effective the local actors access the tacit knowledge, the more successful the system is.
- *The RISs put the innovation on the basis of evolutional development.*

According to the evolutional approach, the RIS consists of five components. Doloreux (2002: 252) lists these components as follows;

- Processes of change are determined by unstable conditions in markets as well as institutional and organizational configurations within economies.
- Externalities and spatial agglomeration factors play an important role in the process of change.
- Innovation is a significant factor in overall economic performance.
- Institutions set up norms, rules and conventions.
- Learning, creation, access, process, and diffusion are seen as fundamental socio-economic imperatives in the system.

RIS consists of subsystems that are in interaction with each other. These systems are knowledge generation and diffusion subsystem, knowledge application and exploitation subsystem and regional policy subsystem (Cooke et al., 2007: 55). These systems and their components are presented in Fig. 3.

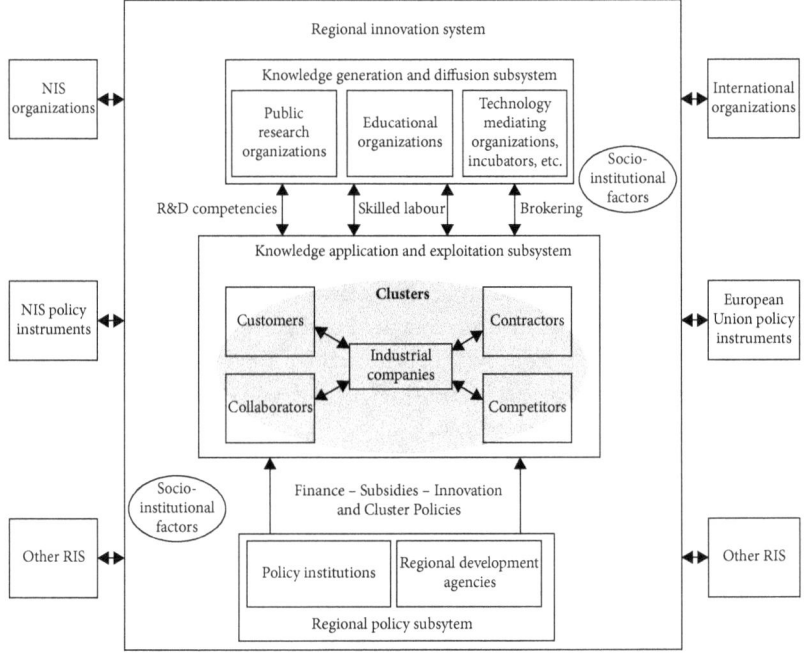

Fig. 3: Interactive Subsystems of Regional Innovation System
Source: Cooke et al., 2007: 55

Knowledge generation and diffusion subsystem lays the foundation of information infrastructure and is the first step to RIS. The most important objective of this subsystem is to trigger and support the enterprises creating the innovation. This system consists of public research institutions, education institutions, and technology intermediaries. The institutions create and diffuse both coded and tacit technological knowledge (Autio, 1998).

Among these institutions, the education institutions and especially the universities play a special role because these institutions both create the information and educate the labor that will produce knowledge. Thus, they provide the human source that the other institutions necessitate. However, as well as the presence of education and research institutions in the region, their quality is also very important. At this point, the education institutions' capacity and understanding of being informed of general conjuncture in the world significantly influences the success of system. Another important factor influencing the success is the other actors' outlook on the research institutions. For instance; "the firms may sometimes not see these supply-side institutions to be insufficient in terms of expertise, knowledge, and support; the relationships between the institutions cannot turn into permanent cooperation because of the lack of confidence" (cited by Aydoğan, 2011). In fact, it is a problem arising from the lack of social capital and it prevents the institutions from interacting with each other. Another important point is the local society's outlook on the science. The innovative perspective would exactly be positively influenced if the local peoples appreciate and internalize the science. This perspective depends on the institutional and cultural characteristics of the region. For this reason, if the technologic innovation is combined with the appropriate institutional and cultural structure, then a holistic development process may be achieved (Kee, 2009).

Knowledge application and exploitation subsystem incorporates firms, firms' clients, suppliers, rivals, and partners. In this system, there are commercial activities inclining to aggregate (Autio, 1998).

The key actors of this subsystem are the firms. For this reason, the outlook of firms on the innovation influences the proper functioning of both this subsystem and whole RIS. The firm may produce innovation by means of its own departments but also outsource it as well.

The factors influencing the outlook of firms on the innovation can be classified into three groups (Doğan and Albeni, 2015: 289–292):

- Entrepreneur-Oriented Determinants: Entrepreneur's age, educational status, gender, human capital, belief in innovation, risk-taking capacity, openness to change, personal specialty, experience, personal learning and knowledge, values, creativeness, and character type.
- Firm-Oriented Determinants: Parameters such as the firm's year of establishment, age, activity period, scale, and regional economic performance. Moreover, the structural complexity, previous innovations, rival orientation, and customer orientation are also classified into this group.
- Environment-Oriented Determinants: The rapid environmental change, the uncertainty arising from this change, and gradually increasing competition are considered within this context.

As listed above, there are many factors influencing the outlook of the firm on the innovation. These factors range between personal characteristics of entrepreneur and firm's quality to the regional and national conditions and international economic relations. In such a complex structure, it is not possible to determine the key common characteristics of innovative firms and to classify the firms as innovative and non-innovative. The important point here is to show the firms the potential advantages of innovation. In other words, it is important to provide them with the culture of innovation.

The most important factor influencing the success of knowledge application and exploitation subsystem is the intensity of network structure among the firms. This intensity is significantly influenced by the clustering. The cluster can be defined as a group consisting of firms and relevant institutions that are geographically close and linked to each other and have common and complementary characteristics (Porter 2000).

The firms trigger the clustering by gathering the forward and backward linkages, suppliers, rivals, and partners in the same location. The cluster formed will then establish a relationship with other industries, research institutions, etc. by progressing the process. The clustering provides the region with knowledge and labor pools. Thus, an economic network incorporating rivals in cooperation with each other may be achieved. However, the establishment of such relationship network is based primarily on the physical capital of region and then on the individuals with entrepreneurial spirit. Moreover, other characteristics (geographical, historical, corporate, demographical, etc.) establishing the region's comparative advantage also influence the region's economic structure. For this reason, the commercialization of knowledge requires the regions to turn their disadvantage into advantage and attract the companies to their region.

Regional policy subsystem refers to ensuring the interaction between firms and institutions, increasing the learning capacity of the region, and mobilizing the internal potential of the region (Dökmen, 2009).

This subsystem consists of political institutions and regional development agencies. The political institutions refer to the central and local administrations and all the other local actors affecting the innovative perspective and cooperation.

In the RISs, the main responsibilities of the central administration and its local organization can be listed as follows;

- Integrating the RISs with the NIS,
- Supporting the innovative actors constituting the system,
- Encouraging the network structure between the actors in the system,
- Encouraging the regional leadership rather than controlling the innovation process in the region,
- Playing entrepreneurial and accelerating role in the innovation process,
- Acting in close cooperation with private sector and other actors in the region.

The central administration plays a supra-regional role for the RIS and it eases the functioning of system. However, the local administration plays a central role in

RIS. The local administrations are the actors shaping the policies by considering the spatial differences and based on the spatial dynamics. They play important role especially in the mobilization of internal dynamics of the region and the implementation of clustering strategies together with the innovation policies (Dökmen, 2009). To what extent the local administrations play role in the system depends on the administrative structure of the country.

These subsystems integrate with each other and constitute the RIS. However, RIS is an open system. For this reason, it depends on and incorporates the NIS, other regional systems in the country and other countries, and international organizations (Cooke et al., 2007).

The RIS depends on the interaction between knowledge generation and diffusion subsystem and knowledge application and exploitation subsystem and the one using and benefiting from them establish different relationships with each other and within themselves depending on the knowledge spillover, source and human capital flows. These relationships are related to the socio-institutional structure (Dökmen, 2009).

The socio-institutional structure establishes the cooperation required for new technologies and changes together with the new technology developed. Fig. 4 illustrates the relationship between technologic change and socio-corporate structure.

The present socio-institutional structure may resist to the change because of the lasting inertia and it delays the adaptation to the new conditions (Perez, 2004). However, the new technological potential both creates new paradigms and applies economic and social pressure for the change in old socio-institutional structure. Thus, in addition to the emergence of a new socio-institutional structure, also the economy grows up. However, the completion of the change is a very difficult process because of the factors laying the foundation of socio-institutional structure.

The socio-institutional structure consists of written documents such as law, codes, regulations, and statutes and the unwritten documents such as region's behavior patterns, routines, cooperation culture, attitude towards innovation and technology, etc. (Trippl, 2006). If the socio-institutional structure is seen as an iceberg, then the legal regulations constitute the visible part. The real structure, which is the informal values, is the philosophy of the region. The factors influencing this philosophy are the geographical, demographical, historical, cultural, religious, and all other aspects. In sum, all the characteristics of a region from past to future referring to their evolutional heritage affect the socio-institutional structure. In other words, it is affected by all the characteristics carried from its own path. And, this structure shapes the innovation system of the region. For this reason, it is not possible to establish a common model or factor set that will ensure the success of RIS for all the regions. However, by comparing the RISs, the differences and similarities can be detected and a typology can be achieved in this parallel. Doloreux (2002) listed five typologies in his work.

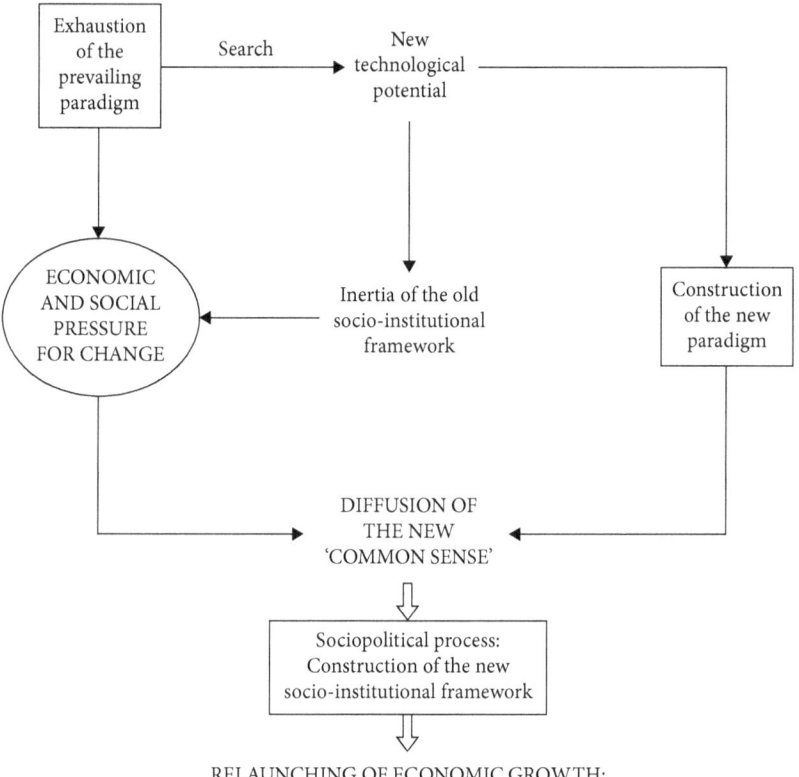

Fig. 4: The Process of Creative Destruction in Long-Wave Transitions
Source: Perez, 2004: 237

As seen above, there are different region types in the world and different innovation systems consisting of the regions. Besides that, it can be seen that RIS ensures success in regions creating a collective order with the characteristics of general associational, cooperative, and trust-dependent. The main factor that will

Tab. 1: Five Typologies Addressing Differences Between RSI

Typologies	Categories
Regional potential	***Region with strong capacity:*** The regions having a strong structure with universities, research institutions, and technology and innovation institutions for technology and innovation. ***Region with medium capacity:*** The regions that have the institutions aiming the innovation but also have weaknesses in terms of innovation support organizations. ***Region with low capacity:*** The regions, in which the cooperation between university and industry cannot be achieved and the organizational interaction does not occur.
Level of regional integration	***Top-down perspective:*** The BIS that is compatible with the national innovation system and corresponds to its smaller form. For this reason, it is not specific to any region and it completely reflects the national system. ***Bottom-up perspective***: The BIS that has region-specific characteristics and relations. Thus, it is specific to the region.
Social cohesion	***Regionalized national innovation system***: The BIS, in which the production structure and corporate infrastructure have been established in the region but which is not a part of NIS from the functional aspect. ***Territorially embedded innovation system***: The BIS, in which the production structure and corporate infrastructure have been internalized in the region.
Governance modes of technology transfer	***Grassroots:*** The region, in which the technology transfer is locally encouraged. ***Network:*** The region, which makes the technology transfer available at different spatial levels (local, regional, national, and global). ***Dirigiste:*** The region, in which the technology transfer is performed outside and top of the region by the central administration.
Regional barriers	***Organizational thinness RSI:*** The region, in which there is no actor to provide the collective learning. ***Fragmented RSI:*** The region, in which there is the lack of local cooperation and mutual trust between the actors. ***Lock-in RSI:*** The region that is an old industrial zone, in which the old-fashioned technologies are dominant.

Source: Doloreux, 2002: 256–258.

establish the collective order is the people living in the region. The society has to create dynamism in a collective order. At this point, by investing in the physical, human and social capital of the region, they should enrich their heritage from history in this time, and thus build the future on a more solid structure.

Conclusion

In the last three decades, the fundamental dynamics of regional development understanding have changed greatly, and in the meantime, by emphasizing on global competition, an innovative perspective based on the information society has come to the fore. In this perspective, the concepts of new era such as information, capacity of creating knowledge, and innovative capacity come to the forefront and they are accepted as the fundamental components making a region more attractive within the global competition. In the period when innovation is seen as the basis of development, many models have emerged to explain the relationship between innovation and regional development. One of these models is the RIS.

RIS is an institutional infrastructure supporting the innovation within the production structure of a region. Based on the cooperation of all actors in the region, RIS mobilizes the existing resources of the region. In addition, the system supports regional clustering, and explores how technological innovation takes place within this cluster. However, RIS does not rely solely on technological innovation, but also on institutional and cultural innovation. In this respect, the RIS reveals a total economic development and bolsters itself with this economic development.

Although RIS is one of the main development strategies of the regions today, this strategy does not have a common model or factor set that will ensure the success of it for all the regions. The main underlying reasons is that RIS varies depending on the spatial components. RIS includes all socio-institutional and cultural characteristics in the region and is influenced by them. These characteristics have emerged with a long historical past and reflect the evolutionary heritage of the region.

Evolutionary heritage can now lead to an increase regional inequalities by giving advantage to some regions to establish a successful RIS. However, this is not a reason for disadvantaged regions to give up. These regions should now enrich what carried from the past in order to create a successful RIS and increase their competitiveness. Thus, instead of leaving their future to chance, regions will build it on the structure laid the foundations of today.

References

Andersson, M. and Karlsson, C. (2006). Regional Innovation Systems in Small and Medium-Sized Regions. In Johansson, B., Karlsson C. and Stough, R. (Eds.), *The Emerging Digital Economy Entrepreneurship, Clusters and Policy* (pp. 55–82). Berlin: Springer.

Asheim, B. T., Lawton Smith, H. and Oughton, C. (2011). Regional Innovation Systems: Theory, Empirics and Policy. *Regional Studies*, 45(7), 875-891.

Asheim, B. T. and Coenen, L. (2005). Knowledge Bases and Regional Innovation Systems: Comparing Nordic Clusters. *Research Policy*, 34, 1173-1190.

Autio, E. (1998). Evaluation of RTD in Regional Systems of Innovation. *European Planning Studies*, 6(2), 131-140.

Aydoğan B. (2011). *Bölgesel Ekonomik Kalkınmanın Yeni Pusulası: Bölgesel İnovasyon Stratejileri (RIS) Mersin Örneği*. (Yayınlanmamış Y. Lisans Tezi). Niğde Türkiye: Niğde Üniversitesi, Sosyal Bilimler Enstitüsü.

Braczyk, H., Cooke, P. and Heindenreich, M. (1998). *Regional Innovation Systems*. London: UCL Press.

Breschi, S. and Malerba, F. (1997). Sectoral Innovation Systems. In Edquist C. (Ed.), *Systems of Innovation: Technologies, Institutions and Organizations*. London: Pinter Publishers.

Cooke, P., Laurentis, C.D., Tödtling, F. and Trippl, M. (2007). *Regional Knowledge Economies Markets, Clusters and Innovation*. Northampton, USA: Edward Elgar.

Cooke, P. (2005). Regionally Asymmetric Knowledge Capabilities and Open Innovation. *Research Policy*, 34(8), 1128-1149.

Cooke, P., Uranga, G. and Exterbarria, G. (1997). Regional Innovation Systems: Institutional and Organizational Dimensions, *Research Policy*, 26, 475-491.

Doğan B. Albeni, M. (2015). Türk İmalat Sanayisinde Firma Düzeyinde Yeniliğin Belirleyicileri Üzerine Bir Araştırma. *Süleyman Demirel Üniversitesi, İktisadi ve İdari Bilimler Fakültesi Dergisi*, C.20(S.2), 287-298.

Doloreux, D. and Parto, S. (2005). Regional Innovation Systems: Current Discourse and Unresolved Issues. *Technology in Society*, 27(2), 133-153.

Doloreux, D. (2002). What We Should Know About Regional Systems of Innovation. *Technology in Society*. 24, 243-263.

Dökmen, G. (2009). *Bölgesel Kalkınmada Yenilik Sistemleri ve Devletin Rolü: Türkiye Örneği*. (Yayınlanmamış Doktora Tezi). İzmir, Türkiye: Dokuz Eylül Üniversitesi, Sosyal Bilimler Enstitüsü.

Freeman, C. and Soete, L. (2003). *Yenilik İktisadı (Çev. E. Türkcan)*. Ankara: TÜBİTAK Yayınları.

Freeman, C. (1995). The 'National System of Innovation' in Historical Perspective. *Cambridge Journal of Economics*, 19, 5-24.

Freeman, C. (1987). *Technology Policy and Economic Performance: Lessons from Japan*. London: Pinter Publishers.

Freeman, C. (1982). Technological Infrastructure and International Competitiveness. Draft paper submitted to the OECD Ad hoc group on Science, technology and competitiveness, August 1982, mimeo.

Fritsch, M. and Slavtchev, V. (2007). What Determines the Efficiency of Regional Innovation Systems. *Jena Economic Research Papers*. Friedrich-Schiller-University and the Max Planck Institute of Economics. Paper No: 2007–006.

İmamoğlu Salih, Z. and Açıkgöz A. (2012). Milli Yenilik Sistemleri ve Türkiye için Öneriler, *Girişimcilik ve İnovasyon Yönetimi Dergisi*, Cilt 1, Sayı 1, ss: 69–96.

Johnson, B., Edquist, C. and Lundvall, B.-Å. (2003). Economic Development and the National System of Innovation Approach. https://smartech.gatech.edu/handle/1853/43154.

Kee, K. H. (2009). Alternative Regional Development Based on Decentralization and Innovation. *6th Global Forum on Reinventing Government*. May 24–27, Seoul. https://www.researchgate.net/publication/254221251_Alternative_Regional_Development_Based_on_Decentralization_and_Innovation.

Kitanovic, J. (2007). The Applicability of the Concept of National Innovation Systems to Transition Economies, *Innovation: Management, Policy & Practice*, 9(1), 28–45.

Kline, S. J. and Rosenberg. N. (1986). An Overview of Innovation. In Landau R. and Rosenberg N. (Eds.), *The Positive Sum Game*. Washington, DC: National Academy Press.

Kumral N. (2008). "Bölgesel Rekabet Gücünü Artırmaya Yönelik Politikalar". Ege University Working Papers in Economics, Paper No: 08/02.

Kumral, N. and Değer, Ç. (2005). Sanayi Rekabet Performansı Endeksi: Türkiye NUTS1 Bölgeleri Örneği. In İçinde Erlat, H. (Ed.), *Bölgesel Gelişme Stratejileri ve Akdeniz Ekonomisi* (ss. 177–197). Ankara: Türkiye Ekonomi Kurumu.

Landabaso, M. and Reid A. (2005). Developing Regional Innovation Strategies: The European Commission as Animateur. In Morgan, K. and Nauwelaers C. (Eds.), *Regional Innovation Strategies: The Challenge for Less-Favoured Regions* (pp. 18–39). London, UK: Taylor & Francis e-Library.

Lenger, A. (2006). Bölgesel Yenilik Sistemleri ve Devletin Rolü: Türkiye'deki Kurumsal Yapı ve Devlet Üniversiteleri. *Ege Akademik Bakış Dergisi*, 6(2), 141–155.

Lundvall, B.-Å. (2007). National Innovation Systems-Analytical Concept and Development Tool. *Industry and Innovation*, 14(1), 95-119.

Lundvall, B.-Å. (1992). *National Systems of Innovation: Towards a Theory of Innovation and Interactive Learning*. London: Anthem Press.

Lundvall, B.-Å. (1988). Innovation as an Interactive Process. from User-Producer Interaction to National Systems of Innovation. In Dosi, G., Freeman, C., Nelson, R., Silverberg, G., and Soete, L. (Eds.), *Technical Change and Economic Theory* (pp. 349-369). London: Pinter.

Lundvall, B.-Å. (1985). *Product Innovation and User-Producer Interaction*. Aalborg: Aalborg University Press.

Nelson, R. (1993). *National Innovation Systems: A Comparative Analysis*. New York: Oxford University Press.

OECD. (1999). *Managing National Innovation Systems*. Paris: OECD Publishing.

OECD. (1998). *Technology, Productivity and Job Creation: Best Policy Practices*. Paris: OECD Publishing.

Özer, Y. E. (2008). Küresel Rekabet-Bölgesel Kalkınma Ajansları ve Türkiye, *Review of Social Economic & Business Studies*, 9(10), 389-408.

Perez, C. (2004). Technological Revolutions, Paradigm Shifts and Socio-Institutional Change. In Reinert, E. S. (Ed.), *Globalization, Economic Development and Inequality: An Alternative Perspective* (pp. 217-241). Cheltenham, UK: Edward Elgar.

Porter, M. E. (2000). Location, Competition, and Economic Development: Local Clusters in a Global Economy. *Economic Development Quarterly*, 14(1), 15-34.

Saatçioğlu, C. (2005). Ulusal Yenilik Sistemi Çerçevesinde Uygulanan Bilim ve Teknoloji Politikaları: İsrail, AB ve Türkiye Örneği, *Anadolu Üniversitesi Sosyal Bilimler Dergisi*, Cilt:5, Sayı:1, ss:179-198.

Sternberg, R. (2007). Entrepreneurship, Proximity and Regional Innovation Systems. *Tijdschrift voor Economische en Sociale Geografie*, 98(5), pp. 652-666.

Trippl, M. (2006). *Cross-Border Regional Innovation Systems*. SRE-Discussion Papers, 2006/05. Vienna: Institut für Regional- und Umweltwirtschaft, WU Vienna University of Economics and Business.

TÜSİAD. (2003). *Ulusal İnovasyon Sistemi, Kavramsal Çerçeve, Türkiye İncelemesi ve Ülke Örnekleri*. Ankara: TÜSİAD publish.

İdil Gülnihal Yazici[1]

Chapter 5 The Process of Regional Development in Turkey and the Interaction of Non-governmental Organizations

Introduction

In the European Union (EU), national qualities and policies are regarded as impulsive powers of development. Since the very beginning of regional policies, equal development of all regions has been one of the essential statements of all the EU policies; however, the disparities between regions in a state were and even now are more than national disparities. "During the last decade of the 20th century, widespread concern was expressed about an integrative role of regional policy and planning in furthering the economic, social, and political coherence of Europe" (Balchin, Sýkora, & Bull, 1999, s. 1). For instance, The Organization for Economic Co-operation and Development (OECD) regions, in terms of noticeable disparities in economic performance like incomes, employment rate, productivity, comparative advantages, levels of development, or public policies, show more disparities than that of OECD states (Keskin & Sungur, 2010, s. 274). Thus, one objective has always been on the agenda: developing underdeveloped regions even in the developed Member States. These regional disparities, unemployment, and lack of infrastructure required new policies. Rather than a centralized one, states focused on more efficient regional systems to be able to change the living standards in poor and disadvantaged regions and to improve developing and developed regions more.

When Turkey realized the relation between regional development and development of a country, it initiated regional development plans. Still, the term "region" mostly meant geographical diversities rather than economic or social ones. "Seven regions were created in the 1940s. They have neither an administrative status nor an institutional structure. Therefore, the regional level did not have political reality" (Bafoil & Kaya, 2009). Regional policies supported different plans for each region. However, as the regions were divided according to their geographical similarities, which seemed irrelevant from time to time, it was hard to identify the exact needs of a specific region. A process started as a

---

[1] Ph. D. Candidate and Lecturer, İstanbul University, 34000, İstanbul/TURKEY

geographical terms shaped regional planning and development in the national plans. This framework that prioritized the underdeveloped and emerging regions affected the whole economic and political process in Turkey.

Regional Development did not have a separate part in Development Plans till 1963; it was only used as means of development of the country as Turkey needed to focus on establishing a new country and making eligible to be able to compete with other countries. Therefore, the main objective of the planning caused regional disparities and industrialization and social service industry was depended on some cities (Keskin & Sungur, 2010, s. 282).

With development plans, Turkey prepared a paper reporting benefits and harms to analyze processes and to improve new ones. From the traditional point to the modern regional development perception, Turkey had eight Five-Year Development Plans (1963–2005) and two Development Plans, which will be referred as Development Plans in general. These plans play an essential role to explore the aim of Turkey both on national and international levels. According to State Planning Organization (SPO), pre-1960 plans followed statist policy while 1960–1980 plans followed mixed capitalism plans and 1980–2000 plans followed liberalist and strategic policies. "The important substitution policies" that had been critical in industrialization before 1980 replaced with "open economy" after 1980 (Devlet Planlama Teşkilatı). The aim was to reduce the burden of the developed and developing cities and move industrialization and goods and services to every region. In this study, it is possible to see the Development Plans and regional development policies of Turkey as the changes in time are visible via Development Plans.

The EU-Turkey relations have changed the concept of regions. Contrary to traditional regionalization in Turkey, a new way was drawn by the EU policies in order to specify the needs of less favored regions. After the Helsinki Summit of 1999, a pre-accession strategy for Turkey was prepared and regional development was part of it. This connection aimed:

- Strengthening the political dialogue, with a particular focus on human rights issues, and involving Turkey in Community positions and activities under the CFSP;
- Coordinating all sources of EU financial assistance in the run-up to accession within a single instrument;
- Providing for Turkey's full participation in Community programs and agencies;
- Adopting an accession partnership, linked to a national program for the adoption of the acquis;

- Establishing mechanisms similar to those in the Europe Agreements for monitoring the implementation of the accession partnership, and starting with Turkey a process of analyzing the acquis with a view to harmonizing legislation and practices (EUR-Lex, 2005).

The importance of non-governmental organizations (NGOs) has changed with the EU legislation. The EU has focused on deepening and widening with the help of subsidiarity principle since the Maastricht Treaty. The more local authorities got involved the more the decision-making process evolved in the EU. Thus, NGOs gained importance in order to develop decentralized policy of development. The subsidiary and transparency policies developed relations with civil societies, and the EU aimed to become an institution not only served by centralized institutions but also shaped by volunteered and eager citizens.

The model of economic process had to change and so did the priorities. As poverty and social inclusion became problematic within the EU, the importance of NGOs was indicated and NGOs were considered to be one of the best actors to deal with the problems. Still, with financial problems, migration, poverty and populist problems the EU needs NGOs more than before. With respect to this understanding, Turkey started indicating the importance of civil society groups and NGOs in Turkey, even in its official statements. However, the improvement of the civil dialogue with NGOs has been harder than the EU process.

This study aims to show the interaction and support of NGOs in regional development process and to analyze the process Turkey has had since the first planned development period. This study focuses on "Regional Policies in the EU" as it is important to understand the structure of the regional policies to be able to analyze the present situation and the expectations of the EU. As the policies for the candidate and potential candidate countries are based on the internal policies of the EU, this chapter clarifies the historical background and financial aid instruments of the EU. The study also shows "Regional Development in Turkey" with its National Development Plans and the EU financial aids in Turkey. The development of regional policies and the role of NGOs in the national plans will reflect the potential movements of Turkey in the future. Also, it clarifies the similarities or differences between the EU and Turkey. Lastly, the study will try to clarify "NGOs and their roles in Turkey" to focus on NGOs and their development in Turkey. Values and the concept of the NGOs in both Turkey and the EU are clarified to analyze the interaction of the NGOs in regional development. It is also essential to analyze relations between the governmental and non-governmental organizations in Turkey.

Regional Policies in European Union

Having considered the reason of its foundation, the EU is mainly an economy-based institution and therefore, regional and social concerns were mostly on the regions of coal and steel trade. The purpose was "reducing the differences existing between the various regions and the backwardness of the less favored regions" (Manzella & Mendez, 2009, s. 5). It was not a supranational attempt but a national one as the Member States were still the one and only authority. The most important aim was to support Member States and their budget to overcome industrialization and infrastructural problems. The focus has changed with the enlargement policies and policies for miscellaneous fields were considered vital to be able to deepen and develop in harmony.

Factors like topographic structures of the regions, the distribution of resources, climate differences, domestic and foreign market distances, and properties create regional differences between the Member States. These differences cause inequalities among the regions in terms of welfare levels and the regional policies address these disparities to create a better and united EU. Therefore, the European Union has focused on building a stronger financial structure for two main reasons. The very first one was to compete with other strong economies in the world and also, to prevent disparities between Member States and even regions in the same country. Creating a common policy in order to balance regional inequalities has been a major purpose. As the European Commission states it, the purpose of EU regional policy is to reduce the significant economic, social, and territorial disparities that still exist between Europe's regions (European Commission, 2009). Disparities between Member States are inevitable, so since the establishment of the community EU's policy has been organized in the communication and decision-making process together with regional partners as well as the Member States. It works to bring out the best option in every region, to make all regions more competitive, and to create more and better jobs. There are three main objectives of EU considering regional development. These are to promote structural adjustment and growth in regions underdeveloped in developing; to promote economic and social transition in the areas facing structural difficulties; and to support modernization and harmonization of education and employment policies (Kahraman, 2008, s. 1732).

Historical Development of Regional Policies in European Union

Treaty of Rome

The Treaty of Rome contains different agreements that are regarded as the founders of European community. Their aim is to reduce regional disparities and backwardness of the less favored regions and to support harmonious development (Manzella & Mendez, 2009, s. 5). Policy setting, the regulation of the markets, setting up organizations and rules to construct were on the leading agenda; however, the main focus was not actually regional development. Besides, "it was the purposeful activities of representatives of national governments" (Sweet, Sandholtz, & Fligstein, 2001, s. 29). Hence, the regional policy is not a direct address; it is mentioned through sectorial policies like agriculture, transport, and state aid. "Despite the recognition of the existence of a "regional issue" in all European countries at the Messina convention of 1955, ..., attention to regional policy in the Treaty of Rome of 1957 was minimal" (Manzella & Mendez, 2009, s. 5–6).

Regional policy was regarded as a sensitive issue as it was questioning the solidarity of the community members and balance of powers between the European countries by building new institutions. Also, economic tradition supported by the Member states supported the idea of regional policies at national level rather than supranational one. Moreover, the foundation of World Bank and great expectations about the capacity of Public Investment Banks prevented development of a separate regional policy. Also, the European Investment Bank (EIB) was designed as an intergovernmental body, owned, and governed by the Member States which was indeed promoted to build regional policies. "Regional policy forms an integral part of the system of internal balances on what the State is based" (qtd. in Manzella & Mendez, 2009, s. 5).

The decisions made in the Treaty were not sufficient to support the regional development in Community. As it was an inevitable fact, in December 1961, "Conference on Regional Economies" was organized and the national administrators with responsibilities in the area and experts in the field participated in the conference. Starting with this conference reflection on the regional policy increased. It was 1964, when the work was, officially, recognized at the institutional level in the Community's First Medium-Term Economic Policy Programme. "The creation of a comprehensive regional policy and the coordination of national initiatives on the basis of regional development programmes" were among the main indicators (qtd. in Manzella & Mendez, 2009, s. 6)

Paris Summit

During the Paris Summit of 1972, the common regional policy was shaped. The Heads of the Government of the European Community decided to make direct contribution to regional development to reduce imbalances between regions (European Documentation, 1975, s. 7). In the Summit, the status quo was stated. For all nations, "hopes for detente and cooperation were emerging" and many developing countries were aware that "the gap widening between them and the industrialized nations, were legitimately claiming increased aid and a more equitable utilization of wealth" (European Community, 1972, s. 15). The Member States were aware that the Community needed new obligations and widening the capabilities of European institutions was essential. The Economic and Monetary Union was essential to build up a stronger Community, which would guarantee "stability and growth" and supply "remedy for regional disparities". In order to find Community solution for regional development developing countries volunteered, "to raise their efforts in aid for and cooperation with the poorest nations" (European Community, 1972).

Here is the decision taken in behalf of regional development policy:

- The Heads of State and Government give top priority to correcting the structural and regional imbalances in the Community, which could hinder the achievement of the Economic and Monetary Union.
- The Heads of State and Government invite the Commission to prepare as soon as possible a report analyzing the regional problems of the enlarged Community and offering suitable proposals.
- Desiring to apply their efforts to a Community solution of regional problems, they ask the Community Institutions to set up a "Regional Development Fund" to be operative by 31 December 1973 (European Community, 1972, s. 15)

Even though there was structural development in regional policies, there seemed to be supervisory mechanism in economy (Karaarslan, 2008, s. 8). Europe had to identify itself with the concerted and better controlled pursuit of the common good with economic resources being reoriented towards the collective interest, a reduction in regional and social inequalities, decentralization and participation in decision making (Karaarslan, 2008, s. 12). Regional policy required a common action and it was definitely more than "a mere compensatory tool for integration spillovers" (Manzella & Mendez, 2009, s. 9). It was important to identify the citizens of Europe and the gravity of the process. The foundation of Regional Development Fund showed that both internal and external actions of the EU were to develop a cooperation, trust, and identification. With the new economies and changes in the world, Europe needed to place itself in a safer place. In addition, to accomplish the main purpose of the Union regional policy was a crucial point.

Single European Act

The European Economic Community (EEC) stated the importance of regional policy and cooperation. However, it was the founding treaty and the problems and objectives of the Treaty were mostly based on the structure of the EEC and the status quo after World War II. Resolution of the founding problems and institutionalization were the major points. Even though it was a weak statement, the importance of regional cooperation and common policies were stated as well. In the following years, European Regional Development policies and the Fund were mostly based on the national basis and it went on like this till the Single European Act (SEA). It is the most concrete step in terms of harmonization and institutionalization after the Treaty of Rome. It is expanded and amended version of the Treaty.

SEA articulated institutions, their relations to one another, their role, and the goals and objectives of policies. The institutions mentioned in the SEA were European Commission, Council of Ministers, the European Parliament, and the Court of Justice. As the amending act of the Rome Treaty, SEA suggested, "the Council shall, acting on a proposal from the Commission, in co-operation with the European Parliament and after consulting the Economic and Social Committee" (Single European Act, 1986, s. 5).

Other than the changing role of institutions and the Member States, there were two prominent points. One of them was the revitalization of regional policy with the support of cohesion policy, which was also stated with the common market. The complete edition of common market introduced relations to cohesion policy. Article 130b emphasized that the implementation of common policies, including internal market, shall take into account the objectives of social and economic cohesion. Importantly, the article referred to the necessity to "redress regional imbalances" through regions "participating in economic development" and undergoing "structural adjustment" (Hübner, 2005, s. 2)

An important process for single market that aimed to create a market between developed and less favored regions started with the SEA. That policy aimed to refer fixed policies between members avoiding national protection of the goods and products in Europe. SEA clarified regional disparities and states that the Commission could take into account the extent of the effort that certain economies showing differences in development will have to sustain during the period of establishment of the internal market and it may propose appropriate provisions (Single European Act, 1986, s. 10). In order to build a strong regional policy, cooperation and dialogues between states are important and necessary. Therefore, the Member States, with the help of the SEA, saw the changing and developing points of the EU and its policies not only in regional aspects but also in environmental, technological, and economic development policies.

Reforms of the Structural Funds

The 1980s were sensitive of economic and social development. The financial agreements of 1988–1993 represented the situation of the Member States and the EU and clarified sources used for increasing the budget for structural operations. The Reforms of the Structural Funds (RSF) introduced national and subnational governments and various interest groups coming together to design and to develop regional policies.

The 1988 reform represents objectives of European Structural Fund (ESF). The implementation of the ESF was based on concentration, operational programming, and the role of partnership and operational programs provided information about how to apply for the structural policies and how to achieve operational values and instruments. Cohesion policy was regarded as a long-term process based on continuity and reinforcement. Concentration stated the objectives of different areas such as lagging regions, industrial areas, and rural development and partnership clarified the importance of cooperation, as it has been important to know the region in order to avoid training or employment problems. As regional and local actors are familiar with the area, they can provide effective support and assistance. Lastly, the EU expenditure is not a substituted expense of national expenditure: the expenditure is like back up for the state that helps developing.

The Maastricht Treaty

In terms of structural and cohesion policies and institutional construction, it was one of the substantial treaties. The Treaty extended the economic and social cohesion and strengthened institutions such as the European Parliament. It was for the first time the Cohesion Fund was introduced in Article 129c to help infrastructural investments of poorer states (Maastricht Treaty, 1992, s. 32). The Maastricht Treaty also established Economic and Monetary Union with extended policies and common market policy. In addition to this, six new policies were established in the Treaty: consumer policy, industrial policy, trans-European network, education, youth, and culture. These policies included both internal and foreign policies of EU.

The main statement of regional policies is in Article 130 c. "The European Regional Development Fund is intended to help to redress the main regional imbalances in the Community through participation in the development and structural adjustment of regions whose development is lagging behind and in the conversion of declining industrial regions" (Maastricht Treaty, 1992, s. 34; Single European Act, 1986). Stating the substantiality of structural and cohesion funds, the Treaty showed once more the importance of cooperation within funds, regions, and nations.

Treaty of Lisbon

"With respect to values, the Treaty begins with an explicit commitment to human dignity, freedom, democracy, equality, the rule of law and the respect for human rights" (Wilson, 2011, s. 1). The interaction of the EU with other institutions in the world and the significance of human rights are stated with these values. These values also refer to the EU's foreign policy as well as internal policies. The substantial point of development and cooperation, once again, is emphasized in a EU Treaty with amending and expanding parts. The Treaty of Lisbon presents more democratic and transparent EU by equalizing national and regional levels, and their rights in EU. The term subsidiarity presented in the Treaty gives a member state to act at national level unless it is essential to execute in the EU level. This creates local and regional autonomy in the EU, helping develop more qualified development policies and change the perception of region.

In terms of regional development, first noticeable point is the territorial cohesion. Although the definition of the term is not given, the Treaty states that the EU "shall promote economic, social, and territorial cohesion, and solidarity among Member States". Accordingly, Title XVII of Part Four of the Treaty on the Functioning of the European Union is now devoted to "economic, social and territorial cohesion", with Articles 174–178 on Regional Policies and Structural Funds replacing former Articles 158–162 "TEC" (Wilson, 2011, s. 5).

Regional development policies throughout the world are stated in the Treaty. Different regions (continents) stated with their own characteristics and the importance of cooperation once again mentioned. The reduction of regional disparities is clarified once again. There are three important points stated in terms of regional policy in the Lisbon Treaty: "The Structural and Cohesion Funds are the main instruments the EU has to increase growth-enhancing investment. Second, embedded in the management system of European regional policy is the concept of ownership. Third, European regional policy is based on a strategic approach" (Hubner, 2005, s. 3–4). Another amending policy is the limitation of regional policy funds. In the Lisbon Treaty, the framework changes as:

Among the regions concerned, particular importance shall be paid to rural areas, areas affected by industrial transition and regions which suffer from severe and permanent natural or demographic handicaps such as the northernmost regions with very low population density and island, cross-border and mountain region (Wilson, 2011, s. 7).

This means the cohesion fund and other regional development funds are no more just for the poorer countries but it is possible for any region that is in need of development. The Lisbon Treaty, in general, provides economic growth and competitiveness, workforce development, increasing personal representation, creating better policies, health care and educational progress, and a big opportunity to develop institutions for better development policies.

Starting with the Treaty of Rome of 1957, EU designed and introduced development policies. Each treaty and plan improved European funds. In 2007–2013 plans, Cohesion Policy is reported as "a new partnership for cohesion: convergence, competitiveness, and cooperation" that supported partnership between Member States, regional competitiveness and employment, and territorial development supporting harmonious and balanced development. The EU regional policy has objectives to work on five key areas:

- investing in people by supporting access to employment, education and social inclusion opportunities
- supporting the development of small and medium size businesses
- strengthening research & innovation through investment and research-related jobs
- improving the environment through major investment projects
- modernising transport and energy production to fight against climate change, with a focus on renewable energy and innovative transport infrastructure (European Union).

After Lisbon Strategy had ended, Europe 2020 was prepared to cope with economic crisis, unemployment, social exclusion and poverty. To find solutions to the well-known problems of the EU and to compete with the leaders in the world, the EU once again tried to state the problematic areas and implement different strategies. As the regional balances kept changing, especially with enlargement policies, and demographic changes, inclusion, environmental issues, employment and competition became major problems. Therefore, it included regional development policies with smart, sustainable and inclusive growth goals (Yazıcı, 2018, s. 444).

Regional Development in Turkey

The Development Plans of Turkey

From traditional point to the modern perception of regional development, Turkey had ten development plans. These ten Development Plans play essential role to explore the aim of the country both on national and international levels by examining the development plan of the country from different perspectives.

When Turkey was introduced into planned development period in 1963, with the first Five-Years Development Plan, it required developing different project in the long term, for at least fifteen years further, in order to state the goals and the initials (Republic of Turkey Prime Ministry State Planning Organization-SPO). It is possible to see development progress from different angles including regional planning and regional development. According to DPT, pre-1960 plans followed statist policy while 1960-1980 plans followed mixed capitalism plans and 1980-2000 plans followed liberalist and strategic policies. "The important substitution policies" that had been critical in industrialization before 1980 replaced with "open economy" after 1980 (T.C. Başbakanlık Devlet Planlama Teşkilatı, 1963). Here are the aims of the each year, before starting to point regional planning and development process.

When historical background of regional development is examined in Turkey, it is possible to see that there are several different development methods and processes; each is generated by a strong centralized management unit. In the development plans, on one hand, functionality in regional growth and eliminating disparities between regions is viewed and on the other hand, the relations between the European Union and Turkey, and effects of this process are possible to examine. According to Keskin and Surgun, these processes show "the need for a new axis in regional development" (Keskin & Sungur, 2010, s. 271-293). This need gives a new perception with the evaluation of regional development tools (used by various parameters) and change in development forms is one of the facts (Keskin & Sungur, 2010, s. 279). 2000 and following years are essential for political transformation of Turkey. Starting with the EU pre-accession adaptation process, Turkey has had many responsibilities including regional development and put essential plans and projects into practice.

Regional policies in Turkey can be divided into three parts. In the first period, 1923-1963 (also known as unplanned period), regional planning was not regarded as an important aim but more like a tool in the process of development. Planning and basic aims were based on layout plans and because of this industrialization and service sector were centered in the developed western regions. In 1963, with the first Development Plan, second part of development process started. This is a period between the first Five-Years Development Plan (FYDP) and 1999, Helsinki Summit. In this period, regional planning policy started to change and became priority in planning process (Keskin & Sungur, 2010, s. 280). With the planned period, integrated plans including social and economic dimensions, was put into action. Third period started after 1999 Helsinki Summit. As negotiations with the EU started, institutional arrangements, including regional development, have been implemented.

The first FYDP was introduced in 1963. FYDP has three parts: the main objectives and goals, the evaluation of status quo, and organization, measurements, and precautions. These aspects show the division of regions, centralized standards, and following objectives. The aim of the plan is "to help inter-regional imbalances in development preventative, resolve problems of urbanization and population, public services, the deployment of a corrective distribution of incomes and the potential wastage of resources will provide an orderly development" (T.C. Başbakanlık Devlet Planlama Teşkilatı, 1963, s. 471–477).

This plan aims to resolve regional disparities with a national solution in a vertical way. The position and the economic and social objectives of the region are important to find the appropriate plan. In order to resolve income disparities, the plan suggests distribution of public service to the regions. The main objective of the plan eliminates both regional and individual disparities.

In order to reach success, the plan divides regions into three categories. First one is a "potential development area" that is shown as Antalya (Mediterranean Region). For the sake of general development, in a potential region "self-sufficient units and the functions of economy are handled as a whole". The second type of region is "underdeveloped regions". In this plan, East and Southern East Anatolia are regarded as underdeveloped regions. As the economic rates are low, cities are put in order according to potential development rate. Increasing support of private sector and reduction of taxes are primary objectives in the region. The last region is "developed regions" which is primarily İstanbul and its neighborhood in Marmara Region. New attraction and growth centers, distribution of population and economic studies, and the creation of industry areas are essential in order to have an optional region other than İstanbul (T.C. Başbakanlık Devlet Planlama Teşkilatı, 1963).

The first FYDP is seen as "an inclusive and comprehensive long term process" as regionalism is a new aspect for both for the state and for the world. The plan suggests that economic growth on national basis is the most important thing; that is why it clearly claims that regional planning is nothing but part of the national planning process and it is hard to separate it from national dimension. Even though the regions are separated according to their level of development, regional distinctions were still based on geographical similarities (T.C. Başbakanlık Devlet Planlama Teşkilatı, 1963).

Objectives, status quo, and policies are once more clarified in the second FYDP (1968). One of the main aspects of this plan is urbanization problem expected because of development. Objectives are to promote balanced development and to lead investments in the regions where development rates are low. Both private and state investments play crucial roles. The plan, also, supports urbanization and facilities of urbanization as an impetus that should be static and supportive in social and cultural fields. As a result, the investments in Eastern Anatolia (underdeveloped region) were increased from 11 % to 23 %. Urbanization in development also means modernization in agriculture and industrialization. The possible differentials in economy and environment would be supported by the state. Here, development rate is not based on cities but regions.

While stating the status quo back then in 1968, there was one major problem according to the second FYDP. The aim was to modernize the economic and social structure of the population and to accelerate the social changes, which meant a regionalization process in Turkey. Before this plan, cities and villages were regarded as separate units; however, with the modernization process they started to work together from a centralized unit. Because of this rapid process, urbanization would have created problems and it had to be balanced. Therefore, policies on this plan were based on urbanization and social sectors. Infrastructural developments in developed and potential developing regions are one of the policies stated in the plan. Regional planning is seen as a tool for balanced development and Antalya, Çukurova, Marmara, Zonguldağ and Keban were sample regions to evaluate the process. The evaluation of the sources and capacities of the region (whether it develops or not) were essential to produce new projects with the potential solutions (T.C. Başbakanlık Devlet Planlama Teşkilatı Müsteşarlığı, 1978, s. 268). Regional policies were still considered with the national development and civic and private sector cooperation to support growth and development were also stated. In this plan, even though there is no sign of regional planning strategy, as the EU did, the need to improve region-specific plans was also mentioned.

The third FYDP (1973) is an essential plan in terms of international relations because for the first time in a development plan international organizations, like EEC, Regional Cooperation for Development (RCD), signed by Pakistan, Iran, and Turkey were stated (T.C. Başbakanlık Devlet Planlama Teşkilatı Müsteşarlığı, 1978, s. 64).

A new perspective for regional planning, "Priority Regions for Development" was put into action and mentioned in detail. With this plan:

- Natural and human resources of the regions that have potential in developing would be specified and according to the tables reflecting socio-economic integration of these regions a list will be created and these regions would be supported by annual plans.

- These regions will be developed with the gradual developing plans, completing each other.
- When these policies are not sufficient for the region, additional policies and precautions would be developed in the annual plans. They would be consistent with the national plans (T.C. Başbakanlık Devlet Planlama Teşkilatı Müsteşarlığı, 1978, s. 947–949).

The fourth FYDP (1979) continues Priority Regions for Development project with a few changes. One of the biggest and national projects, Southeastern Anatolia Project-SAP was mentioned which was all-purpose project for Eastern and Southeastern Anatolia. This plan is supportive of previous plans (T.C. Başbakanlık Devlet Planlama Teşkilatı, 1979, s. 292–292).

The fifth FYDP (1984), Priority Regions for Development project, analyzed the consistent projects in order to specify their essential points for the region. Regional development schemes examined the harmony of the plans and alternatives by evaluating the development ratio. The balance of development between regions was substantial as well as regional development, which was based on the infrastructure projects on building, public goods, and services. Hierarchical settling of regional development was developed in order to identify the differences in the region and develop less favored regions.

The Priority Regions for Development project mostly represents Eastern and Southeastern Anatolia in this plan. As well as the big-scaled project, regional and small-scaled projects were supported. Here are some basic policies of Priority Regions for Development project:

- The main goal is to diminish imbalance between Priority Regions and others by developing priority regions.
- Already existing and potential sources in the region would be supported in order to develop industrialization.
- Incentive measures will be implemented in the region.
- A market system for Middle East would be supported (T.C. Başbakanlık Devlet Planlama Teşkilatı, 1985, s. 161–163).

The sixth FYDP is different from other plans because it changes the term "regional planning" into "regional development". Social and technical infrastructure in metropolitans and industrial development are still among the aims (Keskin & Sungur, 2010, s. 285). Differentiation is not limited to the terms; to improve development rapidly sub-regions are defined to prepare more specific plans for the regions. However, regional specification is still based on geographical regionalism.

During the fifth FYDP period, Turkey, the associate member of the EU, made an application for full EEC membership. In December 1996, Turkey and EU signed the Customs Union agreement. The standardization of products in order to catch EU standards and develop protocols in development gained importance. However, especially in agriculture and textile industry, there were still boundaries for Turkey (T.C. Başbakanlık Devlet Planlama Teşkilatı, 1990, s. 337).

Having different facilities and features of each region located throughout the country made it essential to develop a new approach to deal with the sectorial preferences of spatial analysis in planning. To diminish the imbalance between developing regions, to limit migration, and to develop living conditions in these regions were among the main objectives of the seventh FYDP. The terrorist attacks were seen as a treat to development in Eastern and Southeastern Anatolia and this caused internal migration. For the regions that have common geographical features a new Action Plan was introduced. In 1994, an Emergency Support Plan was put in to action in order to prevent side effects of terror in the region. For the first time in the plan, sustainable development term was used (T.C. Başbakanlık Devlet Planlama Teşkilatı, 1996, s. 170–174)

Turkey has renewed its national and international goals since the beginnings of 1980s. The relations with GATT (later, World Trade Organization), EU and other organizations shaped its development. However, there is no direct link with regional development policy in the plan. The plan tried to fulfill European standards in products and industrial development. Besides, the SAP gained more importance and a detailed project was introduced.

The eight FYDP is important not only in terms of regional development but also of relations with the EU. After the Helsinki Summit of 1999 had announced Turkey as a candidate country, this FYDP is the first plan, prepared with a specific interest of the EU. Different from the previous national development plans, the plan introduced the importance of local dynamics in economic and regional development process and the emphasis was on the increasing role of local authorities. The regional development was the main objective of the FYDP. It states that regional disparities could be eliminated with the cooperative work of national plan, local authorities, and the EU. Regional plans were expected to reflect priorities of national plans, local demands, and connections between different sectors.

The regional development ratio and policies changed in Turkey. "In the application of regional development policies sustainability, inter-regional integration, social and economic balances, improvement in quality of life, equality of opportunities, cultural development and participation will be the main objectives" (T.C. Başbakanlık Devlet Planlama Teşkilatı, 2000, s. 63). The main objectives of the plan, social life and even basic social rights would be analyzed according to the EU standards.

Another important aspect of the plan is the involvement of civil society and local authorities into the regional planning and development process. In order to support increasing working standards of Turkey social dialogue mechanism would be increased and the norms of ILO and the EU would be the basic sources (T.C. Başbakanlık Devlet Planlama Teşkilatı, 2000, s. 225). The participation of society is seen as an important tool for development in the plan. Transparent and open policies of civil society organizations and their objectives are also stated (T.C. Başbakanlık Devlet Planlama Teşkilatı, 2000, s. 202).

For the first time the five-year planning period changes with the improvements of the EU policy. Turkey, stating the importance of globalization and catching modern policies, plans to develop its regional authority and to become one of the developed countries. The Ninth Development Plan is the basis of all regional and national plans, as well as the plans required by the EU Pre-Accession Economic Program and the Strategic Framework for Integration of documents and other programmes that constitute the basis for sectorial and corporate strategy documents. The plan provides the alignment of all planning documents that have different functions. Thus, inter-organizational plan would provide a common understanding and unity of purpose; the legal and institutional changes and the potential of the country by strengthening the connection to the plan-program-budget shall constitute grounds for the use of the upper level (T.C. Başbakanlık Devlet Planlama Teşkilatı, 2006, s. 1). The main objectives of the plan are increasing competitiveness, employment, human development and social solidarity, ensuring regional development, and improving the quality and effectiveness in public (T.C. Başbakanlık Devlet Planlama Teşkilatı, 2006, s. 2).

The last Development Plan states the importance of regional development even in the introduction part. As Turkey needs to be a globally recognized country in the world, regional dynamics that could lead to development should be supported (T.C. Başbakanlık Devlet Planlama Teşkilatı, 2013, s. 1). Globalization, Turkey's relations with other countries and the importance of development are stated. Smart, sustainable and inclusive economic and social development is stated as the main objectives of Turkey. This will be supported by international or national organizations and Turkey is willing to improve its status as a global actor in the world (T.C. Başbakanlık Devlet Planlama Teşkilatı, 2013, s. 1–3). When analyzed it is possible to see the emphasis on regional development in different fields like agriculture, tourism or industrial development. Regional Development Regional Competitiveness Section puts emphasis on the fact that since 2000s, Turkey has been paying extra attention to regional development

(T.C. Başbakanlık Devlet Planlama Teşkilatı, 2013, s. 136). In Article 903, the cooperation of Turkey with Regional Development Agencies, NGOs, local administrations, public institutions and universities are stated. There has been more than 34,000 project applications and of these almost 9,000 of them were found successful and supported; however, the institutions are not specifically mentioned (T.C. Başbakanlık Devlet Planlama Teşkilatı, 2013, s. 139).

Non-governmental Organizations in Turkey

The Structure of NGOs and Their Participation in Regional Development

NGOs in Turkey help develop social relations and solidarity. However, they do not only take part in social and civil movements; their role in policy and decision-making process and development has been effective. In the case of Turkey, they could be regarded as a bridge between the government and the society as the policy is based on indirect representation of people. In addition, as the international organizations do not directly influence the governmental policies, NGOs create a secure field to use the most effective way in terms of development. Before stating the role of NGOs in regional development, or in any kind of development, it is substantial to understand their structure, concept, features, environment, impact, and weaknesses and strength. Strengthened as an important area of social change, communicative and conciliatory part of civil society in organization of public space, the effect of NGOs are deepening and widening.

The development of NGOs dated back to the establishment of the Republic of Turkey in 1923. Back then, an NGO meant social and volunteered involvement rather than a political and effective organ of the society. NGOs did not take part in any political or economic process until 1980s. Since 1980s, and especially after 2000, NGOs have gained importance in local, regional, national, and international levels (Bikmen & Meydanoğlu, 2006, s. 35–36). In 2000, not only the process of democratization and modernization but also, organizational life started in Turkey. Today in Turkey, NGOs are developing in different fields and they become a role model and representatives of their areas. NGOs represent organized fields such as think tanks, trade unions, professional chambers, civic initiatives, and social movements (Bikmen & Meydanoğlu, 2006, s. 35–36). The most common definition of an NGO is the area of voluntary organizations that cannot be dominated by a governmental power. Within the framework of this definition, an NGO is created by a democratic society that does not symbolize the democratization process or does not contribute in policy-making process and it is based on voluntary membership (Bikmen & Meydanoğlu, 2006, s. 38–39). Another definition of an NGO is based on moral and political values: voluntary organization of a society that is not under control of state or the government (Bikmen & Meydanoğlu, 2006). Based on the definition, it could organize itself and hold organizations independent of a state control.

The concept of an NGO is not possible to clarify in Turkey and Turkish because of the name suggested in Turkish. While NGOs directly involve civil society in it, it does not directly refer to non-governmental process, maybe because of the central governance system. Still, it is possible to share some definitions.

NGOs are private and non-profit organizations like think tanks, cultural groups, groups working for the sake of society rather than its members, so on and so forth. Professional and trade associations are composed of member executives. These groups are representatives of their members or of the interests of a particular sector that could act in dominant groups. Some organizations in this group (e.g. TÜSİAD in Turkey) can lead state on economic and political bases and influence social or regional policies. In the modern world, it is hard to separate the role of any NGO. It is an effective long-term solution to problems and an active participant in the policy-making process and the common area separate from the state and established by different voluntary organizations. An NGO could be a descriptive organization of democracy and social and moral values. Being active and working non-governmental are its main concepts. Rather than its thoughts and political level, the contribution in the process and solutions it produces is important in regard of this definition (Bikmen & Meydanoğlu, 2006). An NGO might cooperate with the government or any other political actor. The important objectives are transparency, validity, productivity, and active role of citizens from "micro-regional level" to "macro-national level" (Keyman, 2006, s. 19).

EU defines NGOs as organizations related to public administration or government. These organizations include third sector organizations as well as others. European Economic and Social Committee (EESC) illustrates NGOs as "All organizational structures whose members have objectives and responsibilities that are of general interest and who also act as mediators between the public authorities and citizens" (Commission of the European Communities, 2005, s. 4). All communities are expected to join civil dialogue in EU; "the dialogue includes exchanges between opinion leaders from national and European institutions" (Commission of the European Communities, 2005). This dialogue includes development of a civil society between the EU, candidate, and potential candidate countries. The first aim is to develop existing organizations and their roles in development instead of changing the system.

In 1997, CIVICUS put forward the idea of civil society index and prepared New Civic Atlas, including 60 countries. In order to compare the information in this atlas, a civil society index was prepared and this index led other projects in different countries to be able to create an identity for civil society. CIVICUS started this project in more than fifty countries in 2003 and this project developed the vision of countries including Turkey. The first Project of Civil Society Index (STEP) initiated between January 2004 and December 2005. This project assisted NGOs in Turkey to apprehend their values, strengths, and weaknesses and so on. With two reports presented in 2006 and 2011, with assistance of Third Sector Foundation of Turkey (TUSEV), it became possible to perceive the development of NGOs (Bikmen & Meydanoğlu, 2006, s. 41–42)

In a modern society NGOs are seen as means of direct democracy. The NGOs act in a protective way both in the organization and between organizations. Even though, the structure of NGOs is shaped according to democracy, the individuals think that the leaders are the most important decision-makers of that organization. They directly focus on the issues like thoughts, values, rights, media freedom that is related to democracy. They are, indeed, quite successful in these fields as this report presents (Bikmen & Meydanoğlu, 2006, s. 83–84). Corruption of NGOs was among the biggest bias in Turkey, 2006 Report. The public opinion on reliability was separate from the reality. Contrary to public opinion, an NGO was considered as one of the three least corrupted institutions, as reported by Transparency International (Bikmen & Meydanoğlu, 2006, s. 84–85). In 2011 report, the democratic process is not directly referred, on the contrary, transparency, decision-making process and accountability is referred as elements of democratic process and these elements, even though there is still no binding law in the system, develops in the NGO systems (İçduygu, Meydanoğlu, & Sert, 2011, s. 109).

Participation is one of the most important values of EU policy in any field. Lately, the power the European Parliament gained in the Lisbon Treaty is the biggest sign of the importance of participation. In the process of determining EU policies, participation of all people of European Union either directly or through intermediary institutions that represents interests of these people. The range of participation would shape the policy-making process. Transparency and accountability is important to ensure free flow of information, procedures, and knowledge. In order to ensure this process is applied to all levels and all decision takers, accountability is an essential point. In this process, the decision-makers should be able to present the objectives they work on, the way they use as solidarity mechanism, what affects the policy-making process in the Commission. NGOs, on the other hand, should present what their interests are and how they are represented. Effectiveness is another essential point. It means institutions and their objectives should represent any citizen at any time, so decision-making process in the EU should cover all people of EU. In addition, cohesion, as it is understood with its policies is important in the EU.

The responsibility given to NGOs in the world is increasing, including the EU. However, all the reports stated before has shown that in Turkey, regional development is not considered as a separate or an independent process. Therefore, although it is possible to see the involvement of NGOs in the process, most of the projects are completed via the government or government related institutions. As it can be seen in the previous development plans that decision are mostly central and regions that are specified either according to their geographical positions or the EU norms are still directed from the main center. The Tenth Development Plan did not have a specific part for NGOs and their roles but under the section for Qualified People, Strong Society, their role and importance are specifically mentioned, especially after the war in Syria and migration process (Türkiye Cumhuriyeti Kalkınma Bakanlığı, s. 51).

For Turkey, the Eleventh Development Plan can be considered a unique plan as it involves a specific preliminary report considering NGOs and their roles in the development process. While the term of an NGO is given, the role of it is also clarified in the report (Türkiye Cumhuriyeti Kalkınma Bakanlığı, s. 1). Ministry of Development supports NGOs through three institutions: Southern Anatolia Project-Regional Development Agencies, Social Support Program (SODES) and Development Agencies. The role of the NGOs in the world is defined in the report; however, the process in Turkey and the involvement of NGOs in regional development process is not clearly defined as, there is no common database (Türkiye Cumhuriyeti Kalkınma Bakanlığı, s. 30). Even though the importance of cooperation is emphasized the specific reports are not shared. The role of NGOs in the process is not clear, according to the report, because their aim is not always clear. Sometimes, they may lead something good or bad and it is not always easy to predict. Still, NGOs are seen as the institutions that prevent inequalities and increases equal distribution of things (Türkiye Cumhuriyeti Kalkınma Bakanlığı, s. 34).

Ten Development Plans show the fact that NGOs are present in Turkey; however, their role and involvement in regional development are not clarified. According to the preliminary report for the Eleventh Development Plan, the aim and the role of the NGOs need to be specified first (Türkiye Cumhuriyeti Kalkınma Bakanlığı, s. 54). How to do such things is not the subject of this study, but unless more concrete resolutions are in the agenda, it is not clearly put NGOs in a clarified position.

Conclusion

Following years of World War II, states initiated changes in economics and policies, especially for Europe. States focused on their development plans as war destroyed and reshaped them with their policies. In order to follow stable and proficient plans, one of the substantial aims was to define what region and regionalism represented in the state or union. This created different terms and policies to explain and distinguish regions. Both terms, development and region changed according to the priorities of the states. In nineteenth century, the development would mean "economic development" while at the last quarter of the twentieth century it would refer to "quality of life"; and today that definition also includes "sustainability". Likewise, region and regionalism changed according to the perception of a state or a union. With globalization, regions gained importance as a critical part of economic growth based on innovations. The EU and its policies towards regional development focused on equality and sustainability and aimed to support both Member States and candidate countries to be able to compensate disparities between regions. Turkey, as one of the candidates, had and still has strong relations with the EU and regional development has been part of its FYDPs. The improvement in the plans was seen in the regions as well. However, the interaction of NGOs in regional development was and still is limited. It is important to investigate the impact of NGOs as they have the power to understand regions better. This research aims to show how regional development became part of FYDPs and how NGOs contributed to the process.

As the planned period started in 1963, it took fifty years for Turkey to build the basic needs of the country or Turkey felt responsible to prepare development plans as it intended to improve international relations. The first FYDP put into force in 1963 stated the objectives of Turkey. The plan was traditional, extremely centralized, and nationalist. There were certain boundaries in terms of changing nationalist objectives. Expecting a certain regional development policy in these plans was impossible. The regional planning was used as the means of national growth. Thus, this resulted in regional disparities, and imbalanced cities. Still, the region and regionalism developed, and FYDPs divided regions according to their growth rates and geographical locations.

The EU relations had a rapid impact on regional development policies, though. As the regional development is one of the main objectives of the EU and it did supply financial aids to the related countries, Turkey started using the advantage of being candidate country after the Helsinki Summit of 1999. However, this was not adequate enough for Turkey, as negotiations did not start. Still, from traditional point of view, Turkey began to move towards modern concept of regionalization. The nature and regional development and planning started to move towards decentralize system as the EU expected so. This was initiated with the mobilization of local and regional authorities. The cooperation between national, regional, local, and non-governmental organizations became part of the development plans. The future plans of developing countries, cohesion policy of the EU, and the last development policy of Turkey shared a common sense: the regional development is important for the future of development and the higher values could be caught by using local and civil tools instead of focusing on the nationalist and centralized development plans.

Turkey intended to develop standards in order to work in cooperation with NGOs. However, it caused challenges for the government to build and develop relations with civil society. The potential civil partners of Turkey, universities, local partners, municipalities, civil society organizations, chambers of industry and commerce, and so on, intended to work together with the government. The Council was consulting on the issues the government supported. After, 2005 Turkey started negotiations with the EU and this changed the perspective of the regional development and civil dialogue in development.

It is possible to state that this situation caused regional competitiveness because the regions were not referred to geographical borders any more. They are depended on their growth rate and two cities from different regions could need the financial aid. Here, the actors are NGOs to determine the faith of the region. Financed according to projects, regions needed to promote more projects for their development. The interaction of NGOs is important; however, the effect of NGOs in Turkey is open to discussion. The reason is that the values of the EU are not supported enough in Turkey. Transparency and subsidiary, which are two of the main objectives, are violated. NGOs in Turkey claim to supply information for financial terms but how to reach those sources remains unknown. Even though, one could reach the sources, it is not certain if the information is updated. Furthermore, subsidiary, working with the lowest organization possible is in developing process in Turkey. NGOs are governed from the centers, which are mostly placed in big and developed cities, and this ruins the local authority perspective of one unit.

There are different types of NGOs working for both social and economic means of regional development. Some NGOs like TÜBİTAK, TOBB, KOSGEB work in line with the governmental organizations. They are centralized organizations, but this does not affect their success. However, their relations to governments might affect their policies in the regions. NGOs can refer either to the specific interest groups or to the general purpose of the society. Human rights or education would refer to the general interests while regional development organizations; chambers of industry and commerce would refer to specific interest groups. Still, the aim is to get the utmost beneficiary from the most eligible sources. The important point here is the impact of these NGOs as local actors would know the priorities of the region better than the centralized ones. Thus, as well as the interaction of the NGOs, the participation of the society in the NGO is important to analyze the effects of NGOs on development. The aim of any organization should be to reach society and work for it but if the society were not willing to participate in the progress, again, a NGO would not reach its goals. Unfortunately, this is still one of the major problems of Turkey.

One could conclude that it is difficult to reach the sources about NGOs and to evaluate of those sources. Even the sources are open to the public; it is impossible to evaluate their effectiveness. Thus, even if the NGOs take part in the regional development process, the government is still centralized. It does not want other authorities to be involved in the process whether because of trust issues or because of ineffectiveness of NGOs. That might be the reasons why the NGOs participate in regional development process consist of the ones who are related to governments or have their centralized systems. Still, Turkey seems promising in terms of development. Turkey made a step by changing development plans from centralized to EU standards. Dealing with the ethnic problems of today, trying to catch the standards of the EU and to get a position in the Middle East, Turkey knows that NGOs will play an important role. By giving chance to the NGOs in regional development components can be regarded as a promise for the future development. The governments in Turkey could change laws and systems to make NGOs interact more and more in regional development. However, if the society does not participate in the process, solutions would be temporary. That is why the competitiveness in the regions is a challenging process to keep people aware of their rights in the social and political developments.

References

Bafoil, F., & Kaya, A. (2009). Regional Development and The European Union: A Comparative Analysis of Karabük, Valenciennes, and Katowice. Istanbul: Istanbul Bilgi University Press,.

Balchin, P. N., Sýkora, L., & Bull, G. H. (1999). Regional Policy and Planning in Europe. London: Routledge.

Bikmen, F., & Meydanoğlu, Z. (2006). Türkiye'de Sivil Toplum: Bir Değişim Süreci: Uluslararası Sivil Toplum Endeksi Porjesi Türkiye Ülke Raporu. TUSEV. İstanbul: TUSEV Yayınları.

Commission of the European Communities. (2005, June 29). Civil Society Dialogue between the EU and Candidate Countries COM(2005) 290 final. Brussels.

Devlet Planlama Teşkilatı. (n.d.). Kalkınma Planları. Retrieved May 5, 2019, from Türkiye Cumhuriyeti Cumhurbaşkanlığı Strateji ve Bütçe Başkanlığı: http://www.sbb.gov.tr/kalkinma-planlari/

EUR-Lex. (2005, June 01). Turkey's Pre-Accession Strategy. Retrieved June 1, 2011, from EUR-Lex – Access to European Union law: http://europa.eu/legislation_summaries/enlargement/ongoing_enlargement/community_acquis_turkey/e40113 _en.htm

European Commission. (2009). The EU's Main Investment Policy. Retrieved 2010, from European Commission: https://ec.europa.eu/regional_policy/en/policy/what/investment-policy/

European Community. (1972). Meetings of the Heads of State or Government. Retrieved 06 04, 2011, from University of Pittsburg – Archive of European Integration: http://aei.pitt.edu/1919/2/paris_1972_communique.pdf

European Documentation. (1975). A New Regional Policy for Europe. Retrieved June 15, 2019, from University of Pittsburg – Archive of European Integration: http://aei.pitt.edu/1756/1/regions_brochure_3_1975.pdf

European Union. (n.d.). Regional Policy. Retrieved June 15, 2019, from Official Website of the European Union: https://europa.eu/european-union/topics/regional-policy_en

Hübner, D. (2005, February 3). Regional Policy and the Lisbon Agenda: Challenges and Opportunities. London: London School of Economics.

İçduygu, A., Meydanoğlu, Z., & Sert, D. ş. (2011). Türkiye"de Sivil Toplum: Bir Dönüm Noktası, Uluslararası Sivil Toplum Endeksi Projesi Türkiye Ülke Raporu II. TUSEV. İstanbul: TUSEV Yayınları.

Kahraman, S. (2008). AB-Akdeniz Bölgesel Politikaları ve Türkiye"nin Uyumu. Journal of Yaşar University, 3(12), 1731–1742.

Karaarslan, G. (2008). Avrupa Birliği ve Türkiye"de Bölgesel Politikalar ve Kalkınma Ajansları (Yüksek Lisans Tezi). Ankara: Ankara University.

Keskin, H., & Sungur, O. (2010). Bölgesel Politika Ekseninde Yaşanan Dönüşüm: Türkiye'de Kalkınma Planlarında Bölgesel Politikaların Değişimi. SDÜ Fen Edebiyat Fakültesi Sosyal Bilimler Dergisi, 21, 271–293.

Keyman, F. (2006). Türkiye"de Sivil Toplum Serüveni: Imkansızlıklar İçinde Bir Vaha. Ankara: Sivil Toplum Geliştirme Merkezi.

Maastricht Treaty. (1992). Treaty on European Union. Luxembourg: ECSC-EEC-EAEC.

Manzella, G. P., & Mendez, C. (2009). The Turning Points of EU Cohesion Policy. European Commission. European Policies Research Center.

Single European Act. (1986, February 17). Retrieved March 2010, from http://ec.europa.eu/economy_finance/emu_history/documents/treaties/singleuropeanact.pdf

Sweet, A. S., Sandholtz, W., & Fligstein, N. (2001). The Institutionalization of Europe. Oxford: Oxford: Oxford Press.

T.C. Başbakanlık Devlet Planlama Teşkilatı Müsteşarlığı. (1973). Türkiye Cumhuriyeti Cumhurbaşkanlığı Strateji ve Bütçe Başkanlığı. Retrieved June 21, 2019, from Üçüncü Beş Yıllık Kalkınma Planı 1973-1977: http://www.sbb.gov.tr/wp-content/uploads/2018/11/Üçüncü-Beş-Yıllık-Kalkınma-Planı-1973-1977%E2%80%8B.pdf

T.C. Başbakanlık Devlet Planlama Teşkilatı Müsteşarlığı. (1978). Türkiye Cumhuriyeti Cumhurbaşkanlığı Strateji ve Bütçe Başkanlığı. Retrieved June 21, 2019, from İkinci Beş Yıllık Kalkınma Planı 1968-1972: http://www.sbb.gov.tr/wp-content/uploads/2018/11/İkinci-Beş-Yıllık-Kalkınma-Planı-1968-1972%E2%80%8B.pdf

T.C. Başbakanlık Devlet Planlama Teşkilatı. (1963, January). Kalkınma Planı – Birinci Beş Yıl (1963-1967). Retrieved June 16, 2019, from Türkiye Cumhuriyeti Cumhurbaşkanlığı Strateji ve Bütçe Başkanlığı: http://www.sbb.gov.tr/wp-content/uploads/2018/11/Birinci-Beş-Yıllık-Kalkınma-Planı-1963-1967%E2%80%8B.pdf

T.C. Başbakanlık Devlet Planlama Teşkilatı. (1979, April). Türkiye Cumhuriyeti Cumhurbaşkanlığı Strateji ve Bütçe Başkanlığı. Retrieved June 21, 2019, from Dördüncü Beş Yıllık Kalkınma Planı 1979-1983: http://www.sbb.gov.tr/wp-content/uploads/2018/10/Dorduncu_Bes_Yillik_Kalkinma_Plani-1979-1983.pdf

T.C. Başbakanlık Devlet Planlama Teşkilatı. (1985). Türkiye Cumhuriyeti Cumhurbaşkanlığı Strateji ve Bütçe Başkanlığı. Retrieved June 21, 2019, from Beşinci Beş Yıllık Kalkınma Planı 1985-1989: http://www3.kalkinma.gov.tr/DocObjects/View/13740/plan5.pdf

T.C. Başbakanlık Devlet Planlama Teşkilatı. (1990). Türkiye Cumhuriyeti Cumhurbaşkanlığı Strateji ve Bütçe Başkanlığı. Retrieved June 21, 2019, from Altıncı Beş Yıllık Kalkınma Planı 1990-1994: http://www.sbb.gov.tr/wp-content/uploads/2018/10/Altinci_Bes_Yillik_Kalkinma_Plani-1990-1994.pdf

T.C. Başbakanlık Devlet Planlama Teşkilatı. (1996). Yedinci Beş Yıllık Kalkınma Planı 1996-2000. Retrieved June 23, 2019, from Türkiye Cumhuriyeti Cumhurbaşkanlığı Strateji ve Bütçe Başkanlığı: http://www.sbb.gov.tr/

wp-content/uploads/2018/11/Yedinci-Beş-Yıllık-Kalkınma-Planı-1996-2000%E2%80%8B.pdf

T.C. Başbakanlık Devlet Planlama Teşkilatı. (2000). Uzun Vadeli Strateji ve Sekizinci Beş Yıllık Kalkınma Planı 2001–2005. Retrieved June 25, 2019, from Kalkınma: http://www3.kalkinma.gov.tr/DocObjects/View/13743/plan8.pdf

T.C. Başbakanlık Devlet Planlama Teşkilatı. (2006, July 1). Türkiye Cumhuriyeti Cumhurbaşkanlığı Strateji ve Bütçe Başkanlığı. Retrieved June 26, 2019, from Dokuzuncu Kalkınma Planı 2007–2013: http://www3.kalkinma.gov.tr/DocObjects/View/13744/plan9.pdf

T.C. Başbakanlık Devlet Planlama Teşkilatı. (2013, July 2). Türkiye Cumhuriyeti Cumhurbaşkanlığı Strateji ve Bütçe Başkanlığı. Retrieved June 25, 2019, from Onuncu Kalkınma Planı 2014–2018: http://www3.kalkinma.gov.tr/DocObjects/view/15089/Onuncu_Kalkınma_Planı.pdf

Türkiye Cumhuriyeti Kalkınma Bakanlığı. (2018). Kalkınma Sürecinde Sivil Toplum Kuruluşları 11. Kalkinma Planı Özel İhtisas Komisyonu Raporu. Ankara: Türkiye Cumhuriyeti Kalkınma Bakanlığı.

Wilson, B. (2011). Regional Policy and the Lisbon Treaty: implications for European Union-Asia Relationships. uropean Union Centre at RMIT University. Melbourne: European Union Centre at RMIT University.

Yazıcı, İ. G. (2018). Lizbon Stratejisi ve Avrupa 2020 Hedeflerinde Bölgesel Kalkınma ve Sosyal Politikalar. Uluslararası Yönetim Akademisi Dergisi, 1(3), 436–451.

Esra Doğan[1]

Chapter 6 The Impact of the Change in the Investment Incentive System Application in Turkey on Regional Income Convergence

Introduction

The Investment Incentive System is a mechanism based on the allocation of public resources for the purpose of supporting investments and thus transferring public resources. Although the process of the formation of this mechanism goes as far back as the proclamation of the Republic, it has undergone continuous development and transformation in the historical process. 1923 Izmir Economic Congress, 1927 Industrial Incentive Law, 1961 Constitution and planned development period shaped the legal basis of the investment incentive system. After 1980, investment incentive system became a government regulation means in an environment in which with the change of the overall structure of the liberalization policy there were also free market conditions in the form of transformation of the intrusive nature of the deregulation politics and fiscal policy for capital. In the 1990s, since the general framework of national policies were subjected to regulations in which Turkey was included on the international level, investment incentives also, primarily as part of the World Trade Organization on Subsidies and Countervailing Measures within the scope of provisions relating to international capital mobility, were determined essentially in line with international agreements.

Beyond the international and national structure differentiations, the basic regulations that are already decisive on the existing system in the legal context are the laws and decisions that have been put into force since the 2000s. These regulations include the Law No. 5084 on "the Law on the Promotion of Investments and Employment and Amendments to Certain Laws" in 2004, the Law No. 5350 "Law on the Amendment of the Law on the Promotion of Investments and Employment and Certain Laws" in 2006, Council of Ministers Decree No. 15199 in 2009 and "The Decision of the Council of Ministers on State Aid in Investments" in 2012. Although the current incentive system is based on

---

1 Ph.D., University of Eskişehir Osmangazi, Faculty of Economics and Administrative Sciences, Department of Public Finance, 26000, Eskişehir/TURKEY

the Council of Ministers Decision of 2012, a total of 18 regulations have been made that amended this decision. As a result of the arrangements made, the objective article of the Council of Ministers Decision no. 2012/3305 has become as below:

> "The objective of this Decree is to regulate the principles and procedures to orient savings to investments with high added value, to increase production and employment, to encourage strategic investments and regional and large scale investments which shall increase the international competitive power and which have a high research and development content, to increase international direct investments, to decrease regional development differences, to support investments related to environmental protection and clustering and to support research and development activities related with such investments in conformity with the objectives of development plans and annual programs."

Referring to the current investment incentive system in Turkey, it is seen that the system is constructed in accordance with the determined objectives that support national development in the form of regional incentives for ensuring horizontal equity, technology and large-scale investment incentives aimed at increasing the research and development capacity, incentives for the production of goods with high import dependency. Reducing regional development disparities, categorized to achieve national development and specifically identified as objectives, reveals the instrumentality of the investment incentive system as a regional development policy. As a matter of fact, this spatial-based instrumentality of the investment incentive system has a historical process that extends to the Priority Region in Development practice in 1968 based on the law numbered 202 dated 1963, although the scale changes. Accordingly, the laws of 2004 and 2006 provided for the strengthening of the legal basis of the spatial-based investment incentive mechanism, which started in 1968 with the Decree of the Development Program and the decision of the Council of Ministers to declare 22 Provinces as Priority Development Areas. With the 2009 and 2012 Council of Ministers Decisions, besides the spatial-based mechanism, research and development and production areas aimed at domestic value added were also categorized within the incentive system.

Within the scope of this study, it is aimed to question the spatial-based effect of the investment incentive system, which has distinctly been categorized and organized and assumed an objective specific structure since 2009. The questioning of spatial-based impact will be carried out by evaluating the impact of investment incentive system implementations on the current income levels of provinces with similar socio-economic development levels and therefore with close income levels. The analysis and comparison of inter-spatial income levels within different scales is performed by convergence and divergence analyses that determine whether income imbalance closes or deepens in time. These analyses can be performed in two contexts: Beta convergence, which deals with the specific growth performance of spaces, and Sigma convergence, which deals with the continuity of inter-spatial income distribution. However, due to the criticisms that convergence is not detected correctly with Sigma convergence analysis, Beta convergence analysis is preferred in scientific studies. Accordingly, in this study, in order to evaluate the effect of legal changes in the investment incentive system based on the studies in the literature, whether the income convergence in the spatial and temporal context has emerged is evaluated through Beta convergence analysis.

Theoretical Background

Theoretically, considering convergence as income-based and therefore growth-based is realized in the context of different growth models. These models are divided into four main categories: Solow-Swan Growth Model, Stochastic Solow-Swan Model, Mankiw-Romer-Weil Growth Model, and internal growth model.

Solow-Swan Growth model is based on capital accumulation mechanism such as capital, labor, technology and production function equality (Solow, 1956). Within the model, capital equipment is accepted as the sole determinant of the change in income and it is accepted that there is a relationship between initial capital equipment and income growth. Accordingly, the fact that economic growth is negatively affected by the initial capital stock indicates the convergence.

Stochastic Solow-Swan Growth model is formed by adding random variables to the Solow-Swan Model. Similar to the first model, there is a relationship between the output amount and the initial income, and the fact that this relationship is negative is considered to be convergence and positive relationship is considered as the presence of divergence.

The Mankiw-Romer-Weil Growth Model is an extension of the Solow-Swan models with the addition of human capital fact. Similar to the first two models, the initial income has an impact on the growth rate and the convergence rate is expected to be higher due to the low initial income level in the process. However, due to the fact that the long-term economic growth depends on the countries' own characteristics, it is accepted that the countries with resembling population growth rate, technology equipment and human capital accumulation processes will converge to each other (Mankiw, Romer, & Weil, 1992). Therefore, unlike the absolute convergence approach in the first two models, conditional convergence approach is considered necessary.

Unlike neoclassical exogenous growth models, internal growth models have been developed by adding variables with a potential to affect the growth process to the model internally. In these models where technology is internalized, there is a linear relationship between convergence and technology parameters. In these models, unlike Solow-Swan, it is accepted that there will be convergence only between countries of similar structure, in a way similar to Mankiw-Romer-Weil.

Theoretically, convergence approaches differ in the context of growth models, resulting in different concepts of convergence (Islam, 2003). These concepts include micro-convergence and macro-convergence, capture and convergence, convergence within an economy and convergence between countries, convergence in growth rate and income convergence, β convergence and α convergence, unconditional convergence and conditional convergence, conditional convergence and club convergence, income convergence and total factor productivity convergence, deterministic convergence and stochastic convergence (Rassekh, 1998).

Literature

Although, in the literature, convergence analysis made for Turkey were discussed within different scales as regions and provinces convergence, in these analyses, the effects of different variables on convergence were also considered. Accordingly, in the convergence between regions, the results reached were as follows:

i) In a study examining the effect of deposit accounts, there was convergence between 26 regions (Level 2) on the basis of Nomenclature of Territorial Units for Statistics (NUTS) for 1991–2000 period (Zeren & Yılancı, 2011).

ii) In a study examining the effect of spatial difference (East-West), there was a weak convergence between 12 regions (Level 1) according to NUTS for 1987–2001 period (Ersungur & Polat, 2006).

iii) In a study that examined the effect of the industrial agglomeration and the growth of neighboring provinces, there was convergence between the provinces (73 provinces) for the period 1993–2001, while the convergence process was adversely affected by the agglomeration of neighboring provinces, it was affected positively by the growth of the neighbouring provinces (Karaalp & Erdal, 2012).

iv) In a study examining the impact of population, employment and exports, there was a general convergence between provinces (79 provinces) for the period 2004–2014, and the effect of population, employment and exports on the convergence periodically varied (Soyyiğit, 2018).

However, in studies on the convergence of income between regions where only the temporal change was the basis without including different factors, for the level of 2004–2008 in the Level 2 scale (Abdioğlu & Uysal, 2013) and for the period 1960–2010 (Karaca, 2018) it was concluded that there was no convergence between regions.

On the other hand, in the convergence analyses included in the literature, the effect of direct investment incentives for different scales and periods has been examined. However, these studies are limited in number, and there are studies that mainly examine the impact of investment incentives on regional investment, employment, development and economic growth. Accordingly, it was concluded that investment incentives, i) positively affected the investments across Turkey for the 1980–2003 period (Çakmak-Karaçay & Erden, 2004), the investments in developed regions negatively and the investments in less developed regions positively for the period 1991–2000 (Ay, 2005); ii) in the studies conducted with Turkey scale, in Eastern Anatolia during 1980–2006 (Akan & Arslan, 2008), 1980–2011 period 4 incentive zones (Çiftçi & Koç, 2013), 2002–2011 period in 81 provinces (Karaalp, 2014) 81 provinces in the period 2001–2012 (Selim, Koçtürk, & Eryiğit, 2014) and 1980–2008 period (Yavuz, 2010) had a positive effect on employment, iii) in the studies conducted for the 7 geographical regions in the 2002–2009 period, (Şahin & Uysal, 2011) for the Level 2 scale for the period 2004–2012, (Sevinç, Emsen, & Bozkurt, 2016) for the Level 1 scale in the period 2007–2012 (Bakırcı, Ekinci, & Şahinoğlu, 2014) and in 1970–2000 for the provinces covered and not covered by the Incentive Law No. 5084 (Güven, 2007) could not achieve the purpose of eliminating regional imbalances; however, in a study conducted in 2007 for small and medium-sized enterprises operating in Sivas province, (Gülmez & Yalman, 2010) investment incentives had a positive impact on regional development; iv) in the studies conducted for 7 geographical regions of the period 1980–2006 (Özkök, 2009), for the provinces in the period of 1991–2000 (Gerni, Değer, & Değer, 2009), for 81 provinces in 2000 (Yavan, 2011) and for Level 2 in the period of 2004–2011, (Recepoğlu & Değer, 2016) such incentives affected the income, thus the economic growth positively; however, in the study based on six regions determined by "The Socio Economic Development Ranking of Provinces and Regions Study" in the period of 2004–2014, it was concluded that the investment incentives led to economic growth only in developed regions (Değer & Recepoğlu, 2018). Although the effects of investment incentives on the convergence have been indirectly demonstrated by these studies, the effect of the direct investment incentive system on the convergence was examined in a regional (Level 2) and provincial basis study for the period 2004–2012. In that study, it was concluded that there was no convergence at regional level, but convergence emerged for 2009–2012 period in provinces (Gerni, Sarı, Sevinç, & Emsen, 2015).

In this context, studies in the literature for Turkey considered as a whole, the convergence between regions, unlike the convergence between provinces, occurred in the period preceding the year 2000 and did not occur in the periods before and after 2000 over long periods of time. However, despite the positive impact of the investment incentive system on investment, employment and economic growth in Turkey, it can be said that this effect is not effective in terms of regional imbalances and thus cannot provide convergence. In this study, it is aimed to contribute to the literature by revealing whether the changes made in the investment incentive system legislation in particular have a regional based effect.

Empirical Analysis

Data Set and Method

In this study, the relationship between investment incentives and economic growth is examined at regional level. For the investment incentive data, the investment incentive statistics published by the Ministry of Economy in the report dated 01 June 2018 between 01 January 2001 and 31 May 2018 and for the economic growth data, the national accounts data published by Turkey's Statistics Institute (TUIK) under the Regional Statistics were used. Accordingly, while the fixed investment amount (TL) was used as investment incentive data on a regional basis, regardless of the sector, support class and investment type in the investment incentive data set, the gross domestic product per capita (GDP-TL) statistics included in the national accounts by TUIK were used as economic growth data.

In the use of the data set, a categorical distinction was made in both spatial and temporal dimensions. Accordingly, spatial categorization was established on the basis of six regions determined according to the report "Socio-Economic Development Ranking of Provinces and Regions (SEGE)". With this categorization, it is aimed to determine whether there is a convergence of income between the provinces with socio-economic development level and the effect of investment incentives on the convergence between the provinces having similar structure.

With the categorization in temporal dimension, it is aimed to reveal the effect of the transformation of the investment incentive system in the legal context. However, due to the fact that per capita GDP data was announced by TUIK for 2004–2017, the time dimension of the study was limited to 2004–2017. Accordingly, 2009, which constitutes the fundamental legal break for the period in question, is the basis for the categorical separation of the time dimension of the data set. However, since the 2009 regulation became effective in July 2009, and accordingly it was not possible to separate the data set for 2009 in the context of before and after this regulation, a periodic distinction was made as the period 2004–2009 and 2010–2017.

In the studies in the literature, it has been observed that different empirical methods such as horizontal cross-sectional approach, panel approach, time series approach and distribution approach were applied. As a matter of fact, since the data set in this study had a temporal dimension and therefore dynamic analysis was applicable, a limited application with horizontal cross-sectional analysis was not preferred. However, the time series approach was not feasible because the temporal dimension in question was too limited to allow the use of the time series approach. Accordingly, in this study, it was preferred to apply the panel approach method based on the existing data set in order to determine the effect of investment incentives on the income level differences between provinces and thus to identify a convergence.

Within the scope of the panel approach for convergence analysis, different models are used, but (β) convergence analysis which examines the convergence on the basis of the regional distinction determined within the scope of this study and gained popularity with the work of Barro and Sala-i Martin (1991, 1992) and examines the relationship between the initial income levels and growth rates of the spaces was used. In the beta convergence analysis, there are two distinctions as absolute and conditional, and according to the absolute beta convergence hypothesis, there is a negative relationship between the initial income level and growth, and therefore, it is suggested that poor countries will grow faster. However, it is assumed that there is no inter-spatial structural difference in the absolute beta convergence analysis, and the analysis becomes conditional beta convergence analysis with the inclusion of structural differences between the spaces. Accordingly, according to the conditional beta convergence hypothesis, the negative relationship between the initial income level and growth, and hence the assumption that the poorer countries will grow faster, emerges with the effect of the differences in the structural characteristics of spaces at different income levels.

In this study, beta convergence analysis is examined through the following models.

$$\ln(PGDP_{i,t}/PGDP_{i,t-1}) = \alpha + \beta \ln(PGDP_{i,t-1}) + u_i \qquad (1)$$

$PGDP_{i,t}$, represents gross domestic product per capita in period t for region i, $PGDP_{i,t-1}$, represents the gross domestic product per capita in the period t-1 for region i. Therefore, the dependent variable indicates the growth rate in gross domestic product per capita for region i. In this model, the fact that β is a negative coefficient means that the absolute convergence hypothesis is valid.

$$\ln(PGDP_{i,t}/PGDP_{i,t-1}) = \alpha + \beta \ln(PGDP_{i,t-1}) + \lambda x_{i,t-1} + u_i \quad (2)$$

In addition to the variables in model number one, a control variable is added to model number two $x_{i,t-1}$. This variable is used to measure the structural difference between spaces and represents the investments made within the scope of investment incentive certificate. Also, in this model while β coefficient being negative means that the conditional convergence hypothesis is valid, λ coefficient is also expected to be positive.

OLS method was applied since only dependent variable delay was used in the equation to estimate the equation number one. In the estimation of equation number two, Generalized Moments Method (GMM) developed by Arellano and Bond was preferred due to the dynamic structure of these models and since it takes the first-order differences of the variables and uses the past value of the dependent variable as a tool variable, thus allowing the use of a tool variable for the solution of deviant and inconsistent results. However, for the consistency and validity of the GMM estimation method results, two basic assumptions are required. First, for the reliability of the prediction results, first-order auto-correlation is a problem, but second-order auto-correlation should not be present. As a matter of fact, the presence of auto-correlation indicates that the lagged value of the dependent variable is internal or that the instrument variables are not external. Secondly, the tool variables must be external and suitable for the model. For this purpose, Hansen Excess Determination (Hansen J Test) and Hansen Externality Tests are performed. The second assumption regarding the consistency of the GMM estimation method is also provided by accepting the null hypotheses of these tests as "no over-determination" and "tool variables are external".

Empirical Findings

Within the scope of the study, the findings about Beta convergence analysis estimated with OLS and GMM method by using investment incentive and output statistics for per capita GDP belonging to 81 provinces in Turkey and related to the period of 2004–2017 are shown in the tables below according to the temporal and the spatial categorization established for the purpose of the study.

Regional Income Convergence & Investment Incentive System   127

Accordingly, the estimate results of the absolute β convergence for Equation 1 are evaluated in Tab. 1; and the results of the conditional β convergence estimation using Equation 2 are evaluated for each period of 2004–2009 and 2010–2017 in Tab. 3 and Tab. 4.

Tab. 1: Results of Unconditional β Convergence Estimation for the 6 Region and the Periods of 2004–2009 and 2010–2017

Periods	Regions	Coefficients	Coefficient Estimations	t statistics	p-value	F statistics	F Significance
2004–2009	1	α	10.15134	68.21	0.000	13.17	0.008
		β	-0.0000331	-3.63	0.008		
	2	α	13.1677	12.85	0.000	15.64	0.002
		β	-0.4218299	-3.96	0.002		
	3	α	13.26309	13.79	0.000	17.61	0.001
		β	-0.4508061	-4.20	0.001		
	4	α	13.5465	18.10	0.000	39.56	0.000
		β	-0.5078439	-6.29	0.000		
	5	α	12.01857	18.83	0.000	27.01	0.000
		β	-0.3653553	-5.20	0.000		
	6	α	13.20998	12.74	0.000	22.18	0.000
		β	-0.5624411	-4.71	0.000		
2010–2017	1	α	13.43083	15.83	0.000	13.27	0.008
		β	-0.2976841	-3.64	0.008		
	2	α	12.94094	17.97	0.000	16.18	0.002
		β	-0.2891873	-4.02	0.002		
	3	α	13.37002	17.90	0.000	20.09	0.001
		β	-0.34508420	-4.48	0.001		
	4	α	13.06259	16.57	0.000	18.18	0.001
		β	-0.33293	-4.26	0.001		
	5	α	13.85445	11.14	0.000	11.44	0.004
		β	-0.4371804	-3.38	0.004		
	6	α	13.20738	15.98	0.000	23.55	0.000
		β	-0.4147096	-4.85	0.000		

According to the results of the absolute convergence analysis, where Equation 1 is estimated by OLS method, because for both periods in all 6 regions β coefficient is negative and probability value is significant (p <0.05), it is observed that absolute convergence is present.

Based on the determination of absolute convergence for each region, conditional convergence analysis was conducted in order to reveal the effect of investment incentive system on this convergence. The test results are summarized in the table below in order to determine the reliability of the estimates obtained primarily by GMM method and the suitability of the investments made within the scope of the investment incentive system used as a tool variable.

Tab. 2: Verifications Tests for the Model and the Instrumental Variable for the 6 Region and the Periods of 2004–2009 and 2010–2017

Periods	Tests	Region 1	Region 2	Region 3	Region 4	Region 5	Region 6
2004–2009	AR(1) Test	0.466	0.747	0.913	0.685	0.115	0.773
	AR(2) Test	0.922	0.463	0.459	0.256	0.781	0.062
	Hansen J Test	0.106	0.073	0.104	0.059	0.053	0.087
	Hansen Difference Test	0.906	0.707	0.756	0.696	0.635	0.681
	Number of Groups	8	13	12	17	16	15
	Number of Observation	45	75	68	99	91	82
	Number of Instruments	6	10	10	12	7	10
2010–2017	AR(1) Test	0.230	0.007	0.042	0.001	0.071	0.122
	AR(2) Test	0.258	0.024	0.069	0.091	0.716	0.392
	Hansen J Test	0.195	0.301	0.396	0.202	0.148	0.189
	Hansen Difference Test	0.118	0.801	0.306	0.886	0.629	0.792
	Number of Groups	8	14	14	17	16	15
	Number of Observation	61	101	93	129	125	117
	Number of Instruments	8	13	12	16	14	14

According to the results of AR (1) and AR (2), which provide first- and second-order auto-correlation, it was concluded that in the data set for all 6 regions for 2004–2009 period and in the data set for all regions but the second region (AR

(2) <0.05), there was high probability value, and therefore there was no first and second degree auto-correlation. Accordingly, it can be said that GMM estimation results are reliable. Hansen Excess Determination and Hansen Externality tests were performed to determine the externality of the tool variables and their suitability to the model. According to the results of the test, it was observed that there were no excessive determinations in tool variables in all regional models for 2004–2009 and 2010–2017 periods and that tool variables were external variables. Thus, tool variables are both model-appropriate and suitable for being tool variables. GMM estimation results are summarized in the table below depending on the model and tool variables.

Tab. 3: Results of Conditional β Convergence Estimation for the 6 Region and the Period of 2004–2009

Periods	Regions	Coefficients	Coefficient Estimations	t Statistic	p-Value	F Statistic	F Significance
2004–2009	1	α	13.64618	4.44	0.003	7.96	0.016
		β	-0.5344096	-1.71	0.132		
		λ	0.1749262	3.32	0.013		
	2	α	13.20227	12.95	0.000	8.51	0.005
		β	-0.4226638	-4.12	0.001		
		λ	0.0058463	-0.12	0.906		
	3	α	13.24019	11.85	0.000	6.50	0.014
		β	-0.4439983	-3.60	0.004		
		λ	-0.008057	-0.15	0.881		
	4	α	12.4731	20.98	0.000	17.85	0.000
		β	-0.4060966	-5.95	0.000		
		λ	0.0480891	1.48	0.159		
	5	α	-69.84151	-0.97	0.346	3.75	0.048
		β	9.156589	1.08	0.296		
		λ	0.2706705	2.69	0.017		
	6	α	13.09047	12.16	0.000	11.84	0.001
		β	-0.5565631	-4.54	0.000		
		λ	0.033031	1.09	0.295		

According to the results of the conditional convergence analysis in which Equation 2 is estimated by GMM method, as β coefficient is negative and probability value is significant (p <0.05) in the 2nd, 3rd, fourth and 6th regions, conditional convergence is observed. In the first region, there is no convergence due to the fact that probability value was not significant (0.132> 0.05) and in the fifth region β coefficient is positive, so there is no convergence present. Regarding the effect of investments made based on investment incentive certificate, which is the tool variable, on convergence in the regions where convergence exists, it does not have a significant (p <0.05) and positive effect ($\lambda > 0$), contrary to expectations. As a matter of fact, although it has a positive coefficient in regions 2, 4 and 6, the tool variable does not have a positive effect on the convergence between provinces on a regional basis due to the fact that the coefficient is not significant (p> 0.05).

Tab. 4: Results of Conditional β Convergence Estimation for the 6 Region and the Period of 2010–2017

Periods	Regions	Coefficients	Coefficient Estimations	t Statistic	p-Value	F Statistic	F Significance
2010–2017	1	α	12.66654	3.50	0.010	66.56	0.000
		β	-0.4179201	-1.26	0.248		
		λ	0.2579037	7.15	0.000		
	2	α	12.24303	10.58	0.000	6.65	0.011
		β	-0.2385692	-2.57	0.024		
		λ	0.0290982	0.54	0.598		
	3	α	12.83344	13.48	0.000	12.82	0.001
		β	-0.31130799	-3.59	0.004		
		λ	0.0381983	1.22	0.249		
	4	α	12.41366	20.92	0.000	23.62	0.000
		β	-0.2816697	-5.43	0.000		
		λ	0.0284401	1.14	0.271		
	5	α	13.27128	10.52	0.000	4.76	0.025
		β	-0.3849485	-3.01	0.009		
		λ	0.0161224	0.46	0.650		
	6	α	12.7548	13.65	0.000	9.16	0.003
		β	-0.370717	-4.11	0.001		
		λ	0.0101751	0.26	0.799		

According to the results of the conditional convergence analysis in which Equation 2 is estimated by GMM method, β coefficient is negative and probability value is significant (p <0.05), so there is conditional convergence. In the 1st region, there is no convergence due to the fact that the probability value is not significant (0.248> 0.05). Regarding the effect of investments made based on investment incentive certificate, which is a tool variable, on convergence in the regions where convergence exists, it does not have a significant (p <0.05) and positive effect ($\lambda > 0$), contrary to expectations. As a matter of fact, although the tool variable has a positive coefficient in all regions, the tool variable does not have a positive effect on the convergence between provinces on a regional basis due to the fact that the coefficient is not significant (p> 0.05).

When the results of the conditional Beta convergence estimation for 2004–2009 and 2010–2017 periods were evaluated as a whole, it was concluded that the regulations made in 2004, which focused on regional incentives specifically within the scope of investment incentive system, and in 2009, whose objective specific features such as investments for research and development increased, had no effect on the convergence of provinces based on regions with similar socio-economic development levels. Accordingly, in the context of income convergence, it can be said that the regulations made in 2009 did not produce a different effect from those in 2004. Although there are period and scale differences, these results obtained are similar to the studies in the literature conducted for 7 geographical regions in the period of 2002–2009 which concluded that the investment incentive system did not achieve the aim of eliminating regional imbalances, (Şahin & Uysal, 2011) for the Level 2 scale in the period 2004–2012, (Sevinç, Emsen, & Bozkurt, 2016) for the Level 1 scale for the period 2007–2012, (Bakırcı, Ekinci, & Şahinoğlu, 2014) for provinces covered and not covered by the Incentive Law No. 5084 in the period 1970–2000, (Güven, 2007) and Level 2 scale for the 2004–2012 period, which concluded that there was no convergence at the regional level (Gerni, Sarı, Sevinç, & Emsen, 2015). In order to question the reason of this situation obtained as a result of the analysis in the context of investment incentive system, the distribution of investments supported within the scope of investment incentive system in the period of 2004–2017 is examined in 6 regions.

Fig. 1 shows the distribution of investments supported under the investment incentive system in the period 2004–2017 and the amount of supported investment increases as the colors on the map become darker. According to the map, the highest amount of support (the darkest two colors) is obtained from the provinces in the top three regions with the highest socio-economic level and the lowest amount of support (the lightest color) was obtained by three, four, five and sixth regions. Therefore, a significant portion of the incentives within the scope of investment incentive system went to the provinces with the highest socio-economic development level (first region), while the amount of support to the provinces with the lowest socio-economic development level (sixth region) remained at the lowest level. Although the period is different (2009–2017), a similar result has been reached in a different study (Doğan, 2018) that specifically examines regional investment incentives. However, if all of the strategic, large-scale, regional and general investment incentives are included, it is obvious that the impact on per capita income levels and economic growth of provinces

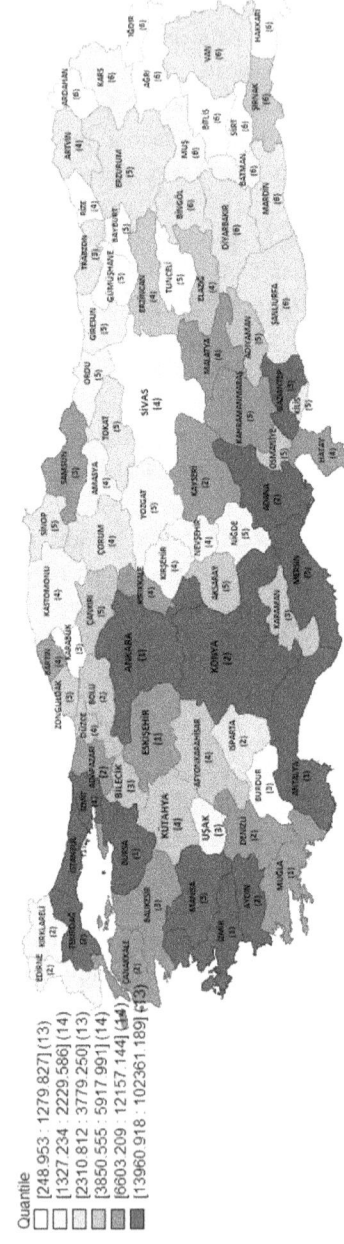

Fig. 1: Regional Dispersion of Induced Investments via Investment Incentive Certificate during the Period of 2004–2017*

*The values in brackets indicate the region where the provinces are indicated according to socio-economic development level.

Source: It is generated by the author via using the GeoDa and Investment Incentives Dataset published by Ministry of Economy.

in each region will be more decisive considering the size of the supported investment amount.

On the other hand, when the amount of support received by the provinces on the basis of socio-economic development level in the context of Fig. 1 is evaluated from the regional context, it can be seen that it includes provinces receiving support from almost all levels except the first region. For example, some of the provinces in the sixth region received the lowest level of support (Bitlis, Siirt, Hakkari, Agrı, Igdır, Ardahan) and some of them were five (Kars, Muş, Batman), four (Van, Bingol, Diyarbakır, Mardin, Şanlıurfa) and third (Şırnak) receives the highest level of support. A similar situation exists for other regions outside the first region. It can be said that this situation has an effect on the differentiation of the growth paths of the provinces on the basis of each region (Gluschenko, 2012), thus having different growth paths even though they have similar income levels and the elimination of the potential convergence in absolute Beta convergence.

Conclusion

Financial incentive system which is one of the basic tools that replaced the interventionist fiscal policy as a tool of regulatory fiscal policy in Turkey, has turned into an objective specific structure, particularly with arrangements made since the 2000s. With this objective specific structure, the investment incentive system has been categorized based on regional, strategic and technological development. However, it is expected that this structure, which emerges in the legal context, will exist in practice for the relevant purpose.

In this study, an empirical analysis was conducted to examine whether the objective of eliminating regional imbalances intended in legal context arises in practice. Based on the objective specific structure of the investment incentive system with the decision of the Council of Ministers numbered 15199 in 2009 and with the aim of revealing the effect of this specific structure, a spatial categorization based on six regions by a periodic distinction between 2004–2009 and 2010–2017 and spatial categorization was made. As a result of the OLS and Beta convergence analyses made on the basis of these categorizations, it was concluded that there is absolute convergence on the basis of each region, but there is no conditional convergence in which the effect of investments made within the investment incentive system is tried to be put forward. This means that the convergence of the provinces in each region to the common growth path on regional basis does not occur in the convergence of the growth path of each province to the growth path of the other provinces in a system including investment incentive system applications. The fact that there is no conditional convergence due to the investment incentive system among the provinces with similar socio-economic characteristics can be evaluated as the fact that the difference in income increase even between these provinces could not be overcome by the investment incentive system applications. This suggests that the aim of eliminating regional imbalances in the allocation of incentives cannot be practiced. Therefore, it can be said that the practical process of the investment incentive system is incompatible with the objective specific structure determined in the legal sense.

As a result, it is seen that the investment incentive system in Turkey remains uncovered practically in the context of the objective specific legislation for the elimination of regional imbalances in Turkey included in the Council of Ministers Decision No. 15199 and 3305 issued in 2009 and 2012. Accordingly, it is deemed necessary to make arrangements in the execution phase of the investment incentive system that will enable the realization of the objective in the legal context. Beyond the determination of the execution phase on the basis of the legal regulation, which constitutes the ideal of these arrangements, it will be possible to solve the problems arising during the execution phase by moving them to the legislative phase. In this context, the incentive elements within the legal context of the investment incentive system should be differentiated on a regional basis as well as allowing for the elimination of imbalances between provinces in each region.

References

Abdioğlu, Z., & Uysal, T. (2013). Türkiye'de Bölgeler Arası Yakınsama: Panel Birim Kök Analizi. *Atatürk Üniversitesi İktisadi ve İdari Bilimler Dergisi, 27*(3), 125–143.

Akan, Y., & Arslan, İ. (2008). Türkiye'de Sektörel Yatırım Teşvik Belgeleri ve İstihdam Analizi: Doğu Anadolu Bölgesi Üzerine Bir Uygulama (1980–2006). *Çalışma ve Toplum, 1*(16), 107–119.

Ay, M. H. (2005). Yatırım Teşviklerinin Sabit Sermaye Yatırımları Üzerindeki Etkisi. *Selçuk Üniversitesi Karaman İktisadi ve İdari Bilimler Dergisi, 5*(2), 176–184.

Bakırcı, F., Ekinci, E. D., & Şahinoğlu, T. (2014). Bölgesel Kalkınma Politikalarının Etkinliği: Türkiye Alt Bölgeler Bazında Bir Uygulama. *Atatürk Üniversitesi Sosyal Bilimler Enstitüsü Dergisi, 18*(2), 281–298.

Barro, R. J., & Martin, X. S.-i. (1991). Convergence Across States and Regions. *Brookings Papers on Economic Activity* (s. 107–182). içinde

Barro, R. J., & Martin, X. S.-i. (1992). Convergence. *Journal of Political Economy, 100*(2), 223–251.

Çakmak-Karaçay, H., & Erden, L. (2004). Yeni Bölgesel Kalkınma Yaklaşımları Ve Kamu Destekleme Politikaları: Türkiye'den Bölgesel Panel Veri Setiyle Ampirik Bir Analiz. *Gazi Üniversitesi İİBF Dergisi, 6*(3), 77–96.

Çiftçi, H., & Koç, M. (2013). İstihdamın Artan Önemi ve Teşvik Belgeli Yatırımlar Etkinlik Analizi. *21. Yüzyılda Eğitim ve Toplum Eğitim Bilimleri ve Sosyal Araştırmalar Dergisi, 2*(6), 19–41.

Değer, M. K., & Recepoğlu, M. (2018). Yerel Ekonomik Büyümede Devletin Rolü: Kamu Yatırım Harcamaları mı Toksa Yatırım Teşvikleri mi? *Çağdaş Yerel Yönetimler Dergisi, 27*(1), 1–22.

Doğan, E. (2018). Bölgesel Nitelikli Yatırım Teşviklerine Yönelik Temel Mantık ve Mekansal Otokorelasyon Yöntemi ile Bir Değerlendirme. *Maliye Araştırmaları Dergisi, 4*(3), 141–158.

Ersungur, Ş. M., & Polat, Ö. (2006). Türkiye'de Bölgeler Arasında Yakınsama Analizi. *Atatürk Üniversitesi Sosyal Bilimler Enstitüsü Dergisi, 8*(2), 335–343.

Gerni, C., Değer, M. K., & Değer, Ö. S. (2009). Provincial Economic Growth in Turkey: Cross-Section Analyses. *İktisat, İşletme ve Finans, 24*(282), 54–81.

Gerni, C., Sarı, S., Sevinç, H., & Emsen, Ö. S. (2015). "Bölgesel Dengesizliklerin Giderilmesinde Yatırım Teşviklerinin Rolü ve Başarı Kriteri Olarak Yakınsama Analizleri: Türkiye Örneği", International Conference on Eurasian Economies, 311–320.

Gluschenko, K. (2012). *Myths About Beta-Convergence*. Michigan: William Davidson Instute.

Gülmez, M., & Yalman, İ. N. (2010). Yatırım Teşviklerinin Bölgesel Kalkınmaya Etkileri: Sivas İli Örneği. *Atatürk Üniversitesi İktisadi ve İdari Bilimler Dergisi, 24*(2), 235–257.

Güven, A. (2007). Türkiye'de İller Arası Gelir Eşitsizliğinde Teşvik Politikasının Rolü: Bir Ayrıştırma Analizi. *Akdeniz İ.İ.B.F. Dergisi, 14*, 20–38.

Islam, N. (2003). What Have We Learnt From The Convergence Debate. *Journal of Economic Surveys, 17*(3), 306–362.

Karaalp, H. S. (2014). The Effect of Public Investment and Firm-Based Investment Incentives On Employment: A Panel Data Analysis for Turkey. *Journal of Economic and Social Development, 1*(1), 74 85.

Karaalp, H. S., & Erdal, F. (2012). Sanayileşmenin Bölgesel Yığılması ve Komşu İllerin Büyümesi Gelir Farklılıklarını Artırır mı? Türkiye için Bir Beta Yakınsama Analizi. *Ege Akademik Bakış, 12*(4), 475–486.

Karaca, O. (2018). Türkiye'de Bölgesel Yakınsamanın 50 Yılı: Yeni Veri Seti ve 1960–2010 Dönemi Analizi. *Sosyoekonomi, 26*(35), 207–228.

Mankiw, N., Romer, D., & Weil, D. N. (1992). A Contribution to the Empirics of Economic Growth. *The Quarterly Journal of Economics, 107*(2), 407–437.

Özkök, Y. (2009). Türkiye'de Yatırım Teşviklerinin Bölgesel Gelişmişlik Bazında Değerlendirilmesi. *Gaziantep Üniversitesi Sosyal Bilimler Enstitüsü Yüksek Lisans Tezi.*

Rassekh, F. (1998). The Convergence Hypothesis: History, Theory and Evidence. *Open Economies Review, 9*, 85–105.

Recepoğlu, M., & Değer, M. K. (2016). Türkiye'de Bölgesel Yatırım Teşviklerinin Bölgesel Ekonomik Büyüme Üzerine Etkisi: Düzey 2 Bölgeleri Üzerine Panel Veri Analizleri (2004–2011). *Kastamonu Üniversitesi İktisadi ve İdari Bilimler Fakültesi Dergisi, 14*, 6–21.

Selim, S., Koçtürk, O. M., & Eryiğit, P. (2014). Türkiye'de Yatırım Teşvikleri ve Sabit Yatırımların İstihdam Üzerine Etkisi: Panel Veri Analizi. *Ege Akademik Bakış, 14*(4), 661–673.

Sevinç, H., Emsen, Ö. S., & Bozkurt, E. (2016). Yatırım Teşvik Politikalarının Bölgesel Belirleyicilerine Yönelik Bir Analiz: Türkiye Örneği. *Çankırı Karatekin Üniversitesi İktisadi ve İdari Bilimler Fakültesi Dergisi, 6*(1), 525–556.

Solow, R. (1956). Contribution to the Theory of Economic Growth. *Quarterly Journal of Economics, 70*(65).

Soyyiğit, S. (2018). Türkiye'de Kriz Öncesi ve Sonrası Dönemde İl Bazında Yakınsama Analizi. *Social Sciences Studies Journal, 4*(16), 1279–1287.

Şahin, M., & Uysal, Ö. (2011). Bölgesel Kalkınma Çerçevesinde Yaırım Teşviklerinin Shift-Share Analizi. *Maliye Dergisi, 160*, 111–138.

Yavan, N. (2011). Teşviklerin Bölgesel Ekonomik Büyüme Üzerindeki Etkisi: Ampirik Bir Analiz. *Ekonomik Yaklaşım, 22*(81), 65–104.

Yavuz, A. (2010). Bir Maliye Politikası Aracı Olarak Yatırım Teşviklerinin Rekabet Koşulları Altında Özel Kesim Yatırımları ve İstihdam Üzerine Etkisi: Ekonometrik Bir Analiz. *Süleyman Demirel Üniversitesi İktisadi ve İadri Bilimler Fakültesi Dergisi, 15*(1), 83–101.

Zeren, F., & Yılancı, V. (2011). Türkiye'de Bölgeler Arası Gelir Yakınsaması: Rassal Katsayılı Panel Veri Analizi Uygulaması. *Business and Economics Research Journal, 2*(1), 143–151.

Necmettin Çelik**

Chapter 7 The Division and Specialization Proposals to Regions in Line with the Spatial and Sectoral Concentration Patterns of Turkey

Introduction

The balanced and comprehensive regional development is closely associated with the main issues of economics such as full employment, effective use of resources and rapid economic growth. Since, the serious and ongoing problem of regional disparities pressures on the developed regions via several channels such as immigration as well as it damages on the self-sufficiency dynamics of undeveloped regions. It puts some obstacles on the potential growth process because of using of resources inefficiently and imperfectly. Therefore, the regional policies toward balanced and comprehensive regional development process are crucial at least national policies.

Being able to minimize of regional disparities issue requires a division and specialization having substitution perspective among regions. It is based on exposing of the strategic and competitive aspects of own regions. Thus, all regions will be able to use their own resources effectively and perfectly; and also, they reach rapid growth abilities by establishing the macroeconomic policies in consistent with their own strategic or competitive advantages.

In this direction, the regional disparities are ongoing and structural issue despite the partial and ignorable improvements in Turkey according to the variation coefficients estimating regional disparities (Deliktaş and Çelik, 2018a: 387; 2019: 30). Accordingly, the industries which are being exhibited advantages strategically and competitively or potentially in 26 NUTS-II Regions[1] in Turkey over 2009-2015 have been identified by Location Quotients (LQ) based on the number of firms, employees and amount of investments. Indeed, this methodology has been mainly used in the literature to identify strategic or competitive sectors in any regions or locations such as TÜSİAD, Kazancık (2007), İZKA (2010), GEKA (2011), BEBKA (2012), Dinçer and Karakayacı (2012), KUZKA, BAKKA (2013),

---

* * Asst. Prof., Department of Economics, İzmir Katip Çelebi University, İzmir-Turkey, Necmetttin.Celik@ikc.edu.tr
1 The detailed information about that regions could be seen in Appendix 1.

KUZKA (2014), FKA (2014), BAKKA (2014), Ünal, Sungur (2015), Seçilmiş (2015), Lazaretti et al. (2014), ÇKA (2017), Akgüngör et al. (2017), Akgüngör et al. (2018a), Akgüngör et al. (2018b), Çiftçi (2018), Deliktaş and Çelik (2018a, 2019), Çelik et al. (2019). Finally, the specific policies toward regions have been proposed in the light with empirical findings of the investigation.

Methodology and Analysis

In the estimation of the LQ that measure sectoral specializations in a specific region, the proportion of the regional share of sectors to national share in terms of several proxies, such as number of employees, has been used. Then the concentration degree of that sector could be estimated. LQ is defined as (Miller and Blair, 1985):

$$LQ_L = \frac{L_i^R}{L_R} / \frac{L_i^N}{L_N} \quad (1)$$

Where L_i^R stands for the employment level of sector i in a region, and L_R stands for the total employment level of that region, while L_i^N stands for the national employment level of sector I, and L_N stands for total national employment level. The LQ values higher than 1 refer to specialization of a sector in a region over the national average.[2]

However, estimating of the spatial concentration patterns by the number of employees only is not effective because of the differences between industries in terms of their capital- or labor-intensive structure. Indeed, the spatial concentration patterns of the capital intensive industries that have crucial potential as the number of capital or the amount of investment they receive will not be identified by the LQ values based on the number of employees. On the other hand, the confidence level of investigations could be decreased due to the alternative indicators that do not have similar importance at the specialization level (BAKKA, 2014: 24). Therefore, alternative LQ values based on the number of capital and the amount of investment was taken into consideration. They are defined as:

$$LQ_C = \frac{C_i^R}{C_R} / \frac{C_i^N}{C_N} \quad (2)$$

---

2   In some studies such as Çelik et al. (2019), Deliktaş and Çelik (2019), Akgüngör et al. (2018), Akgüngör et al. (2017) 1,25 threshold took into account.

$$LQ_I = \frac{I_i^R}{I_R} / \frac{I_i^N}{I_N} \tag{3}$$

Where C_i^R stands for the number of firms performing in sector i in a region, C_R stands for the total number of firms in that region while C_i^N stands for the number of firms performing in sector i in nation and C_N stands for the total number of firms in nation.
Where I_i^R; stands for the amount of investments toward sector i in a region, I_R stands for the total the amount of investments in that region while I_i^N stands for amount of investments toward sector i in the nation and I_N stands for the total amount of investment in the nation.

In the sectoral investigation process, there are 17 industries that perform in Turkey and have continuous statistics which are "Agriculture, Forestry and Fishing", "Mining", "Manufacturing", "Energy", "Water Supply, Sewerage, Waste Management and Remediation Services", "Construction", "Wholesale and Retail Trade and Repair Services of Motor Vehicles and Motorcycles", "Logistic", "Tourism", "Information and Communication", "Real Estate Services", "Professional, Scientific and Technical Services", "Management and Support Services", "Education", "Human Health and Social Work Services", "Culture, Art and Sport Services" and "Other Services". In addition, "Finance and Insurance Services" including insurance, reinsurance and pension funding services and services auxiliary to financial services and "Public Administration and Defense Services; Compulsory Social Security Services" provided by government and public administrations could not be considered due to lack of data. Tab. 1 includes detailed information about the main activities in these industries.

Empirical Findings

Fig. 1 includes 26 NUTS-II Regions that have LQ values 1,25 or higher LQ values based on all criteria such as the number of employees, firms and the amount of investment in 17 industries.[3] When findings are evaluated as a whole, the regions 20 to 26 in NUTS-II have spatial concentration of the industries 12 to 17 that are strategically or competitively while the regions TR31, TR63, TR71, TR83, TR90 and TRC2 do not have concentration patterns that indicates a specialization level in any of the industries in Turkey.

---

3 The detailed information about the LQ values of regions in strategically specialized sectors could be seen in Appendix 2.

Tab. 1: NACE-2 Industries and Activities

NACE 2 Code	Industries	Activities
A	Agriculture, Forestry and Fishing	It includes crop and animal production, hunting and related service activities
B	Mining and Quarrying	It includes mining of coal, lignite, metal ores; extraction of crude petroleum and natural and mining support service activities
C	Manufacturing	It includes manufacture of several products such as food, beverages, tobacco, textiles, wearing apparel, leather and related products, wood, paper and paper products, coke and refined petroleum, chemicals and chemical products, basic pharmaceutical, rubber and plastic, other non-metallic mineral products, basic metals, fabricated metal products (except machinery and equipment), computer, electronic and optical products, electrical equipment, machinery and equipment n.e.c., motor vehicles, trailers and semi-trailers, other transport equipment, furniture, etc.
D	Energy	It includes production, transmission, distribution and trade of electricity and gas; and also, steam and air conditioning supply
E	Water Supply, Sewerage Waste Management and Remediation Services	It includes water collection, treatment and supply, sewerage and waste collection, etc.
F	Construction	It includes construction of buildings, civil engineering and specialized construction activities
G	Wholesale and Retail Trade and Repair Services of Motor Vehicles and Motorcycles	It includes wholesale and retail trade and repair of motor vehicles and motorcycles activities
H	Logistic	It includes land, water and air transport and transport via pipelines; warehousing and support activities for transportation and postal and courier activities
I	Tourism	It includes accommodation and food and beverage service activities
J	Information and Communication	It includes several activities such as publishing, programming and broadcasting, telecommunications, computer programming, consultancy and related activities, information service activities, etc.

Tab. 1: (continued)

NACE 2 Code	Industries	Activities
L	Real Estate Services	It includes buying and selling of own real estate, renting and operating of own or leased real estate and real estate activities on a fee or contract basis
M	Professional, Scientific and Technical Services	It includes legal and accounting activities, activities of head offices; management consultancy activities, architectural and engineering activities; technical testing and analysis, scientific research and development, advertising and market research and other professional, scientific and technical activities, etc.
N	Administrative and Support Service Activities	It includes rental and leasing activities, employment activities, travel agency, tour operator reservation service and related activities, security and investigation activities, office administrative, office support and other business support activities, etc.
P	Education	It includes pre-primary, primary, secondary, higher and other education and educational support activities
Q	Human Health and Social Work Services	It includes human health activities such as hospital, general and specialist medical practice activities, residential care activities and social work activities without accommodation
R	Culture, Art and Sport Services	It includes creative, arts and entertainment activities; libraries, archives, museums and other cultural activities; gambling and betting activities; sports activities and amusement and recreation activities
S	Other Services	It includes activities of membership organizations, repair of computers and personal and household goods and other personal service activities

Source: Eurostat, https://ec.europa.eu/eurostat/documents/3859598/5902521/KS-RA-07-015-EN.PDF

When findings are evaluated at the sectoral and regional levels, the region TR10 (Istanbul) has a strategic role in the information and communication industry that is consistent with the findings in Türkcan (2019) and Çelik et al. (2019) while exhibiting a competitive advantage in the several service activities such as education, health and real estate. On the other hand, logistics, especially, based on water and air transportation might be considered as a key sector for

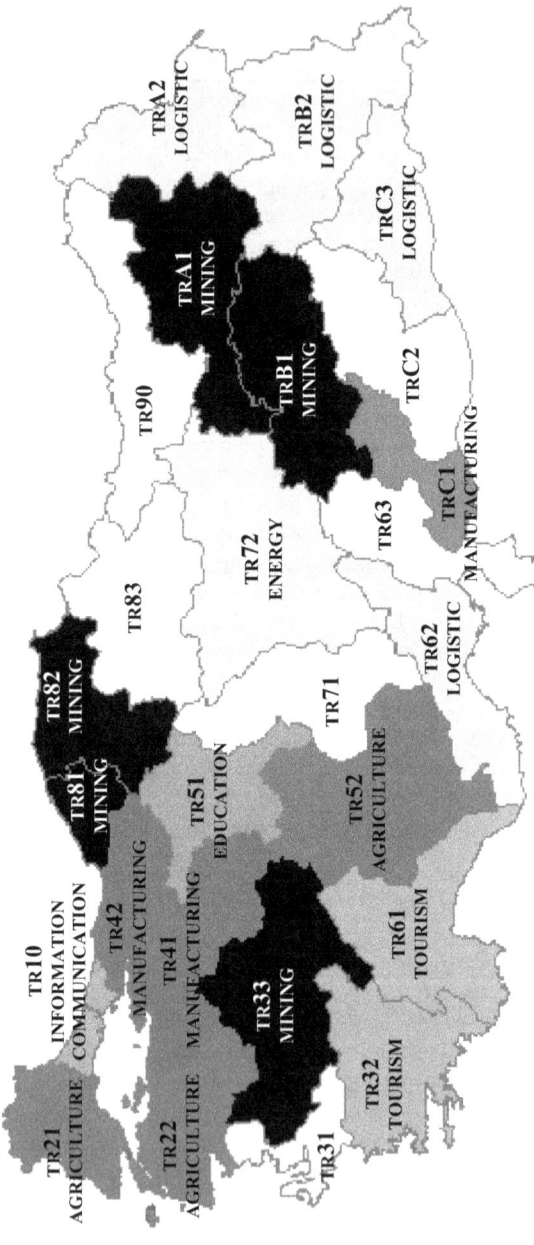

Fig. 1: The Sectoral Concentration Patterns of Regions (1,25 or Higher LQ Values in All Criteria)
Source: It has been compiled over TSI Annual Industry and Service Statistics by the Author

the region TR10 because it has the largest port capacity[4], domestic and foreign passengers and freight traffic[5] thanks to its geopolitical location and existing capacity. Similarly, logistics is a strategic sector for the region TR62 (Adana) which has Mersin Port, the region TRA2 (Ağrı) which has the border gates to Azerbaijan, Georgia, Iran and Iraq; and also, the regions TRB2 (Van) and TRC3 (Mardin) which are on the route for Economic and Social Commission to Asia and the Pacific (ESCAP).

Manufacturing, recognized as a key to economic growth, is concentrated mainly in the regions TR41 (Bursa) and TR42 (Kocaeli) compared to the national level; therefore, it could be considered as a strategic sector for these regions. This is consistent with the findings in Çelik et al. (2019). On the other hand, the concentration patterns of manufacturing in the regions TR33 (Manisa) and TRC1 (Gaziantep) are quite complicated especially in terms of the number of employees and amount of investment rather than the number of firms. Therefore, it could be evaluated as potentially strategic or competitive sector for these regions.

Tourism is another crucial source of growth thanks to its added value, employment and foreign currency capacity which has a strategic importance for the regions TR61 (Antalya) and TR31 (Aydın) that are known to be the largest tourism destinations in Turkey and it could be reached competitive aspects in the region TR22 (Balıkesir), especially in terms of the number of employees and firms. Findings are consistent with the tourism capacities of the regions TR61, TR32 and TR22 respectively, since, especially, the regions TR61 and TR32 stand out as coastal tourism destinations thanks to their tourism centers and geographical structures;[6] and also, the Region TRB2 has several strong aspects in terms of a tourism center such as a highly accessible and a rich cultural background

---

4 According to General Directorate of Maritime Trade Statistics, in 2018, the Ambarlı Port has a the largest foreign trade capacity as the number of container in water transportation with 28,2 % share in Turkey. https://atlantis.udhb.gov.tr/istatistik/istatistik_konteyner.aspx, Access Date: 22.07.2019

5 According to General Directorate of State Airports Authority statistics, in 2018, 78 % of total passengers and freight traffic over Turkey was occurred in Atatürk and Sabiha Gökçen Airports, https://www.dhmi.gov.tr/sayfalar/istatistik.aspx, Access Date: 22.07.2019

6 According to statistics compiled from Tourism Centers List which are published by Republic of Turkey Ministry of Culture and Tourism, the region TR61 has 35, the region TR32 has 33 and the region TR22 has 18 to 270 tourism centers in Turkey. In other words, these regions reflect almost the 32 % of tourism potential in Turkey alone. http://yigm.kulturturizm.gov.tr/TR-9669/ktkgb-ve-turizm-merkezleri.html, Access Date: 22.07.2019

(Gökdeniz, 2015). On the other hand, the food industry based on agriculture and fishing activities could also reach a competitive structure where the tourism industry has a strategic importance. Indeed, findings indicate that the food industry has competitive advantages in the tourism destinations of TR61, TR32 and TR22. And also, the food industry based on agriculture, forestry and fishing activities is a strategic sector for the regions TR52 (Konya), TR21 (Tekirdağ) and TR22 (Balıkesir) respectively because of their geographic and climatic characteristics that are better than other potential regions.

Education is another sector that is concentrated spatially which leads to a strategical specialization level in Turkey. According to findings, the education sector, including pre-primary, primary, secondary, higher and other education and educational support activities, has a strategic importance for the region TR51 (Ankara) and it is a competitive aspect of the region TR10 (İstanbul). Findings are consistent with the human capital dynamics of the regions TR51 and TR10, which are respectively, the first and second largest regions in Turkey in terms of the share of college or faculty graduates in total population which are 21,5 % and 17,4 % (Çelik, 2017: 30).

Finally, mining and energy are the sectors that are concentrated spatially in Turkey. Findings indicate that mining concentrates spatially in the regions TR33 (Manisa), TR81 (Zonguldak), TR82 (Kastamonu), TRA1 (Erzurum) and TRB1 (Malatya) which could reach a sectoral specialization level. They are consistent with the natural resources of these regions. For instance, the region TR33 (Manisa) has rich mineral diversity and reserves such as titanium, boron and uranium; which are, respectively, 100 %, 50 % and 37 % of Turkey's total reserves (ZKA, 2012: 8). And also, the copper and marble are the main reserves of the Region TR82 (KUZKA, 2013: 101); mining activities are mainly shaped by the iron-steel industry which are the most added value sources of the Region TR81 (BAKKA, 2013: 12; 2014: 25) and the metal-ore mining is mainly concentrate on the region TRB1 (FKA, 2014: 107). On the other hand, findings are mainly consistent with the findings of local development agencies such as ZKA (2012), BAKKA (2010, 2013) and FKA (2014). Furthermore, the energy industry will be a strategic aspect of the region TR72 (Kayseri) which has a crucial uranium-thorium reserve, when the planned nuclear facilities become active in Turkey. Indeed, the region TR72 (Kayseri) having about 53 % of total uranium reserves in Turkey, could be a crucial energy-supply center in terms of nuclear energy thanks to its mining reserves (Deliktaş and Çelik, 2018b: 437). Similarly, the energy sector could be a crucial competitive structure for the region TRA1 (Erzurum) located in Baku-Tbilisi-Erzurum Natural Gas Pipeline route.

Conclusion

The solution to the regional disparities that are the crucial and structural ongoing problems in Turkey is depend on the specialization of regions on their sectors that have specific strategic and competitive advantages and regional macro-economy shaped by these dynamics. This requires the identification of the key sectors as strategic or competitive in a region and connecting them to specified regional policies complementarily. Thus, the positive externalities could be revealed by minimizing human and physical regional disparities. In this direction, this study aims to identify the strategic and competitive sectors in 26 NUTS-II Regions and to determine a specified policy proposal for them in Turkey. For this purpose, LQ based on the number of firms, employees and amount of investments have been calculated for the 17 major industries performing in 26 NUTS-II Regions in Turkey over 2009–2015 periods.

When findings that show the spatial concentration of the industries 12 to 17 in NUTS-II regions 20 to 26 are taken into consideration at the national level, Turkish economy is mainly shaped by geographical, geopolitical and climatic circumstances such as logistics, mining, agriculture and tourism; additionally, the manufacturing industry which is known for being the key to economic growth is concentrated in almost restricted areas where the production has low and medium-low tech along with knowledge-intensive patterns, in Turkey. When findings are taken into consideration at the regional level, the region TR10 (İstanbul) differs from other regions in terms of both sectoral diversity and concentration level. Indeed, it exhibits both strategic and competitive advantages in, respectively, the logistics, information and communication, education, health and real estate sectors compared to other regions. On the other hand, the logistics industry is mainly concentrated in the regions TRA2, TRB2, TRC3 that have border gates; the regions TR10 and TR62 that have the largest ports in terms of handling capacity in Turkey, the tourism industry in the regions TR61 and TR32 thanks to their geographical features; the agriculture and food industries in the regions TR52, TR21 and TR22; the manufacturing industry in the regions TR41, TR42 and TRC1; the education industry in TR51; and the mining industry in the regions TR33, TR81, TR82, TRA1 and TRB1 in terms of the level of strategic or competitive advantages. Finally, when the plans for construction of nuclear facilities are considered, the energy industry could be a strategically crucial sector in the region TR72 which has about 53 % of total uranium reserves in Turkey.

In the light of the findings, the policies that give incentive to improve the highway network and infrastructure of the regions TRA2, TRB2 and TRC3 which are the strategic points of international roads, and the handling capacity of ports located in the regions TR10, TR62 and TR31 that are considered to be the centers in international waterway transportation could decrease the costs of logistic activities.

On the other hand, when the positive and strong forward-backward linkages among tourism and food industries are taken into consideration, the policies to strengthen the tourism sector in the regions TR61, TR32 and TR22 could increase the potential effects of this industry both on regional and national economy. In addition, although the low added value patterns of agriculture, the importance of autarky has been increasing because of the rising population and food security awareness. Therefore, thanks to the concentration and specialization of agricultural activities especially in specific regions exhibited strategic advantages, use of resources and regional development could be more effective and balanced. In this direction, thanks to the policies in the regions TR52 (Konya), TR21 (Tekirdağ) and TR22 (Balıkesir) that turn them into agricultural production centers; the potential effects of food industry on regional economy could increase.

Also, the manufacturing clusters that are located strategically in the regions TR41 (Bursa) and TR42 (Kocaeli), and, potentially, in the regions TR33 (Manisa) and TRC1 (Gaziantep) might be supported and the incentive policies might be implemented to transfer the manufacturing sector to medium-high and high-tech industries from low and medium-low tech industries to rise sectoral and spatial spillovers.

On the other hand, mining activities are generally located in specific regions that have mining reserves because of the reserve structure, high transportation costs and security risks. Therefore, the mining must be considered as a potentially competitive sector for those regions which do not have any other potential. In this perspective, the sectoral incentives for extracting and mining in the regions TR33 (Manisa), TR81 (Zonguldak), TR82 (Kastamonu) and TRB1 (Malatya) that turn natural resources into added value for these regions could be effective. Indeed, the specialization of these regions on mining industry might be considered a geographical requirement. However, alternative strategic and competitive sectors for these regions could be determined by the finite and scarce characteristic of all mineral reserves. In this perspective, the manufacturing and food industries for the region TR33; tableland or winter tourism for the region TR82 might be considered alternative specialization activities. However, when their current capacities are taken into consideration, the regions TR81 and TRB1 do not have any alternative other than the mining industry.

Finally, the policy proposals could be offered to six other regions which do not concentrate on any industry as a specialization level when their economic structures are considered. For instance, the region TR31 (İzmir) could specialize on logistics especially in water way transportation because of its geopolitics location. And also, the health sector has an importance in terms of the number of firms and the amount of investment in the region TR31. Therefore, medical tourism could become a competitive sector in the process. This is consistent with the findings in Mirza (2016). On the other hand, textile clusters are dominant in the region TR63 (Hatay) (Çelik et al., 2019: 15). For this reason, manufacturing of textile products could be a competitive sector, potentially, in this region as well as the logistics industry because of its location which is a secondary road of ESCAP route. Furthermore, the region TR71 (Kırıkkale) exhibits competitive advantages in the agriculture sector while the region TR83 (Samsun) in wholesale and retail trade sector. When the awareness about tourism potentials of the region TR90 (Trabzon) could be arisen, tourism will be a competitive sector, and logistics industry, depending, especially, on passenger transportation, will provide a considerable added value for this region. Finally, service activities regardless of the location could be an added value and an employment source for the region TRC2 (Şanlıurfa) which do not have any specialized industry even potentially. In this perspective, locating the call centers of the companies that operate in the service industry such as the finance, telecommunication, health, logistics, information and trade sectors in Diyarbakır and Şanlıurfa, coded 82.2 NACE-2, call center activities in the administrative and support service could be a crucial added value and employment source for these regions.

References

Aküngör, S., Çelik, N. and Kumral, N. (2018a), "Türkiye'de Endüstriyel Kümelenmeler ve Bölgesel Uzmanlaşma", "Bölgesel Kalkınma ve Bölge Bilimi Üzerine Yazılar", Ankara: Nobel Akademik Yayıncılık.

Akgüngör, S., Kumral, N. and Çelik, N. (2018b). "Türkiye'de Bölgesel Uzmanlaşmanın Teknoloji ve Bilgi Yoğunluğu Açısından Değerlendirilmesi", *18. Ulusal Bölge Bilimi ve Bölge Planlama Kongresi (BBTMK2018) Bildiri Özetleri*, İstanbul.

Akgüngör, S., Kumral, N. and Çelik, N. (2017). "Türkiye'de Sektörel İleri – Geri Bağlantılar, Kümelenmeler ve Bölgesel Uzmanlaşma", *17. Ulusal Bölge Bilimi ve Bölge Planlama Kongresi (BBTMK2017) Bildiri Özetleri*, Burdur-Türkiye.

BAKKA (2014). "TR81 Düzey 2 Bölgesinin Sektörel Yapı ve Rekabet Gücünün Girdi Çıktı Modeli ile Analizi", *Batı Karadeniz Kalkınma Ajansı*, Zonguldak.

BAKKA (2013). "TR81 Düzey 2 Bölgesi Sektör Tanımlama, Önceliklendirme ve Rekabet Analizi Raporu", *Batı Karadeniz Kalkınma Ajansı*.

BEBKA (2012). "TR41 Bölgesi İlleri Kümelenme Analizi", *Bursa Eskişehir Bilecik Kalkınma Ajansı.*

BAKKA (2010). "2010–2013 Batı Karadeniz Bölge Planı", *Bat Karadeniz Kalkınma Ajansı.*

ÇKA (2017). "RIS+Mersin Yenilik İhtiyaç Analizi Raporu", *Çukurova Kalkınma Ajansı*, Şubat.

Çelik, N., Akgüngör, S. and Kumral, N. (2019). "An Assessment of the Technology Level and Knowledge Intensity of Regions in Turkey", *European Planning Studies*, 27(5): 952–973.

Çiftçi, M. (2018), "Türkiye'de Bölgelerarası Sektörel Verimliliğin Analizi", *İşletme Araştırmaları Dergisi*, 10(1): 551–580.

Çelik, N. (2017). "Türkiye'de Bölgesel Kalkınma Sorunsalı ve Bölgelere Özgü Politika Önerileri" Ege Üniversitesi Sosyal Bilimler Enstitüsü, Yayımlanmış Doktora Tezi, 1–165.

Deliktaş, E. and Çelik, N. (2018). "Yozgat Bölgesi Sektörel Uzmanlaşma Analizi", *III. Uluslararası BOZOK Sempozyumu*, Yozgat, Mayıs.

Deliktaş, E. and Çelik, N. (2018). "TR72 Bölgesi Sektörel Uzmanlaşma Analizi", III.Uluslararası Bozok Sempozyumu, Bölgesel Kalkınma ve Sosyo-Kültürel Yapı.

Deliktaş, E. and Çelik, N. (2019), "TRB2 Bölgesi'nde Rekabetçi Sektörlerin Belirlenmesi", *İzmir Katip Çelebi Üniversitesi İktisadi ve İdari Bilimler Fakültesi Dergisi*, 2(1): 29–44.

Dinçer, İ. S. and Karakayacı, Ö. (2012) "Sanayi Kümelerinde Firma Özellikleri, Bilgi Ağları ve Yenilikçilik", *YTÜ Sigma Journal of Engineering and Natural Sciences*, 4: 22–36.

FKA (2014). "2014–2023 TRB1 Bölge Planı", *Fırat Kalkınma Ajansı*, Aralık.

GEKA (2011). "TR32 Düzey II Bölgesi'nde Kümelenme Yaklaşımı", *Güney Ege Kalkınma Ajansı.*

Gökdeniz, A. (2015). "Turizmde Kümelenme ve Bölgesel Kalkınma Üzerindeki Etkileri", *Uluslararası Sosyal ve Ekonomik Bilimler Dergisi*, 5(1): 37–48.

İZKA (2010). "İzmir Kümelenme Analizi", *İzmir Kalkınma Ajansı.*

Kazancık, L. (2007). Bölgesel Gelişme ve Sektör-Bölge Yığınlaşmaları, 2. Bölgesel Kalkınma ve Yönetişim Sempozyumu Bildiriler Kitabı, TEPAV, İzmir.

Kuzey Anadolu Kalkınma Ajansı (2013). "TR82 Düzey 2 Bölgesi (Kastamonu, Çankırı ve Sinop İlleri) Bölge Planı 2014–2023", KUZKA, Ağustos 2013.

KUZKA (2014). "TR82 Bölgesi 3 Yıldız Küme Analiz Çalışması", *Kuzey Anadolu Kalkınma Ajansı.*

Lazzeretti, L., Capone, F. and Seçilmiş, İ.E. (2014), Türkiye'de Yaratıcı ve Kültürel Sektörlerin Yapısı", *Maliye Dergisi*, 166: 195-220.

Mirza, N., (2016), "İzmir Medikal Turizm Kümelenme Potansiyeli", *Dokuz Eylül Üniversitesi Sosyal Bilimler Dergisi*, 18(4): 743-768.

Miller, R. and Blair, P. (1985). Input-Output Analysis – Foundations and Extensions. Cambridge, UK: Prentice-Hall.

Seçilmiş, İ. E. (2015), "Türkiye'de Yaratıcı Endüstrilerin Kümelenmesi", *Ege Akademik Bakış Dergisi*, 15(1): 9-18.

Sungur, O. (2015), "TR61 (Antalya, Isparta, Burdur) Bölgesinde Sektörel Yoğunlaşmanın ve Yoğunlaşma Dinamiklerinin Analizi", *Yönetim ve Ekonomi Araştırmaları Dergisi*, 13(3): 316-341.

Türkcan, B. (2019), *"Türkiye'de Endüstriyel Bölgeler ve Bölgesel Gelişme"*. Ankara: Endüstri 4.0 ve Türkiye Ekonomisi, Orion Kitapevi.

ZKA (2012). "TR33 Bölgesi Mevcut Maden Kaynakları ve Stratejiler", *Zafer Kalkınma Ajansı*, Kütahya.

https://atlantis.udhb.gov.tr/istatistik/istatistik_konteyner.aspx, Access Date: 22.07.2019

https://www.dhmi.gov.tr/sayfalar/istatistik.aspx, Access Date: 22.07.2019

http://yigm.kulturturizm.gov.tr/TR-9669/ktkgb-ve-turizm-merkezleri.html, Access Date: 22.07.2019

https://www.enerji.gov.tr/tr-TR/Sayfalar/Dogal-Gaz-Boru-Hatlari-ve-Projeleri, Access Date: 27.07.2019

Appendix 1: NUTS Classification in Turkey

NUTS 1		NUTS 2		NUTS 3	
Code	*Region*	*Code*	*Region*	*Code*	*Region*
TR 1	Istanbul Region	**TR10**	**Istanbul Region**	TR100	Istanbul
TR 2	West Marmara Region	**TR21**	**Tekirdag Region**	TR211	Tekirdağ
				TR212	Edirne
				TR213	Kırklareli
		TR22	**Balikesir Region**	TR221	Balıkesir
				TR222	Çanakkale
TR 3	Aegean Region	**TR31**	**Izmir Region**	TR310	İzmir
		TR32	**Aydin Region**	TR321	Aydın
				TR322	Denizli
				TR323	Muğla
		TR33	**Manisa Region**	TR331	Manisa
				TR332	Afyonkarahisar
				TR333	Kütahya
				TR334	Uşak
TR 4	East Marmara Region	**TR41**	**Bursa Alt Bölgesi**	TR411	Bursa
				TR412	Eskişehir
				TR413	Bilecik
		TR42	**Kocaeli Region**	TR421	Kocaeli
				TR422	Sakarya
				TR423	Düzce
				TR424	Bolu
				TR425	Yalova
TR 5	West Anatolia Region	**TR51**	**Ankara Region**	TR510	Ankara
		TR52	**Konya Region**	TR521	Konya
				TR522	Karaman
TR 6	Mediterranean Region	**TR61**	**Antalya Region**	TR611	Antalya
				TR612	Isparta
				TR613	Burdur
		TR62	**Adana Region**	TR621	Adana
				TR622	Mersin
		TR63	**Hatay Region**	TR631	Hatay
				TR632	Kahramanmaraş
				TR633	Osmaniye

Division and Specialization Proposals to Regions of Turkey 151

Appendix 1: (continued)

NUTS 1		NUTS 2		NUTS 3	
TR 7	Central Anatolia Region	TR71	Kirikkale Region	TR711	Kırıkkale
				TR712	Aksaray
				TR713	Niğde
				TR714	Nevşehir
				TR715	Kırşehir
		TR72	Kayseri Region	TR721	Kayseri
				TR722	Sivas
				TR723	Yozgat
TR 8	West Black Sea Region	TR81	Zonguldak Region	TR811	Zonguldak
				TR812	Karabük
				TR813	Bartın
		TR82	Kastamonu Region	TR821	Kastamonu
				TR822	Çankırı
				TR823	Sinop
		TR83	Samsun Region	TR831	Samsun
				TR832	Tokat
				TR833	Çorum
				TR834	Amasya
TR 9	East Black Sea Region	TR90	Trabzon Region	TR901	Trabzon
				TR902	Ordu
				TR903	Giresun
				TR904	Rize
				TR905	Artvin
				TR906	Gümüşhane
TR A	Northeastern Anatolia Region	TRA1	Erzurum Region	TRA11	Erzurum
				TRA12	Erzincan
				TRA13	Bayburt
		TRA2	Agri Region	TRA21	Ağrı
				TRA22	Kars
				TRA23	Iğdır
				TRA24	Ardahan

(*continued on next page*)

Appendix 1: (continued)

NUTS 1		NUTS 2		NUTS 3	
TR B	Central Eastern Anatolia Region	TRB1	Malatya Region	TRB11	Malatya
				TRB12	Elazığ
				TRB13	Bingöl
				TRB14	Tunceli
		TRB2	Van Region	TRB21	Van
				TRB22	Muş
				TRB23	Bitlis
				TRB24	Hakkari
TR C	Southeastern Anatolia Region	TRC1	Gaziantep Region	TRC11	Gaziantep
				TRC12	Adıyaman
				TRC13	Kilis
		TRC2	Sanliurfa Region	TRC21	Şanlıurfa
				TRC22	Diyarbakır
		TRC3	Mardin Region	TRC31	Mardin
				TRC32	Batman
				TRC33	Şırnak
				TRC34	Siirt
TOTAL 12		26		81	

Source: Government Gazette, 2002/4720 Decree

Appendix 2: The Strategic (Key) and Competitive Sectors in NUTS-II Regions

Region Code	NACE Code	Industries	Statute	LQ$_{COMPANY}$ 2009–2015	LQ$_{LABOR}$ 2009–2015	LQ$_{INVESTMENT}$ 2009–2015
TR 10	J	Information and Communication	STRATEGIC	1,33	1,55	2,03
	M	Professional, Scientific and Technical Services	COMPETITIVE	1,32	1,33	1,76
	R	Culture, Art and Sport Services	COMPETITIVE	1,52	1,34	1,67
	N	Administrative and Support Service Activities	COMPETITIVE	1,38	1,20	2,18
	Q	Human Health and Social Work Services	COMPETITIVE	1,62	1,13	1,29
	L	Real Estate Services	COMPETITIVE	1,22	1,28	1,24
	H.50	Logistic (Waterway Transportation)	STRATEGIC	1,79	2,22	2,65
	H.51	Logistic (Airway Transportation)	STRATEGIC	2,01	2,73	2,29
TR 21	A	Agriculture, Forestry and Fishing	STRATEGIC (P)	3,42	0,68	1,72
	C	Manufacturing	COMPETITIVE (P)	0,77	1,71	2,00
TR 22	A	Agriculture, Forestry and Fishing	STRATEGIC	5,20	6,77	2,81
	B	Mining	COMPETITIVE (P)	1,84	2,40	2,89
	D	Energy	COMPETITIVE (P)	1,01	1,23	1,63
	I	Tourism	COMPETITIVE	1,59	1,40	0,50

(continued on next page)

Appendix 2: (continued)

Region Code	NACE Code	Industries	Statute	LQ_{COMPANY} 2009–2015	LQ_{LABOR} 2009–2015	LQ_{INVESTMENT} 2009–2015
TR 31	H	Logistic	STRATEGIC (P)	0,72	0,92	0,81
	Q	Health	COMPETITIVE (P)	1,28	0,96	1,33
	TR 32	I	Tourism	STRATEGIC	1,46	1,94
3,51		A	Agriculture, Forestry and Fishing	COMPETITIVE	1,12	1,75
4,57		B	Mining	COMPETITIVE	1,36	1,61
1,38		D	Energy	COMPETITIVE (P)	0,80	1,02
1,78	TR 33	B	Mining	STRATEGIC	1,55	4,86
5,63		D	Energy	COMPETITIVE	0,56	1,25
0,95	TR 41	C	Manufacturing	STRATEGIC	1,25	1,65
1,81		B	Mining	COMPETITIVE	1,36	1,13
1,29	TR 42	C	Manufacturing	STRATEGIC (P)	0,96	1,52
1,97	TR 51	P	Education	STRATEGIC	1,54	1,45
1,28		J	Information and Communication	COMPETITIVE	1,34	1,76
1,08		B	Mining	COMPETITIVE	1,49	1,02
1,61		D	Energy	COMPETITIVE	2,36	2,33
1,22	TR 52	A	Agriculture, Forestry and Fishing	STRATEGIC	4,02	2,14

Division and Specialization Proposals to Regions of Turkey 155

1,98		G	Wholesale and Retail Trade and Repair Services of Motor Vehicles and Motorcycles	COMPETITIVE (P)	1,12	1,22
1,37		C	Manufacturing	COMPETITIVE (P)	1,15	1,13
1,36	TR 61	I	Tourism	STRATEGIC	1,06	3,14
8,73		A	Agriculture, Forestry and Fishing	COMPETITIVE	3,00	1,86
3,89	TR 62	H.52	Logistic (Storage and Supportive Activities)	STRATEGIC	1,44	1,66
1,67		G	Wholesale and Retail Trade and Repair Services of Motor Vehicles and Motorcycles	COMPETITIVE (P)	1,08	1,25
1,49	TR 63	H	Logistic	COMPETITIVE (P)	1,19	1,40
0,89	TR 71	I	Tourism	STRATEGIC (P)	1,01	1,04
0,89		A	Agriculture, Forestry and Fishing	COMPETITIVE (P)	0,59	1,56
3,11		B	Mining	COMPETITIVE (P)	1,29	0,98

(*continued on next page*)

Appendix 2: (continued)

Region Code	NACE Code	Industries	Statute	$LQ_{COMPANY}$ 2009–2015	LQ_{LABOR} 2009–2015	$LQ_{INVESTMENT}$ 2009–2015
1,53	TR 72	D	Energy	STRATEGIC	1,56	1,42
0,73		B	Mining	COMPETITIVE	1,83	1,60
2,01	TR 81	B	Mining	STRATEGIC	2,18	11,23
4,26		D	Energy	COMPETITIVE (P)	0,61	1,25
0,42		I	Tourism	COMPETITIVE (P)	1,49	1,01
0,37	TR 82	B	Mining	STRATEGIC	1,52	1,62
3,08		H	Logistic	COMPETITIVE (P)	1,40	1,18
0,51	TR 83	G	Wholesale and Retail Trade and Repair Services of Motor Vehicles and Motorcycles	COMPETITIVE (P)	1,08	1,30
1,55	TR 90	I	Tourism	STRATEGIC (P)	1,27	1,20
0,59		H	Logistic	COMPETITIVE (P)	1,59	1,35
0,62	TR A1	D	Energy	STRATEGIC	1,71	1,94
1,71		B	Mining	COMPETITIVE	1,74	1,65
3,91		H	Logistic	COMPETITIVE	1,36	1,29
1,23	TR A2	H	Logistic	STRATEGIC	1,62	2,25
3,24		D	Energy	COMPETITIVE (P)	1,34	0,80

Division and Specialization Proposals to Regions of Turkey 157

Region			Sector	Type		
TR B1	1,42	B	Mining	STRATEGIC	1,74	1,85
	2,30	D	Energy	COMPETITIVE (P)	0,94	1,36
TR B2	1,16	H	Logistic	STRATEGIC	1,87	1,93
	1,96	D	Energy	COMPETITIVE (P)	1,09	1,78
	1,44	B	Mining	COMPETITIVE (P)	0,99	0,57
TR C1	1,45	C	Manufacturing	COMPETITIVE (P)	1,16	1,34
TR C2	1,81	H	Logistic	COMPETITIVE (P)	1,62	1,38
	0,68	G	Wholesale and Retail Trade and Repair Services of Motor Vehicles and Motorcycles	COMPETITIVE (P)	1,06	1,01
TR C3	1,53	H	Logistic	STRATEGIC	1,70	2,32
	1,61					

(P), refers that regions exhibit strategic or competitive advantages potentially in that sector.

Source: They are calculated by Author over TSI Annual Industry and Service Statistics

Murat Çiftçi[1]

Chapter 8 Regional Clustering in Social Service Workers: An Application with Three Star Analysis (2008-2017)

Introduction

Social policy, social security and social services are three interrelated disciplines. Social policy, which aims to combat disadvantageousness, includes social security, which aims to protect against social risks which cause disadvantageousness. The discipline of social security includes the discipline of social service that provides non-premium social protection. Therefore, social work is a sub-branch of both social policy and social security disciplines.

There are many professions that carry out social service activities. However, among these professions, social service experts/social workers constitute the main element. It is generally the social worker who listens to the applicant, determines the situation and determines the application contents. Many occupations operate in the dispatch and management of social workers, from psychologists to child development specialists.

The complexity of social service activity makes it too many occupation members to operate, thus making it difficult for social workers to be quantitatively sorted out of service providers. In addition, the majority of social workers are procured from non-social service graduates. For this reason, it is difficult to determine who is a social worker and who is not.

Turkey has a vibrant socio-economic life. This feature increases social problems. Inequalities in income and wealth distribution, social gender pressure, population aging, urbanization, internal and external migration, refugee problem, problems in working life, increasing crime rates, divorce, bringing disabled people to work and social life are among the first application areas of social service. The need for social workers or other occupation members performing this function in the solution of social problems in such a wide field increases day by day.

---

[1] Assoc. Prof., Trakya University, Faculty of Economics and Administrative Sciences, Department of Labour Economics and Industrial Relations, Edirne/TURKEY, muratciftci@trakya.edu.tr

In this study, it was focused on the determination of interregional clusters of the employees in the social service activity field employed by the employment contract. The preferred statistical method in the study is the three-star analysis used in regional cluster detection. Data were obtained from the Social Security Institution's statistic annuals. The implementation period is ten years between 2008 and 2017.

Firstly, social services and operator personnel's development in Turkey and in the world is examined. Secondly, the theory of regional clustering is introduced. Thirdly, the literature on three-star analysis is summarized. Fourthly, information about the data set and method used in statistical application is given. Fifthly, the findings which are acquired from the application are reported.

Modern Social Services and Operator Personnel

The main purpose of social work is to fulfill social justice. Social workers should understand the impact of social structure and social policy on social service users to support social justice. They also should be actively involved in social policy formation (Weiss et al., 2006: 789). This feature leads social workers to become human rights workers (Williams, 2004: 50).

The social worker examines the person's life as a whole before applying anything. Its main purpose is the holistic development of the life of the service recipient. With this feature, social work focuses on life skills, family functioning and personal relationships (Clark, 2006: 78).

The social workers profession includes many disciplines, philosophies, theories and groups within itself. In this intradisciplinary profession, it is seen that a large number of disciplines, philosophies, theories and groups were brought to the forefront according to time (Brashears, 1995: 693). It has expertise in personal development and overcoming interpersonal barriers. In addition, clinical social workers are capable to make biopsychosocial evaluations and make differential diagnosis. They are trained to detect mental illness, alcohol and drug addictions and problematic families (Caspi, 2005: 360).

The occupations in the field of social work are therefore very diverse. In the 1940s, legal studies related to professional competence established in the UK generally required certification from universities for institutionalized social workers, such as Hospital Almoning, Family Casework and Mental Deficiency Work. However, in most other branches there was no such standardization (Eyden, 1950: 433). Diversity in occupations that assume the role of social workers increases, especially in the case of social services in disaster situations such as war. For example, in the aftermath of World War II, there were so many people in Germany who needed social work, such as widows, orphans, unemployed, homeless, refugees, etc. that educated and expert social workers remained incapable to provide services. Clergymen, doctors, teachers, psychologists and employers took on the role of social workers. In fact, foreign social workers also worked in Germany against the inadequacy (Social Work, 1952: 732–733). Therefore, the more confusion and disadvantage, the more diversification occurs in occupations that are social workers.

Van Driel (1937: 435) emphasizes that the nature and the function of social work requires adaptation to changing needs. According to him, changes in the political, economic and social conditions in the society lead to changes in requirements. This leads to the rapid change of social services as a profession. This profession is relatively new comparing with the most of other occupations and the body of professional technical knowledge is not fully established yet. There is also a heterogeneous social group characteristic among social workers. This heterogeneity leads to differences of opinion on the function of social work. In addition, the social worker group cannot always make full use of professional technical knowledge. Opinion differences among professionals encourage the development of the profession.

Due to the nature of social work, social workers have to choose between alternative intervention methods in every encounter with individuals, families and groups that they serve. This is a chronic problem that is constantly encountered in social studies (Rosen and Connawayi, 1969: 89). Thus, no matter how many standards have been developed, the profession is highly complex and requires special expertise.

In the past, social work was carried out by voluntary organizations (Eyden, 1950: 434). In the modern sense, the history of social work is new. Social work practices were carried out under the rule of the Charity Organization Society (COS), which came to the United States from England in the 1870s. According to this organization, the cause of poverty was personal failure. The first generation of social work practices was shaped by supporting the more efficient work of the poor. In the 1880s, the notion that poverty was caused by individual failure was replaced by the idea that individuals have very little control in poverty. The change in perspective has transformed social work from individual-oriented to community-oriented (Abramovitz, 1998: 513–514).

Poverty and inequality in the US, accompanied by rapid urbanization and long-distance migration, led to the need for social work. In the first phase between 1890 and 1920, the focus of social work was; dwelling, public welfare, public health and education. In addition, it was emphasized that cooperation between social classes should be ensured (Reisch, 1998: 163). Other topics focused on social work were poverty, child and family welfare, unemployment, discrimination and social justice. Progressivism, which emerged in response to industrialization and expansionism in the first phase, dominated social work. This movement was commenced in the early twentieth century mainly by female social workers (Murdach, 2010: 81-83).

Social workers achieved great successes during the twentieth century. They played an active role in the solution of many social problems caused by social transformation, rapid urbanization and economic instability. Between the years 1910-1921 in the United States with the newly established children's office newborn deaths has halved. During the Great Depression, for millions of unemployed people jobs found and millions of poor families were helped (Uehara et al., 2013: 165).

In the US, however, social assistance and service activities until the Great Depression were left to the initiative of local units. Until 1931, the responsibility of the states was essential and there were wide differences in practices between the states. The creation of a legal framework at the federal level was through the Social Security Act of 1935 (Bruno, 1936: 263). After the Great Depression, more attention was paid to social work skills and social work in general. At the same time, people in need of social work understood social workers more and demanded more social work. Social resistance to the profession decreased (Clarke, 1944: 179). Starting from the late 1930s, the majority of social workers became public servants (Abramovitz, 1998: 516). However, the positions and job descriptions of social workers in the state administration were not clear yet (Khan, 1943: 6).

The second major legal change in social service activities took place in 1967. With the adopted legal regulations, social welfare activities started to be carried out in public welfare with separating income maintenance from family welfare activities. Until this separation, social service specialists were helping families to budget their scarce resources; they also began to provide care services for family's dependent children. In addition, the profession of social work expertise was brought to the legal standards requiring education at the level of higher education (Austin et al., 1996: 85-86).

During the welfare state, almost every country experienced rapid development in the field of social work and increased professional prestige. For example, in England, social workers played a central role in decisions on local social service practices (Dickens, 2011: 23-24). Despite the increasing importance, profession was very complicated and difficult. In the last period of welfare state, the turnover among people who work in the field of social service activity field was very high in the USA. Few of those who worked in this field and quit were moving to a new job in the same field. This was also seen as a problem in the relevant units of the state, and solutions were sought to reduce the turnover rate. Because, it is aimed for the employees who provide services for the elderly from child care, health care to other related fields to work longer. In this period, the social worker profession began to become a career profession (Knapp et al., 1981: 422–424).

Attacks on social work took place as part of the restructuring of the Welfare State. This change was especially felt by those who excluded from the economic and social sphere. Social workers were also deprived of the budget that they needed to carry out the charitable activities. Ideologically, precise lines have been removed. Not only the social work budget was reduced, but also individualism, familyism, volunteering and private initiatives were brought to the fore instead of the state's social service activities. In the new conservatism, the state's responsibilities were replaced by the argument of individual and familial responsibility. It was claimed that social service activities increased dependence on the state and weakened individual and familial responsibilities (Jones and Novak, 1993: 196–197).Therefore, social work hit the rock bottom with Reagan by declining since the Nixon rule in the 1970s (Murdach, 2010: 85). For example the increase in the welfare which will be formed by economic growth and the increase in the odds of poor mothers to find jobs were cited as the reasons of the cut back on social welfare providing practices for women and children in need (Pelton, 2001: 433). Similarly, poverty in the UK reached 1/3 of the population in the 1980s and social exclusion became widespread. Unemployment, low qualification, high crime rates, inadequate dwelling, poor health, and family deterioration were diversified as causes of social exclusion (Craig, 2002: 672).

In the new service model, it was aimed to expand the cooperation of social service activities with other services. For this purpose, removal of social services from institutional activities and its systematic shift to social care was foreseen as beneficial. It was aimed to develop common practices in connection with voluntary services. To the activities such as the protection of social minorities were tried to ensure the participation of more communities (Walton, 2005: 588).

The neoliberal point of view also leads to drastic changes in the point of view of social workers. According to researches, social workers in the UK no longer consider poverty as the main problem affecting other disadvantages. With this point of perspective, fight against poverty is no longer the focus. Opinion that the main source of disadvantage is biased psychiatric and family based has become widespread (Krumer-Nevo et al., 2009: 227). Therefore, the decline in the tendency of the state to take part in social service activities in the neoliberal period is legitimized.

The need for social workers continues by increasing more in the twenty-first century. Global poverty, extreme inequalities, sustainability problems in health and human services increase the need for social services. These problems lead social workers to be in need of unprecedented problem-solving skills and collaboration that has never seen until this day. Even if global problems are overcome and a bright world is created for everyone in the new age, social work can play a more central, transformative and cooperative role in society (Uehara et al., 2013: 165).

The complexity of current social work activities and the necessity of structuring in collaboration with other disciplines is a result of the expansion of their fields of activity. For example, palliative care is new to the field of social work compared to other practices. With the aging of the population on a global scale, this need is increasing day by day. As Small (2001: 962) points out, palliative care has been one of the fields of activities for social workers. In this field, all kinds of activities are carried out towards increasing the quality of life of the patient and his/her family towards death. The complexity and difficulty of this activity makes it possible for the social worker to implement with a multidisciplinary team and holistic approach.

The need variety for social workers to provide social services to the elderly and especially to the woman elderly is increasing. According to this, broad and complex responsibilities from nursing homes to the organization of day care services, from home visits to the rehabilitation of poor widows and mobile geriatric services are loaded up on social workers (Gopal, 2006: 4483).

As in the case of the United States, occupational social work is also increasing day by day in western countries. Sociological reasons such as the widespread use of alcohol and drugs among high-income workers, the problems caused by the additional obligations of women to participate in business life and the increase in divorce rates were effective in this increase. In addition, companies began to demand more social services in order to increase the productivity of their employees by combating these sociological problems.

In some areas assigned to cooperation with other departments, the success of social service activities seems to be difficult. For example, in the US, social workers have been actively assigned to homeless families. The social work for homeless families, which tripled in number between 1980 and 1990 and reached 150.000, is structured to support other departments in local institutions. This situation has led social workers to be adhered to stereotype practices. Studies on the success of social work for homeless families were also divided into two, and there was no clear conclusion whether it is a success or failure (Stewart and Stewart, 1992: 273, 285).

While analyzing social services in Turkey, there can be seen the presence of a long history of interest based on the Ottoman period. During the classical Ottoman period, social and municipal services were provided through foundations (see Çiftçi, 2011). After the Tanzimat, the state itself became a practitioner. The first social studies carried out by the state during the Ottoman period can be considered the one9.s that are special for orphans since the end of the nineteenth century. The dominance of social protection for orphans in social work continued for a long time even after the republic period (see Reçber, 2019: 727-729). With the opening of the Turkish Grand National Assembly, social services and assistance in social protection were implemented based on four models. These are:

- Experience of publicly supported citizen organization,
- Integrated presentation of social services and assistance with social medicine practices,
- Integrated presentation of social services and assistance with social security in a single ministry,
- Independent presentation of social services and assistance (Gençler and Çiftçi, 2013: 11).

The social service disciplines in the modern sense of history in Turkey are based on nearly half a century (Sevim and Altun, 2017: 53). Under the leadership of the United Nations Social Welfare Counselor, studies were initiated about the professional organization of social services with the participation of ministries and public-private organizations (Yiğit, 2017: 156-157). Social service discipline, which started to institutionalize in the 1960s, has become a practice-oriented discipline (Aysan and Kaya, 2008: 241). Professional social work training started in 1961. The first graduates in 1965 were given the title of "Social Service Specialist". When the Social Work Department was established in 1967, also a separate graduation title was given in 1971 with the title of "Social Worker". Therefore, due to two different titles given to graduates from two schools between 1971and 1983, the topic of what should be the title of this profession is discussed (Karakus, 2015: 170-173).In addition, a significant number of social workers working in the ministry from past to present are not graduates of the social service department (Yıldırım and Şahin, 2019: 2541-2542). This could have been attributed to the numerical shortage of social work graduates in the past. However, there is a significant acceleration in the number of social service graduates today. Until 2003, Hacettepe University Department of Social Service was the only school in this field. Since 2011, many new departments have been opened, including open education. Student quotas are also increasing rapidly each year (Sevim and Altun, 2017: 53).

Social service practices provided by public were removed from the state monopoly with the effect of the neoliberal experience after 1980. Non-governmental organizations, companies, families and groups started to take an active role in social service practices. With the support of increasing graduates, social workers have become laborers in the labor market as well as being public employees. We know the numerical volume of the members of the social service profession working according to the employment contract at the provincial level from Social Security Institution's 2009–2017 dates. In 2008, 3851 people worked in the field of social work activities, which increased to 51981 in 2017. This increase reached 13.5 times the amount in 2008. In the same period, the number of employees working under employment contract increased 64.5 % from 8.8 million to only 14.5 million (see Tab. 1).

Regional Clustering: Regional Glance

For more than half a century, the question of how space and geographic location affects economic development has been sought. From the mid-1950s to the mid-1970s, models were tried to be developed based on statistical analysis. From the mid-1970s to the late 1980s, studies were focused on using the Marxist historical materialism method. On the other hand, Krugman and Fujita developed the economic discipline called new economic geography in order to understand uncertain spatial economic development (Garretsen and Martin, 2010: 128–129). The change in the spatial economy in recent years is very rooted. There is a serious change in every regional scale. For example, East Asia accounted for 23 % of world production in 1980, while this weight increased to 70 % in 2000. Also, in most high-income countries, production was also clustered in remote small cores of the country (Fujita and Mori, 2005: 377–378).

In fact, in the selection and clustering of the production site, spatial economy has a long-established history. Von Thünen's (1826) analysis of land rent was based on Ricardo's theory of comparative advantages. Other prominent works were formed by Weber, Cristaller, Lösch, Isard and Handersen. Krugman, in 1991, developed a new approach by improving past studies with a new economic geography approach. The model strategy is based on the regional cluster of most economic activities. In the regional cluster centripetal forces are; market sizes, thick labor markets and pure external economies. On the other hand, centrifugal forces are immobile factors, land rents and pure external ineconomies (see Krugman, 1998: 7–8). External economies refer to

Tab. 1: Employment in the Field of Social Work Activity Contract and Development in General Employment

Years	Employment of Social Workers	2008=100	General Employment	2008=100
2008	3851	100,0	8.802.989	100,0
2009	9135	237,2	9.030.202	102,6
2010	22.308	579,3	10.030.810	113,9
2011	25.200	654,4	11.030.939	125,3
2012	30.268	786,0	11.939.620	135,6
2013	32.426	842,0	12.484.113	141,8
2014	38.554	1001,1	13.240.122	150,4
2015	41.664	1081,9	13.999.398	159,0
2016	45.165	1172,8	13.775.188	156,5
2017	51.981	1349,8	14.477.817	164,5

economies of scale at the level of the industry branch, not on the basis of an industrial organization. Alfred Marshall stated that these economies are clustered regionally and that clustering is not shaped by access to natural resources. According to him, there should be strong suppliers to support the cluster for the formation of regional clusters, geographic labor market should be formed and geographic clustering should support the information dissemination of the industry. Marshall cited cutlery manufacturers in Sheffield and socks manufacturers in Northampton as examples of non-clustering regional clusters around natural resources. Today, in the semiconductor industry, the Silicon Valley in California, New York in investment banking, and Hollywood for the entertainment industry can be given as examples (Krugman and Obstfeld, 2003: 147). Factor prices (transportation costs, wages, land-building costs) are the determinant of the regional cluster here, and firms can create clusters by moving to more favorable regions (Schmutzler, 1999: 356). Consider the interaction of goods and the labor market. If workers are clustered in a region, the change in spending resulting from the cluster will attract firms to the new regional cluster. Similarly, if firms are clustered in a region, the fall in goods prices attracts workers to the new regional cluster. Therefore, even from the perspective of goods and labor market interaction, effect of an interaction based on factor prices on spatial cluster formation can be seen (see Redding, 2010: 297–298).

Today, in developing countries like China, localization (regional clustering) is based on exportation. This is like England in the nineteenth century (Krugman,

2011: 6). Fundamentally speaking, it is anticipated that industries will provide greater spatial clustering with the reduction of transportation costs and the integration of the world economy. In other words, globalization and localization feed each other in the new economic geography approach (see Fujita et al., 1999: 319)

Global integration promotes localization but in the other hand it also brings theoretical complexity. Apart from access to the natural resources, the determinants of factor costs in the regional cluster are no longer effective on their own. Because there isn't any absolute rationality for economic actors. Networks between individuals and institutions, mutual exchange of information and trust have entered into the shapers of relational economic geography (Sunley, 2008: 3–4).

Perroux's approach to growth poles is the study that can be considered as a milestone in a spatial economy. This approach was the key to the development of regional clustering approaches. The concept of "growth poles" was introduced in the economic literature in 1950. The concept of "growth poles" which reached global popularity after that, became a subject of publication guarantee during the 1950s (Darwent, 1969: 5). The loose definition of the growth poles, which was a useful concept for social policy in the period of question, prevented the criticism of the concept in implementation failures. In the event of failure, the means and means of implementation responsible for the failure were shown (Lasuen, 1969: 137). In developed and developing countries, this concept was applied in urban, regional and national development plans in the late 1960s and early 1970s. In the mid-1960s, the growth poles were seen as spatially repulsive, as cities that included growth companies, and as regional growth providers (Erickson, 1974: 127). But from the late 1970s to the late 1980s, there was a reaction shown to the growth poles. Later, since the 1990s, again poles of growth approach have improved (Christofakis and Papadaskalopoulos, 2011: 5).

This theory was based on an unbalanced approach to growth and this theory assumed that economic expansion was at the poles of growth (Erickson, 1974: 127). Perroux's "growth poles" approach was actually an adaptation of Schumpeter's theory of innovation to the abstract economic field. Accordingly, the industrial group associated with input-output connections around the prominent industry branch constituted the growth pole (Richardson and Richardson, 1975: 163). Even though, regional development theory is not necessary for development influenced by the driving industries, but there is also a need for the theory of growth poles to be theorized geographically (Moseley, 1973: 143). This approach gained popularity among planners interested in regional development programs and popularity increased further in transition economies in developing regional growth strategies (Keith Semple et al., 1972: 591).

Perroux's original growth poles approach had no regional content (Casetti et al., 1971: 377). Hirshman argued in 1958 that a growing economy should develop itself in one or more regional economic power centers, referring to Perroux's the growth poles approach. Including spatial dimension to this approach was reinforced by Boudaville's definition of the cities as the driving force sector (Cambell, 1974: 43). Bourdaville made a triple geographical area classification consisting of homogenous region, polarized region and plan region. Accordingly, the homogeneous region is composed of equivalent geographical areas. The polarized region is based on the hierarchy of cities and interrelations. The plan region refers to the geographical area in which the sectoral investments are determined spatially by national and regional planning by the political authority. In other words, it is the geographical region which is subject to regional and urban planning (Gauthier, 1971: 337–338).

Perroux and King (1953: 203) argued that the world economic field was formed by raw materials, energy resources, transportation networks and strategic industrial poles. They stated that communication and cooperation between the poles will globalize the economy despite national monopolies. They were against the creation of growth poles in existing developed regions. They argued that there is a regional compromise between potential production areas and needs. According to them, the definition of world development region would be reached. Thus, the importance and advantages of national borders would be reduced. They cited the Middle East as an example, although the GDP per capita was between $ 50 and $ 90, but pointed out that the creation of oil production centers as an economic group would support cooperation with existing poles. According to them, the waterless regions will be irrigated with the cooperation between the growth poles on a global scale and local poverty would diminish. The transformation into international credit bodies and exchange centers would take place through transportation and communication networks. This transformation was incompatible with the nation-state.

In summarizing the functioning of the growth pole, Porter's approach to the industrial development of the new generation regional clusters is illustrative. Porter (1998: 184) argues that industrial change does not take place at the firm level by pieces. Because the industry is an interconnected system. A change in the structure of the industry leads to changes in other areas as well. For example, an innovation in marketing develops a new buyer segment and brings innovation in production techniques.

In terms of regional economics, the growth pole was perceived as a center of growth that transmits growth to its hinterland. In short terms, the growth pole was accepted as the center of urban growth. In this case, however, two questions have to be answered: 1) What are the mechanisms and processes that lead to the growth centers? 2) What is the spatial dimension of the hinterland where growth is transmitted? (Keith Semple et al., 1972: 591).

The creative cities approach has come to the forefront among the current regional economics approaches overlapping with the growth pole approach. The concept of "creative cities" is a concept brought forward by city planners and policy-makers. The definitions of "creative industries" and "creative classes" remains popular, and local authorities are focused on exploring the creative features of their cities. Supranational organizations, such as UNESCO, supported this formation through initiatives such as the "network of creative cities" (Atkinson and Easthope, 2009: 65).

The foundations of the creative cities approach can be briefly summarized as follows: The introduction of telegraph, telephone, automobile and airplane into our lives has created the myth that geography has been dead for man and economy since the nineteenth century. However, this thought did not actualized. The new economy like the new people in the new economy, has settled in geographical areas and has continued to grow in the geographical areas. Silicon Valley is an example (Florida, 2003: 4). Local economic development policies, urban transformation and revival brought about cultural transformation in urban and regional policies. This period is also called as renaissance of cities (Ponzini and Rossi, 2010: 1039). The source of urban development in modern society is based on production and work. However, the source of urban development was not limited to labor and capital accumulation. It also included many social, cultural and political developments. Localized commodity and labor markets crystallized before urbanization and all elements of urban life constantly affected each other. If this interaction wouldn't have been mutual, than cities would have been very different simple service centers than they are today. The complexity of modern cities stems from this mutual interaction (Scott, 2006: 2). In the new urban areas, there only isn't a single center and 50–100 miles of growth corridors have emerged (Batten, 1995: 314). Modern transportation technologies have increased the movement radius of the city dwellers. For example, while people travel in the Netherlands in the seventeenth century on average of 40 km per year, today this distance is the daily travel distance of people (Bertolini and Dijst, 2003: 28). Since the 1980s, economic researches have focused on regional competition conditions, shaped by the innovative behavior of firms. Cities and regions have also become key element to economic decision-making. Locality and globalization also complemented each other. The new growth theory became important for regional growth theory (Nijkamp, 2003: 396). The average size of urban areas increased with technology. The increase in the urban population was supported by creativity and human capital and scientific solutions. These modern cities, which develop in quality and quantity, have been labeled as "smart cities" (Caragliu et al., 2011: 66). "Smart city" mainly refers to cities that have creative capabilities and can produce new and sustainable solutions. It is the main parameter that innovative urban spaces produce internal advantages (Kourtit and Nijkamp, 2012: 93).

Urbanization took place in three revolutionary periods. The first urbanization took place in rural-urban development in ancient age. The second revolutionary urbanization took place with the industrial revolution. During this period, the population and spread of the city increased with huge industrial enterprises. The third and the last revolutionary urbanization is taking place from after the World War II until today. In this period, the function of the cities changed and shaped with people who created creative and innovative city potentials instead of passive human settlement (Kourtit et al., 2012: 229).

Porter (1998: 80) points out that clusters are critical to competitiveness. By sharing common technology with the regional cluster; information, inputs, cluster-specific institutions, and industries within the cluster is affected (Delgado et al., 2012: 3).

Regional clustering is the geographical concentration of production. This makes the regional cluster central to the discipline of economic geography. In the regional cluster, Marshall looked at input-output links, regional labor market and firm cost-efficiency advantages. In time, this scope expanded and local demand conditions, specialization institutions, regional business organizations and social networks became the supporters of the cluster (Delgado et al., 2014: 2). During the first half of the twentieth century, the importance of the minimization of spatial costs approach decreased with the development of information and transportation technologies. Today, the importance of geography has been questioned due to the decrease in factor costs caused by the increase in productivity. However, the regional demand volume still supported maintaining importance of geography. In the regional approaches in the economy, state's continuing support to the "baby industries", state's continuing focus on RD activities and state's continuing emphasize to the internal dynamics gained importance (Porter and Porter, 1998: 8). In summary, over the past seventy years, the regional cluster has continued to express competitive power in economic activity.

Regional Clustering Literature

Three-star analysis is widely used by public institutions and organizations in our country to determine regional clustering and regional competitiveness' force. Mostly, regional development agencies generate annual reports using this analysis. The literature in chronological order can be summarized as follows:

Erkek and Öselmiş (2011) on behalf of GEKA for TR32 region, Bursa Eskişehir Bilecik Development Agency (2012) for TR41 region, Trakya Development Agency (2012) for Thrace region, Karadeniz Development Agency (2013) for TR81 region, Mevlana Development Agency (2013) for Konya Karaman region, İzmir Development Agency (2013) for İzmir, and Doğu Anadolu Development Agency (2013) used three-star analysis for clustering in TRB2 region.

Oran Development Agency (2014, 2015) for TR72 region and for Kayseri and Sivas provinces, Zafer Development Agency (2014) for Manisa, Batı Akdeniz Development Agency (2014) for TR61, İpekyolu Development Agency (2015) for Adıyaman, Karacadağ Development Agency (2015) for the TRC2 region, the Ministry of Development (2017) used in the EAP region's clustering, Çukurova Development Agency (2017) for the innovative cluster in Mersin, and the Güney Marmara Development Agency (2017) used for the clustering in the TR22 region.

Economic Enterprise of Technology Development Foundation of Turkey (2016) have benefited from this innovative cluster analysis method in the DAP region. Republic of Turkey Ministry of Industry and Technology, Doğu Karadeniz Project Regional Development Administration (2019) examined the cluster in small cattle, which is occurring in DOKAP region, with the three-star analysis.

Numerous regional clustering studies have been performed by Development Bank of Turkey's experts. Keskin and Önen (2012) for clustering in Konya, Şahinkaya (2013) for clustering in defense industry in TR72 region, Ertuğrul (2013, 2014) for clustering in manufacturing industry for construction and for construction machinery sector in Ankara and for health sector in TR72 region, Bayraktar and Sekmen (2014a, b) for clustering in Amasya and TR83 region, Karaca and Bayrak (2017) for clustering in Bayburt, Çelebi Deniz (2014) for clustering in TRC2 sub-region; used three-star analysis for detection. Türkcan et al. (2016) used this analysis to determine the clustering in cultural economies.

Gökçen Dündar (2016a, b) identified the regional clustering in the cultural industry in three metropolises by three-star analysis.

Other examples in the literature are: Şen and Sandal (2017) applied this analysis to determine the regional clustering in Gaziantep. Sevimli Deniz and Çelik (2017) applied three-star analysis for clustering in TRB2 Region. Seki and Arslan (2018) determined the clustering in TRC2 region by using three-star analysis. Seki et al. (2018) used this analysis for the regional clustering in Çanakkale. Çiftçi (2018) determined the clustering in the Trakya sub-region using three-star analysis. Demirdöğen (2018) used this analysis to determine the clustering in the TRA1 sub-region. Ceyhan and Özcan (2018) used this analysis to measure the level of clustering in the shoemaking sector in Bartın. İyem et al. (2018) determined the clustering in the TR32 region by three-star analysis. Merdan (2018) used this analysis to determine the clustering in the beekeeping sector in Gümüşhane.

Data Design and Method

In practice, the number of social service providers by provinces is based on. Those who work in social activities are those who provide social services to the elderly, disabled, children and other unclassified groups without boarding. These employees are dependent employees who are socially insured under the status of 4–1/a on the basis of the employment contract. The application data were compiled from Social Security Institution's statistical annuals between 2008 and 2017 (SGK, 2008–2017).

The statistical analysis method is three-star analysis. In general, this analysis is based on employment data. Sometimes applications can be made according to the number of working places. The three-star analysis was developed by ECO "European Cluster Observatory" which is funded by European Commission. This feature supports it being an international official indicator such as the Human Development Index. This analysis consists of three parts. When the threshold value is exceeded in each part, a star is given to that region. The geographical unit is called the mature cluster if there are three stars, the potential cluster if there are two stars, and the candidate cluster if there are three stars. Accordingly, the competitiveness force of the regional unit in that field of activity is demonstrated. The three components of the analysis are size, focus and specialization.

Size: If the employment in the province reaches the threshold in the employment in the whole of the country, the activity field has a significant weight in the country. In this case 1 star is given. The activity field coefficient for magnitude is formulated as in Equation 1:

$$SQ_{i,j} = {L_{i,j}} \Big/ {\sum L_{i,j}} \quad (1)$$

Accordingly, $SQ_{i,j}$ symbolizes magnitude coefficient in activity field in province i, $L_{i,j}$ symbolizes the employment in activity field in province i, and $\sum L_{i,j}$ symbolizes the employment in activity field in the whole country.

Focus: Indicates whether the employment in the activity branch within the province has a significant share compared to the total employment in the province. If significant weight has been achieved, there is a focus on the area of activity within the province and 1 star is given. The coefficient of activity field for dominance is formulated as in Equation 2:

$$FQ_{i,j} = {L_{i,j}} \Big/ {\sum L_i} \quad (2)$$

Accordingly, $FQ_{i,j}$ symbolizes focusing coefficient in activity field in province i, $L_{i,j}$ symbolizes the employment in work/activity field in province i, and $\sum L_i$ symbolizes the total employment in province i.

Specialization: If a branch of activity within the province is more specialized than the national economy, it supports that the specialization is capable of attracting it from other provinces towards the branch of activity in that province. Therefore, this branch of activity in the province becomes a regional or national scale attraction area. The specialization coefficient, also known as the location coefficient, is formulated as in Equation 3:

$$LQ_{i,j} = \left(\frac{L_{i,j}}{\sum L_i} \Big/ \frac{\sum L_j}{\sum L} \right) \quad [(3)]$$

Accordingly, $LQ_{i,j}$ symbolizes specialization coefficient in work/activity field in province i, $L_{i,j}$ symbolizes the employment in j work/activity field in province i, and $\sum L_j$ symbolizes the total employment in work/activity field province i, $\sum L$ symbolizes total employment in the country and $\sum L_i$ symbolizes the total employment in province i.

Critical for all three coefficients in the three-star analysis is the determination of the threshold value that must be exceeded to get the star. In the preliminary studies, the threshold value in magnitude and dominance coefficients varies according to the number of activity groups in which employment is materialized. This number should be divided into 100 according to the number of activity branches to reach the ratio of the volume of employment in an activity group that must exceed the percentage weight of the province's employment. For example, if there are 50 fields of activity, the threshold value for magnitude and dominance should be 2 % (100 % / 2 = 2 %). In this study, since there are 88 operating branches, the threshold values are calculated as 1,364 %.

The threshold value to be exceeded in the specialization coefficient is considered as 2 in the ECU. In this study, the threshold value is considered as 2 based on the ECU approach.

Findings

The three-star analysis is conducted for a ten-year period from 2008 to 2017. In spite of the 64.5 % increase in the number of employees through a service contract across the country and there is a 1249.8 % increase in the number of social workers. However, there was no significant increase in regional clustering among 81 provinces. In the ten-year period, the number of provinces without any regional clusters ranges from 48 to 62. The highest regional clustering was realized in 31 provinces in 2013. However, it has started to decrease after this date. In general, around 30 provinces there is a various levels of regional clustering.

The second remarkable situation is that the regional clustered provinces predominantly have single star for becoming candidate clusters. Accordingly, the number of candidate clusters varies between 16 and 31 in 2008–2017. The number of provinces, which are potential clusters by taking two stars, is between 2 and 4. The only province showing three mature cluster features is valid only for Şanlıurfa in 2012. Apart from this, the mature cluster feature could not be reached in any province and in any year. The annual details for the ten-year period are as follows:

- In 2008, no regional clustering was observed in 62 provinces. On the other hand, 16 provinces became the candidate cluster by receiving one star and 3 provinces became the potential cluster by receiving two stars.
- In 2009, no regional clustering was observed in 52 provinces. On the other hand, 25 provinces became the candidate cluster by receiving one star and 4 provinces became the potential clusters by receiving two stars.
- In 2010, no regional clustering observed in 52 provinces. On the other hand, 26 provinces became the candidate cluster by receiving one star and 3 provinces became the potential cluster by receiving two stars.
- In 2011, no regional clustering was observed in 57 provinces. On the other hand, 25 provinces became the candidate cluster by receiving one star and 3 provinces became the potential cluster by receiving two stars.

- In 2012, no regional clustering was observed in 51 provinces. On the other hand, 29 provinces received a single star and one province became a mature cluster by receiving three stars for the first time.
- In 2013, no regional clustering was observed in 48 provinces. On the other hand, 31 provinces became the candidate cluster by receiving one star and 2 provinces became the potential cluster by receiving two stars.
- In 2014, no regional clustering was observed in 52 provinces. On the other hand, 26 provinces became the candidate cluster by receiving one star and 3 provinces became the potential cluster by receiving two stars.
- In 2015, no regional clustering was observed in 54 provinces. On the other hand, 24 provinces became the candidate cluster by receiving one star and 3 provinces became the potential cluster by receiving two stars.
- In 2016, no regional clustering was observed in 51 provinces. On the other hand, 26 provinces became the candidate cluster by receiving one star and 4 provinces became the potential cluster by receiving two stars.
- In 2017, no regional clustering was observed in 55 provinces. On the other hand, 23 provinces became the candidate cluster by receiving one star and 3 provinces became the potential cluster by receiving two stars.

In the three-star analysis, the most important reason why provinces cannot become mature clusters with the exception of one year and one province with three stars is that the field of activity has not been strengthened yet. It is noteworthy that the employment of social workers within the provincial employment volume does not reach sufficient maturity. This makes it difficult to exceed the critical threshold of 0.0114 of the coefficient of dominance (see Tab. 3).

In the absence of mature clusters, the accumulation of social worker employment in a small number of provinces is also effective. Accordingly, the magnitude coefficient falls below the critical threshold of 0.0114, with the exception of a small number of provinces. However, in provinces where the threshold value in the magnitude coefficient is exceeded, the threshold values in the dominance and specialization coefficients have not been exceeded. This prevents the formation of mature clusters (see Tab. 4, Tab. 5).

There are ten stable provinces each year that have the characteristics of regional clusters in the employment of social workers every ten years. These provinces are Adana, Ankara, Antalya, Bursa, Gaziantep, Istanbul, Izmir, Kocaeli, Konya and Şanlıurfa. It can be seen that all this ten provinces are developed provinces. Three metropolises (Ankara, İstanbul, İzmir) showed regional clustering every year. In the industrial cities of Bursa, Kocaeli and Konya, social worker employment has created a regional clustering every year. Adana, Gaziantep and Şanlıurfa draw attention with their proximity to Syria. Antalya has a different character as a tourism center (see Tab. 2).

Conclusion and Suggestions

Social service activity area is a new employment area with a history of approximately one century. The modern sense of origin in Turkey is limited to 50–60 years. This discipline continues to evolve both in Turkey and globally with each passing day. Many reasons such as the dominance of rights-based approach, aging population, increase in inequalities, and refugees seem to increase employment in the field of social work activity in the twenty-first century.

Turkey is a dynamic country with increased need for social work practice every day. It harbors numerous social problems like; gender, income and wealth inequalities, unemployment, increase in divorce rates, population aging, congregation, refugee influx from Syria. As a result of these problems, there is a steady increase in social service activities.

According to the regional units on the number of social workers and other personnel involved in social service activities in the public sector (NUTS1, NUTS2, NUTS3, NUTS4), there is no data. However, the only relevant data are available for 2008–2017 according to NUTS3which is formal labor force amounts in SSI statistical annuals. As a result of the performed three-star analysis, no mature clusters (three stars) were found with the exception in Şanlıurfa in 2012. The number of provinces with potential cluster characteristics was not more than 4 in any year. In some years it has dropped even to 2. The number of provinces in the candidate cluster has changed between 16–31 provinces. Therefore, it is seen that the regional clustering and regional competitive structure have not yet been materialized in employment in the field of social service activities. This situation also supports the increasing demand for labor in this field despite the increasing number of graduates. As a result, there has been more than eight-fold increase in employment in the ten-year period compared to the change in employment across the country. Nevertheless, the volume of employment that could lead to a serious regional cluster has not yet been achieved. Therefore, the number of provinces receiving stars in terms of focus and size is extremely small. In recent years, in provinces that received stars for their focus and their size, there is generally an intensive refugee flow. In economic centers such as Istanbul, Ankara, Izmir and Bursa, where inequality, professional problems, crime, divorce and other social problems are intense, being a candidate cluster could not be vaccinated. Therefore, it should be expected that the demand for labor will continue to increase for many years in the field of social work.

Tab. 2: The Result of Three Stars Analysis

Provinces	2008	2009	2010	2011	2012	2013	2014	2015	2016	2017
Adana	★	★	★	★	★	★	★	★	★	★
Adıyaman										
Afyon										
Ağrı	★	★	★	★						
Amasya										
Ankara	★★	★★	★	★	★	★	★	★	★	★
Antalya	★	★	★	★	★	★	★	★	★	★
Artvin										
Aydın	★	★	★		★	★	★	★★	★	★
Balıkesir		★								
Bilecik			★							
Bingöl	★			★	★	★	★★			
Bitlis		★	★	★	★	★	★	★	★	
Bolu										
Burdur		★		★	★	★	★	★		
Bursa	★	★	★							
Çanakkale									★	★
Çankırı				★	★	★	★			
Çorum			★							
Denizli		★							★★	★★
Diyarbakır									★	
Edirne										

Regional Clustering in Social Service Workers

	Elazığ	Erzincan	Erzurum	Eskişehir	Gaziantep	Giresun	Gümüşhane	Hakkari	Hatay	Isparta	Mersin	İstanbul	İzmir	Kars	Kastamonu	Kayseri	Kırklareli	Kırşehir	Kocaeli	Konya	Kütahya	Malatya	Manisa	K.maraş	Mardin
				★				★	★	★	★	★				★	★								
				★	★			★	★	★	★	★				★	★								
					★			★	★	★	★	★				★	★								
				★	★			★			★	★	★	★		★	★								
	★			★	★		★	★	★	★	★	★	★			★	★								
				★	★			★	★	★	★		★	★		★	★	★							
				★	★					★	★	★	★	★★	★		★	★	★						
				★	★					★★	★	★	★	★			★	★	★★						
				★	★	★		★	★	★				★	★	★									
	★	★		★	★	★				★	★	★			★	★								★	

(continued on next page)

Tab. 2: (continued)

Provinces	2008	2009	2010	2011	2012	2013	2014	2015	2016	2017
Muğla	**	*	*					*	*	*
Muş		*	*	*				*	*	**
Nevşehir		**								
Niğde			*							
Ordu										
Rize										
Sakarya					*	*	*	*	*	*
Samsun		*	*	**	*	*	*	**	*	*
Siirt			*	*	*	*	*	*	**	**
Sinop			*	*	*		*	*		
Sivas		**			*	*				
Tekirdağ		*								
Tokat										
Trabzon		*								
Tunceli	*		*		*	**	**	**	**	**
Şanlıurfa	**	**	**	**	***	**	**	**		
Uşak					*	*	*	*	*	
Van				*	*		*		*	
Yozgat				*						
Zonguldak			*							
Aksaray						*	*		*	
Bayburt										

Karaman
Kırıkkale
Batman
Şırnak
Bartın
Ardahan
Iğdır
Yalova
Karabük
Kilis
Osmaniye
Düzce

References

Abramovitz, Mimi, Social Work and Social Reform: An Arena of Struggle, Social Work, Vol. 43, No. 6, 1998, pp. 512–526.

Atkinson, Rowland and Hazel Easthope, The Consequences of the Creative Class: The Pursuit of Creativity Strategies in Australia's Cities, International Journal of Urban and Regional Research, Vol. 33, No. 1, 2009, pp. 64–79.

Austin, Michael J., Jude MaryAntonyappan and Leslie Leighninger, Federal Support for Social Work Education: Section 707 of the 1967 Social Security Act Amendments, Social Service Review, Vol. 70, No. 1, 1996, pp. 83–97.

Aysan, Mehmet Fatih and Ali Kaya, Türkiye'de Sosyal Politika Disiplininin ve Uygulamalarının Gelişimi, Türkiye Araştırmaları Literatür Dergisi, Vol. 6, No. 11, 2008, pp. 223–250.

Batı Karadeniz Kalkınma Ajansı, TR81 Düzey-2 Bölgesi Sektör Tanımlama, Önceliklendirme ve Rekabet Analizi Raporu, 2013.

Batı Akdeniz Kalkınma Ajansı, Bölge Planı 2014–2023 TR61 Düzey 2 Bölgesi Antalya-Isparta-Burdur, Antalya 2014.

Batten, David F. Network Cities: Creative Urban Agglomerations for the 21st Century, Urban Studies, Vol. 32, No. 2, 1995 313–327

Bayraktar, Fulya and Faruk Sekmen, Amasya Uygun Yatırım Alanları Araştırması, Türkiye Kalkınma Bankası AŞ, Ankara 2014b.

Bayraktar, Fulya and Faruk Sekmen, TR83 Bölgesi Amasya Uygun Yatırım Alanları Araştırması, Türkiye Kalkınma Bankası AŞ, Ankara 2014a.

Bertolini, Luca and Martin Dijst, Mobility Environments and Network Cities, Journal of Urban Design, Vol. 8, No. 1, 2003, pp. 27–43.

Brashears, Freda, Supervision as Social Work Practice: A Reconceptualization, Social Work, Vol. 40, No. 5, 1995, pp. 692–699.

Bruno, Frank J., Social Work Aspects of the Social Security Act, The Southwestern Social Science Quarterly, Vol. 17, No. 3, 1936, pp. 263–273.

Bursa Eskişehir Bilecik Kalkınma Ajansı, TR41 Bölgesi İlleri Kümelenme Analizleri, Bursa 2012.

Campbell John, Note on Growth Poles, Growth & Change, Vol 5, No. 2, 1974, pp. 43–45.

Caragliu, Andrea, Chiara Del Bo and Peter Nijkamp, Smart Cities in Europe, Journal of Urban Technology, Vol. 18, No. 2, 2011, pp. 65–82.

Casetti, E L, J King, and J Odland, The Formalization and Testing of Concepts of Growth Poles in a Spatial Context, *Environment and Planning A*, Vol. 3, No. 4, 1971, pp. 377–382.

Caspi, Jonathan, Coaching and Social Work: Challenges and Concerns, Social Work, Vol. 50, No. 4, 2005, pp. 359-362.

Çelebi Deniz, Zuhal, TRC2 Bölgesi'nde Yerel Ekonominin İtici Gücü Temel Sanayi Sektörlerinin Analizi, Karacadağ Bölgesel Kalkınma, Vol. 4, No. 5, 2014, pp. 17-20.

Ceyhan, Said and Sema Özlem Özcan, Bölgesel Kalkınmada Kümelenmelerin Rolü: Bartın İli Ayakkabıcılık Sektörü Örneği, AİBÜ Sosyal Bilimler Enstitüsü Dergisi, Vol. 18, No. 1, 2018, pp. 141-163.

Chris Jones and Tony Novak Social Work Today, The British Journal of Social Work, Vol. 23, No. 3, 1993, pp. 195-212.

Christofakis, Manolis and Athanasios Papadaskalopoulos, The Growth Poles Strategy in Regional Planning: The Recent Experience of Greece, *Theoretical and Empirical Researches in Urban Management*, Vol. 6, No. 2, 2011, pp. 5-20.

Çiftçi, Murat, Osmanlı İmparatorluğu Döneminde Özel Mülkiyet ve Yapısal Özellikleri, Turkish Studies, Vol. 6, No, 3, 2011, pp. 623-644.

Çiftçi, Murat, Trakya Alt Bölgesindeki Faaliyet Gruplarında İstihdama Dayalı Bölgesel Kümelenme, Diyalegtolog, No. 17, 2018, pp. 1-15.

Clark, Chris, Moral Character in Social Work, The British Journal of Social Work, Vol. 36, No. 1, 2006, pp. 75-89.

Clarke, Helen I. Social Work Today, Social Forces, Vol. 23, No. 2, 1944, pp. 178-187.

Craig, Gary, Poverty, Social Work and Social Justice, The British Journal of Social Work, Vol. 32, No. 6, 2002, pp. 669-682.

Çukurova Kalkınma Ajansı, RIS+Mersin Yenilik İhtiyaç Analizi Raporu, Mersin 2017.

Darwent, D.F., Growth Poles and Growth Centers in Regional Planning, A Reviewt, Environment and Planning, Vol. 1, 1969, pp. 5-32.

Delgado, Mercedes, Michael E. Porter and Scott Stern, Clusters, Convergence, and Economic Performance, Nber Working Paper Series, Cambridge 2012.

Delgado, Mercedes, Michael E. Porter and Scott Stern, Defining Clusters of Related Industries, Nber Working Paper Series, Cambridge 2014.

Demirdöğen, Serkan, Kümelenme Potansiyeli Gösteren Sektörlerin Belirlenmesi: TRA1 Düzey 2 Bölgesi Üzerine Bir Uygulama, AİBÜ Sosyal Bilimler Enstitüsü Dergisi, Vol. 18, No. 4, 2018, pp. 85-113.

Dickens, Jonathan, Social Work in England at a Watershed – As Always: From the Seebohm Report to the Social Work Task Force, The British Journal of Social Work, Vol. 41, No. 1, 2011, pp. 22-39.

Doğu Anadolu Kalkınma Ajansı, TRB2 Bölgesi Mevcut Durum Analizleri, Erzurum 2013.

Edwina Uehara, Marilyn Flynn, Rowena Fong, John Brekke, Richard P. Barth, Claudia Coulton, King Davis, Diana DiNitto, J. David Hawkins, James Lubben, Ron Manderscheid, Yolanda Padilla, Michael Sherraden and Karina Walters, Grand Challenges for Social Work, Journal of the Society for Social Work and Research, Vol. 4, No. 3, 2013, pp. 165–170.

Erickson, Rodney A., The Regional Impact of Growth Firms: The Case of Boeing, 1963–1968, Land Economics, Vol. 50, No. 2, 1974, pp. 127–136.

Erkek, Dilşad and Gülşah Öselmiş, TR32 Düzey II Bölgesi'nde Kümelenme Yaklaşımı, GEKA publishing, Aydın 2011.

Ertuğrul, Erdal, Ankara İş ve İnşaat Makineleri Sektör Analizi, Türkiye Kalkınma Bankası AŞ, Ankara 2014.

Ertuğrul, Erdal, TR72 Bölgesi (Kayseri, Sivas, Yozgat) Sağlık Sektörüne Yönelik İmalat Sanayi Raporu, Türkiye Kalkınma Bankası AŞ, Ankara 2013.

Eyden, J. L. M., Training for Social Work, Social Work (1939–1970), Vol. 7, No. 3, 1950, pp. 433–437.

Florida, Richard, Cities and the Creative Class, City & Community, Vol. 2, No. 1, 2003, pp. 3–19.

Fujıta, Masahisa and Tomoya Mori, Frontiers of The New Economic Geography, Papers in Regional Science, Vol. 84, No. 3, 2005, pp. 377–405.

Fujita, Masahisa, Paul Krugman, Anthony J. Venables, The Spatial Economy – Cities, Regions, and International Trade, The MIT Press, Cambridge, MA/London, England 1999.

Garretsen, Harry and Ron Martin, Rethinking (New) Economic Geography Models: Taking Geography and History More Seriously, Spatial Economic Analysis, Vol. 5, No. 2, 2010, pp. 127–160.

Gauthier, Howard L., Geography, Transportation, and Regional Development, Publication Series (Conference of Latin Americanist Geographers), Vol. 1, Geographic Research on Latin America: Benchmark 1970 (1971), pp. 333–342.

Gençler, Ayhan and Murat Çiftçi, Genel Olarak ve Türkiye Açısından Sosyal Politika Analizi, pp. 4–24, Edt. Hakan Acar, Nilüfer Negiz and Elvettin Akman, Sosyal Politika ve Kamu Yönetimi Bileşenleriyle Sosyal Hizmet, Maya Akademi publishing, Ankara 2013.

Gökçen Dündar, Şebnem, Kültür Ekonomisi Açısından İzmir'in Akdeniz'deki Yeri, Meltem: İzmir Akdeniz Akademisi Kitabı, İzmir 2016b, pp. 73–87.

Gökçen Dündar, Şebnem, Kültür Endüstrileri ve Bölgesel Kalkınma, Bölgesel Kalkınmada Yeni Trendler, Edt. Zekeriya Mızırak and Birol Mercan, Çizgi publishing, Konya 2016a, pp. 247–272.

Gopal, Meena, Gender, Ageing and Social Security, Economic and Political Weekly, Vol. 41, No. 42, 2006, pp. 4477–4486.

Günay Marmara Kalkınma Ajansı, TR22 (Balıkesir, Çanakkale) Güney Marmara Bölgesi İmalat Sanayi Stratejisi Ve Eylem Planı, Balıkesir 2017.

İpekyolu Kalkınma Ajansı, Adıyaman Hazır Giyim Konfeksiyon Raporu 2015, Gaziantep 2015.

İyem, Cemal, Derya Gül Öztürk and Fatma Zehra Yıldız, Clustering and Clustering Potential in TR 32 Regions Province, International Journal of Academic Research in Accounting, Finance and Management Sciences, Vol. 8, No. 3, 2018, pp. 336–345.

İzmir Kalkınma Ajansı, "İzmir Kültür Ekonomisi Gelişme Stratejisi: İzmir 2012 Kültür Ekonomisi ve Kültür Altyapısı Envanteri" İZKA İzmir Bölge Planı 2014–2023 Bölgesel Analizleri, İzmir 2013.

Kahn, Dorothy C., Social Work in The Security Program: Administrative Integration of Social Work in A Social Security Program Which Includes Social Insurance, The Compass, Vol. 25, No. 1 (November 1943), pp. 3–6, 24–26.

Karaca, Mehmet Emin and Faruk Bayrak, Bayburt Uygun Yatırım Alanları Araştırması, Türkiye Kalkınma Bankası AŞ, Ankara 2017.

Karacadağ Kalkınma Ajansı, TRC2 Diyarbakır Şanlıurfa Bölgesi Bölge Planı 2014–2023 Analiz ve Genel Değerlendirme, Diyarbakır 2015.

Karakuş, Bülent, Sosyal Hizmet Mezunlarının Kadro ve Unvanı "Sosyal Hizmet Uzmanı/Sosyal Çalışmacı", Toplum ve Sosyal Hizmet, Vol. 26, No. 2, 2015, pp. 169–190.

Keskin, Filiz and M. Oğuzhan Önen, Konya Uygun Yatırım Alanları Araştırması, Türkiye Kalkınma Bankası AŞ, Ankara 2012.

Knapp, Martin, Kostas Harissis and Spyros Missiakoulis, Who Leaves Social Work? The British Journal of Social Work, Vol. 11, No. 4, 1981, pp. 421–444.

Kourtit, Karima and Peter Nijkamp, Smart cities in the innovation age, Innovation: The European Journal of Social Science Research, Vol. 25, No. 2, 2012, pp. 93–95.

Kourtit, Karima, Peter Nijkamp and Daniel Arribas, Smart cities in perspective – a comparative European study by means of self-organizing maps, Innovation: The European Journal of Social Science Research, Vol. 25, No. 2, 2012, pp. 229–246.

Krugman, Paul R. and Maurice Obstfeld, International Economics – Theory and Policy, Sixth Edition, Addison Wesley Press, Boston etc., 2003.

Krugman, Paul, The New Economic Geography, Now Middle-aged, Regional Studies, Vol. 45, No. 1, 2011, pp. 1–7.

Krugman, Paul, What's New About the New Economic Geography? Oxford Review of Economic Policy, Vol. 14, No. 2, 1998, pp. 7–17.

Krumer-Nevo, Michal, Idit Weiss-Gal and Menachem Monnickendam, Poverty-Aware Social Work Practice: A Conceptual Framework For Social Work Education, Journal of Social Work Education, Vol. 45, No. 2, 2009, pp. 225–243.

Lasuen, J. R., On Growth Poles, *Urban Studies*, Vol. 6, No. 2, 1969, pp. 137–161.

Merdan, Kurtuluş, Yerel Kalkınmada Gümüşhane İli Arıcılık Sektörünün Kümelenme Yaklaşımı İle Değerlendirilmesi, Journal of Social And Humanities Sciences Research, Vol. 5, No. 25, 2018, pp. 1936–1947.

Mevlana Kalkınma Ajansı, Konya Karaman Bölgesi İmalat Sanayi Sektörel Rekabet Edebilirlik Analizi, Konya 2013.

Moseley, Malcolm J., Growth Centres: A Shibboleth?, Area, Vol. 5, No. 2, 1973, pp. 143–150.

Murdach, Allison D., Does American Social Work Have a Progressive Tradition?, Social Work, Vol. 55, No. 1, 2010, pp. 82–89.

Nijkamp, Peter, Entrepreneurship in a Modern Network Economy, Regional Studies, Vol. 37, No. 4, 2003, pp. 395–405.

Oran Kalkınma Ajansı, Kayseri ve Sivas İllerinde Öne Çıkan Sektörler İçin Rekabet Gücü Analizi, Kayseri 2014.

Oran Kalkınma Ajansı, TR72 Bölgesi'nde Öne Çıkan Sektörler, Kayseri 2015.

Pelton, Leroy H., Social Justice and Social Work, Journal of Social Work Education, Vol. 37, No. 3, 2001, pp. 433–439.

Perroux, Francois and Leon King, From The Avarice of Nations to an Economy for Mankind, Cross Currents, Vol. 3, No. 3, 1953, pp. 193–207.

Ponzini, Davide and Ugo Rossi, Becoming a Creative City: The Entrepreneurial Mayor, Network Politics and the Promise of an Urban Renaissance, Urban Studies, Vol. 47, No. 5, 2010, pp. 1037–1057,

Porter, Michael E., Clusters and the New Economics of Competition, Harvard Business Review, November–December 1998, pp. 77–89.

Porter, Michael E., Competitive Strategy: Techniques for Analyzing Industries and Competitors With a new Introduction, The Free Press, New York, 1980.

Porter, Michael E. and Michael P. Porter, Location, Clusters, and the "New" Microeconomics of Competition, Business Economics, Vol. 33, No. 1, 1998, pp. 7-13.

Reçber, Bircan, Sosyal Hizmetin Gelişiminde Türkiye'nin Konumu: Teorik Bir Analiz, Toplum ve Sosyal Hizmet, Vol. 30, No. 2, 2019, pp. 715-738.

Redding, Stephen J., The Empirics of New Economic Geography, Journal O F Regional S Cience, Vol. 50, No. 1, 2010, pp. 297-311

Reisch, Michael, The Sociopolitical Context and Social Work Method, 1890-1950, Social Service Review, Vol. 72, No. 2, 1998, pp. 161-181.

Richardson, Harry W. and Margaret Richardson, The Relevance of Growth Center Strategies to Latin America, *Economic Geography*, Vol. 51, No. 2, 1975, pp. 163-178.

Rosen, Aaron and Ronda S. Connaway, Public Welfare, Social Work, and Social Work Education, Social Work, Vol. 14, No. 2, 1969, pp. 87-94.

Şahinkaya, Serdar, TR72 Bölgesi (Kayseri, Sivas, Yozgat) Savunma Sanayine Yönelik İmalat Sanayi Raporu, Türkiye Kalkınma Bankası AŞ, Ankara 2013.

Schmutzler, Armin, The New Economic Geography, Journal of Economic Surveys, Vol. 13, No. 4, 1999, pp. 355-379.

Scott, Allen J., Creative Cities: Conceptual Issues and Policy Questions, Journal of Urban Affairs, Vol. 28, No. 1, 2006, pp. 1-17.

Seki, İsmail and Mahmut Arslan, TRC2 (Diyarbakır - Şanlıurfa) Bölgesi Kümelenme Potansiyeli Analizi, Al-Farabi Uluslararası Sosyal Bilimler Dergisi, Vol. 1, No. 1, 2018, pp. 32-53.

Seki, İsmail, Mahmut Arslan and Selahattin Bektaş, TR22 Çanakkale Bölgesi Kümelenme Analizi, Uluslararası Yönetim ve Sosyal Araştırmalar Dergisi, Vol. 5, No. 10, 2018, pp. 15-27.

Semple, R. Keith, Howard L. Gauthier and Carl E. Youngmann, Growth Poles in Sao Paulo, Brazil, Annals of the Association of American Geographers, Vol. 62, No. 4, 1972, pp. 591-598.

Şen, Ömer and Ersin Kaya Sandal, Gaziantep İlinde Üç Yıldız Analizi Yöntemi İle Endüstriyel Kümelenme Analizi, Doğu Coğrafya Dergisi, Vol. 22, No. 38, 2017, pp. 39-62.

Sevim, Kaan and Fatih Altun, Sosyal Hizmet Bölümü Öğrencilerinin Geleceğe Yönelik Mesleki ve Akademik Beklentileri, AÇÜ Uluslararası Sosyal Bilimler Dergisi, Vol. 3, No. 2, 2017, pp. 51-65.

Sevimli Deniz, Serpil and H. Eray Çelik, TRB2 Bölgesinde Kümelenme Potansiyeli Olan Sektörlerin Belirlenmesi, Van Yüzüncü Yıl Üniversitesi Sosyal Bilimler Enstitüsü Dergisi, No. 36, 2017, pp. 109-118.

SGK, İstatistik Yıllığı 2008, Ankara 2009.
SGK, İstatistik Yıllığı 2009, Ankara 2010.
SGK, İstatistik Yıllığı 2010, Ankara 2011.
SGK, İstatistik Yıllığı 2011, Ankara 2012.
SGK, İstatistik Yıllığı 2012, Ankara 2013.
SGK, İstatistik Yıllığı 2013, Ankara 2014.
SGK, İstatistik Yıllığı 2014, Ankara 2015.
SGK, İstatistik Yıllığı 2015, Ankara 2016.
SGK, İstatistik Yıllığı 2016, Ankara 2017.
SGK, İstatistik Yıllığı 2017, Ankara 2018.
Small, Neil, Social Work and Palliative Care, The British Journal of Social Work, Vol. 31, No. 6, 2001, pp. 961–971.
Social Work (1939–1970), Social Work in Germany, Vol. 9, No. 4, 1952, pp. 727–733.
Stewart, Gill and John Stewart, Social Work with Homeless Families, The British Journal of Social Work, Vol. 22, No. 3, 1992, pp. 271–289.
Sunley, Peter, Relational Economic Geography: A Partial Understanding or a New Paradigm? Economic Geography, Vol. 84, No. 1, 2008, pp. 1–26.
T.C. Kalkınma Bakanlığı DAP Bölge Kalkınma İdaresi Başkanlığı, 2017 Girişimcilik ve Yenilikçilik İhtiyaç Analizi ve Kümelenme Çalışmaları, Ankara 2017.
T.C. Sanayi ve Teknoloji Bakanlığı Doğu Karadeniz Projesi Bölge Kalkınma İdaresi Başkanlığı, DOKAP Bölgesi Tarımsal Üretim ve Tarımsal Sanayi Yatırım Potansiyeli Araştırma Projesi DOKAP Bölgesi Küçükbaş Hayvancılık Kümelenme Raporu, Ankara 2019.
Trakya Kalkınma Ajansı, Rekabet Analizi, Tekirdağ 2012.
Türkcan, Burcu, Gülçin Gürel Günal, and Neşe Kumral, An Empirical Analysis of Cultural Economy in Turkey's Metropolitan Regions, *Anadolu Üniversitesi Sosyal Bilimler Dergisi*, Vol. 16, No. 4, 2016, pp. 53–66.
Türkiye Teknoloji Geliştirme Vakfı İktisadi İşletmesi, DAP Bölgesi Yenilikçilik ve Girişimcilik İhtiyaç Analizi Projesi Ön Raporu, 2016.
Van Driel, Agnes, Personnel in Social Security, Social Service Review, Vol. 11, No. 3, 1937, pp. 434–445.
Von Thünen, J. H., "Die isolierte Staat in Beziehung auf Landwirtshaft und Nationalökonomie". Pergamon Press, New York, 1826.
Walton, Ron, Social Work as a Social Institution, The British Journal of Social Work, Vol. 35, No. 5, 2005, pp. 587–607.

Weiss, Idit, John Gal and Joseph Katan, Social Policy for Social Work: A Teaching Agenda, The British Journal of Social Work, Vol. 36, No. 5, 2006, pp. 789-806.

Williams, John, Social Work, Liberty and Law,The British Journal of Social Work, Vol. 34, No. 1, 2004, pp. 37-52.

Yiğit, Talip, Türkiye'de Sosyal Hizmet Eğitim/Öğretiminde Kalite Güvence Sistemi ve Akreditasyon Standartlarına İlişkin Bir Model Çerçeve Önerisi, Toplum ve Sosyal Hizmet, Vol. 28, No. 1, 2017, pp. 151-168.

Yıldırım, Buğra and Fatih Şahin, Esping-Andersen'in Refah Devleti Sınıflandırması ve Makro Sosyal Hizmet Uygulamaları Temelinde Türkiye'nin Konumu, OPUS Uluslararası Toplum Araştırmaları Dergisi, Vol. 11, No. 16, 2019, pp. 2525-2554.

Zafer Kalkınma Ajansı, Manisa İli Yerel Ekonomik Gelişme Programı, Manisa 2014.

Appendix

Tab. 3: Value of Size (2008–2017)

Provinces	2008	2009	2010	2011	2012	2013	2014	2015	2016	2017
Adana	**0,019**	**0,017**	**0,017**	**0,016**	**0,019**	**0,019**	**0,024**	**0,021**	**0,026**	**0,025**
Adıyaman	0,002	0,001	0,004	0,004	0,003	0,003	0,005	0,005	0,005	0,006
Afyon	0,001	0,002	0,004	0,007	0,005	0,005	0,006	0,005	0,005	0,005
Ağrı	0,005	0,006	0,005	0,004	0,003	0,002	0,002	0,002	0,003	0,003
Amasya	0,000	0,005	0,003	0,004	0,003	0,004	0,005	0,004	0,005	0,005
Ankara	**0,258**	**0,203**	**0,125**	**0,149**	**0,128**	**0,116**	**0,116**	**0,116**	**0,117**	**0,116**
Antalya	**0,037**	**0,021**	**0,028**	**0,028**	**0,031**	**0,038**	**0,037**	**0,037**	**0,039**	**0,041**
Artvin	0,000	0,002	0,002	0,002	0,002	0,002	0,002	0,002	0,002	0,002
Aydın	**0,020**	**0,012**	**0,014**	0,008	**0,012**	**0,015**	**0,015**	**0,023**	**0,015**	**0,014**
Balıkesir	0,011	**0,012**	0,007	0,007	0,010	0,009	0,009	0,011	0,010	0,010
Bilecik	0,005	0,003	0,002	0,002	0,003	0,003	0,002	0,002	0,003	0,003
Bingöl	0,003	0,001	0,003	0,002	0,003	0,002	0,004	0,003	0,003	0,003
Bitlis	0,000	0,006	0,005	0,004	0,003	0,004	0,004	0,003	0,003	0,003
Bolu	0,001	0,002	0,003	0,003	0,003	0,003	0,003	0,003	0,003	0,002
Burdur	0,003	0,008	0,003	0,003	0,004	0,004	0,004	0,004	0,003	0,003
Bursa	**0,024**	**0,024**	**0,028**	**0,021**	**0,019**	**0,023**	**0,025**	**0,025**	**0,025**	**0,023**
Çanakkale	0,011	0,010	0,005	0,006	0,005	0,005	0,005	0,006	0,007	0,006
Çankırı	0,000	0,002	0,001	0,001	0,002	0,002	0,001	0,001	0,001	0,001
Çorum	0,003	0,003	0,003	0,003	0,006	0,003	0,003	0,003	0,003	0,002
Denizli	0,010	**0,013**	**0,015**	**0,014**	**0,012**	**0,016**	**0,022**	**0,011**	**0,012**	**0,011**
Diyarbakır	0,004	0,001	0,004	0,005	0,009	0,009	0,008	0,009	**0,014**	**0,017**

Edirne	0,004	0,005	0,002	0,001	0,001	0,003	0,005	0,003	0,003	0,002
Elazığ	0,000	0,001	0,005	0,004	0,005	0,011	0,005	0,006	0,007	0,007
Erzincan	0,000	0,001	0,001	0,001	0,001	0,001	0,001	0,002	0,002	0,003
Erzurum	0,009	0,007	0,008	0,007	0,007	0,007	0,008	0,009	0,008	0,008
Eskişehir	0,006	**0,017**	**0,015**	**0,013**	**0,013**	**0,012**	**0,011**	0,010	**0,012**	0,010
Gaziantep	**0,013**	**0,025**	**0,021**	**0,022**	**0,023**	**0,023**	**0,022**	**0,025**	**0,026**	**0,029**
Giresun	0,002	0,004	0,001	0,002	0,004	0,005	0,005	0,006	0,006	0,005
Gümüşhane	0,002	0,003	0,002	0,002	0,001	0,002	0,002	0,002	0,001	0,001
Hakkari	0,000	0,000	0,000	0,000	0,000	0,000	0,000	0,000	0,000	0,000
Hatay	0,011	0,004	0,010	0,010	**0,012**	**0,013**	**0,015**	**0,017**	**0,019**	**0,020**
Isparta	0,000	0,007	0,003	0,001	0,006	0,005	0,004	0,005	0,005	0,005
Mersin	**0,017**	**0,028**	**0,046**	**0,029**	**0,012**	**0,012**	**0,011**	**0,015**	**0,017**	**0,017**
İstanbul	**0,251**	**0,210**	**0,258**	**0,246**	**0,210**	**0,207**	**0,187**	**0,176**	**0,172**	**0,165**
İzmir	**0,060**	**0,033**	**0,036**	**0,048**	**0,052**	**0,045**	**0,056**	**0,056**	**0,060**	**0,056**
Kars	0,002	0,005	0,003	0,004	0,003	0,004	0,003	0,004	0,004	0,004
Kastamonu	0,005	0,002	0,008	**0,011**	0,010	0,009	0,007	0,006	0,006	0,006
Kayseri	0,000	0,003	0,007	**0,013**	**0,013**	**0,016**	**0,017**	**0,018**	**0,017**	**0,017**
Kırklareli	0,001	0,003	0,002	0,001	0,002	0,002	0,002	0,002	0,003	0,002
Kırşehir	0,004	0,005	0,003	0,005	0,004	0,002	0,004	0,004	0,004	0,003
Kocaeli	**0,013**	**0,012**	**0,024**	**0,020**	**0,025**	**0,029**	**0,032**	**0,027**	**0,027**	**0,029**
Konya	**0,015**	**0,026**	**0,015**	**0,018**	**0,025**	**0,029**	**0,037**	**0,030**	**0,020**	**0,022**
Kütahya	0,002	0,008	**0,014**	**0,012**	0,011	0,011	0,009	0,010	0,010	0,009
Malatya	0,005	0,011	0,009	0,007	0,007	0,006	**0,012**	0,010	0,010	0,010
Manisa	0,003	0,010	**0,015**	**0,016**	**0,016**	**0,017**	**0,018**	**0,017**	**0,018**	**0,017**
K.maraş	0,011	0,010	0,004	0,005	0,008	0,009	0,008	0,009	0,009	0,010

(continued on next page)

Tab. 3: (continued)

Provinces	2008	2009	2010	2011	2012	2013	2014	2015	2016	2017
Mardin	0,006	0,006	0,005	0,005	0,008	0,008	0,007	0,006	0,008	0,009
Muğla	**0,024**	**0,013**	**0,012**	0,010	**0,013**	**0,012**	0,011	**0,012**	**0,012**	**0,012**
Muş	0,001	0,004	0,004	0,003	0,003	0,003	0,003	0,004	0,004	0,011
Nevşehir	0,004	**0,012**	0,005	0,005	0,005	0,004	0,004	0,004	0,004	0,004
Niğde	0,003	0,003	0,006	0,005	0,004	0,005	0,004	0,004	0,004	0,004
Ordu	0,005	0,004	0,007	0,008	0,010	0,010	0,009	0,009	0,010	0,010
Rize	0,002	0,002	0,004	0,005	0,005	0,005	0,004	0,004	0,005	0,005
Sakarya	0,010	0,008	0,009	0,010	**0,013**	**0,013**	**0,014**	**0,015**	**0,013**	**0,012**
Samsun	0,004	**0,015**	**0,021**	**0,023**	**0,022**	**0,021**	**0,020**	**0,024**	**0,018**	**0,018**
Siirt	0,000	0,001	0,005	0,004	0,006	0,006	0,004	0,006	0,006	0,006
Sinop	0,003	0,002	0,005	0,005	0,005	0,004	0,005	0,004	0,003	0,003
Sivas	0,002	**0,014**	0,009	0,010	0,011	0,011	0,009	0,009	0,009	0,007
Tekirdağ	0,004	**0,013**	0,007	0,007	0,011	0,011	0,010	0,009	0,010	0,011
Tokat	0,001	0,006	0,004	0,004	0,003	0,003	0,005	0,005	0,006	0,007
Trabzon	0,006	**0,018**	0,005	0,008	0,007	0,008	0,008	0,008	0,008	0,009
Tunceli	0,002	0,001	0,001	0,001	0,002	0,002	0,001	0,002	0,001	0,001
Şanlıurfa	**0,015**	**0,038**	**0,035**	**0,035**	**0,045**	**0,027**	**0,026**	**0,030**	**0,030**	**0,030**
Uşak	0,007	0,006	0,005	0,008	0,007	0,005	0,004	0,004	0,004	0,004
Van	0,003	0,002	0,006	0,003	0,006	0,007	0,009	0,007	0,009	0,010
Yozgat	0,003	0,003	0,005	0,006	0,007	0,006	0,006	0,009	0,008	0,008
Zonguldak	0,009	0,007	0,004	0,004	0,006	0,007	0,007	0,007	0,008	0,009
Aksaray	0,005	0,002	0,002	0,002	0,004	0,004	0,004	0,005	0,004	0,004
Bayburt	0,001	0,001	0,002	0,002	0,002	0,002	0,001	0,001	0,001	0,001
Karaman	0,000	0,001	0,008	0,006	0,005	0,006	0,006	0,009	0,009	0,008

Kırıkkale	0,004	0,005	0,002	0,002	0,003	0,003	0,002	0,004	0,003	0,003
Batman	0,001	0,001	0,002	0,001	0,004	0,004	0,003	0,003	0,003	0,004
Şırnak	0,002	0,001	0,000	0,000	0,000	0,001	0,001	0,000	0,003	0,004
Bartın	0,002	0,004	0,002	0,001	0,001	0,001	0,001	0,001	0,001	0,001
Ardahan	0,001	0,000	0,002	0,002	0,002	0,002	0,003	0,002	0,002	0,002
Iğdır	0,000	0,002	0,002	0,001	0,001	0,001	0,001	0,001	0,001	0,001
Yalova	0,005	0,002	0,002	0,002	0,001	0,002	0,002	0,003	0,003	0,004
Karabük	0,001	0,001	0,004	0,005	0,004	0,005	0,004	0,005	0,004	0,003
Kilis	0,000	0,001	0,002	0,002	0,002	0,010	0,007	0,003	0,004	0,005
Osmaniye	0,006	0,006	0,003	0,004	0,006	0,004	0,005	0,008	0,005	0,004
Düzce	0,001	0,000	0,010	0,007	0,007	0,007	0,006	0,008	0,008	0,007

Tab. 4: Location Quotient (2008–2017)

Provinces	2008	2009	2010	2011	2012	2013	2014	2015	2016	2017
Adana	0,94	0,78	0,79	0,72	0,89	0,87	1,11	0,99	1,19	1,17
Adıyaman	0,51	0,21	1,12	1,17	0,84	0,78	1,49	1,48	1,47	1,54
Afyonkarahisar	0,08	0,28	0,65	1,12	0,76	0,85	0,95	0,82	0,84	0,82
Ağrı	3,62	3,99	2,76	2,75	1,78	1,50	1,50	1,56	1,95	1,75
Amasya	0,00	1,69	0,95	1,18	1,11	1,34	1,78	1,30	1,61	1,56
Ankara	3,03	2,28	1,44	1,76	1,50	1,38	1,36	1,33	1,33	1,47
Antalya	1,16	0,66	0,86	0,85	0,93	1,10	1,07	1,08	1,24	1,27
Artvin	0,00	1,12	1,03	0,91	1,01	1,13	0,99	1,29	1,23	1,03
Aydın	1,97	1,21	1,35	0,81	1,18	1,49	1,46	**2,08**	1,34	1,20
Balıkesir	0,95	0,98	0,62	0,59	0,83	0,78	0,77	0,89	0,86	0,86
Bilecik	1,53	0,83	0,57	0,71	0,77	0,83	0,68	0,81	0,86	0,80
Bingöl	**2,61**	1,19	**2,24**	1,42	1,81	1,62	**2,71**	1,53	1,83	1,78
Bitlis	0,00	**4,43**	**3,58**	**3,38**	**2,57**	**3,14**	**2,63**	**2,05**	**2,20**	1,53
Bolu	0,30	0,38	0,65	0,69	0,61	0,76	0,70	0,68	0,65	0,61
Burdur	1,19	**3,10**	1,30	1,13	1,54	1,57	1,55	1,47	1,32	1,07
Bursa	0,49	0,50	0,59	0,43	0,40	0,49	0,53	0,53	0,52	0,48
Çanakkale	1,92	1,84	0,87	1,08	0,96	0,89	1,00	1,05	1,15	1,01
Çankırı	0,00	0,94	0,80	0,75	0,85	0,91	0,78	0,60	0,56	0,63
Çorum	0,74	0,66	0,72	0,68	1,49	0,77	0,81	0,74	0,60	0,58
Denizli	0,66	0,91	1,06	1,01	0,89	1,09	1,54	0,82	0,91	0,83
Diyarbakır	0,47	0,16	0,46	0,49	0,92	1,06	0,86	0,97	1,48	1,68
Edirne	1,00	1,11	0,54	0,26	0,33	0,79	1,12	0,75	0,74	0,56
Elazığ	0,05	0,16	0,91	0,75	1,14	**2,41**	1,11	1,30	1,59	1,37
Erzincan	0,00	0,37	0,33	0,59	0,55	0,51	0,48	1,11	1,18	1,14

Erzurum	1,54	1,14	1,30	1,28	1,28	1,34	1,43	1,61	1,44	1,31
Eskişehir	0,51	1,35	1,18	1,05	1,06	0,97	0,91	0,83	0,94	0,84
Gaziantep	0,86	1,59	1,25	1,25	1,19	1,15	1,10	1,28	1,34	1,44
Giresun	0,48	1,09	0,36	0,52	1,04	1,52	1,44	1,55	1,60	1,39
Gümüşhane	2,64	3,11	1,96	1,82	1,18	2,03	1,77	1,45	1,49	1,23
Hakkari	0,00	0,00	0,08	0,00	0,22	0,20	0,00	0,02	0,00	0,13
Hatay	1,10	0,40	0,90	0,93	1,13	1,14	1,32	1,45	1,70	1,72
Isparta	0,06	1,80	0,86	0,26	1,52	1,22	0,92	1,12	1,23	1,19
Mersin	1,12	1,76	2,90	1,71	0,73	0,73	0,68	0,90	0,98	0,95
İstanbul	0,82	0,70	0,87	0,83	0,71	0,69	0,62	0,60	0,58	0,58
İzmir	0,89	0,51	0,55	0,73	0,81	0,71	0,89	0,91	0,95	0,89
Kars	1,76	3,68	2,15	2,63	1,94	3,03	2,21	2,54	2,51	2,20
Kastamonu	1,68	0,70	2,35	3,42	2,95	2,97	2,17	1,75	1,75	1,67
Kayseri	0,00	0,18	0,46	0,79	0,83	0,96	1,05	1,16	1,10	1,11
Kırklareli	0,21	0,53	0,32	0,23	0,45	0,53	0,44	0,35	0,55	0,31
Kırşehir	2,20	2,49	1,72	2,44	2,03	1,25	1,93	1,97	1,97	1,74
Kocaeli	0,38	0,37	0,70	0,61	0,75	0,85	0,93	0,81	0,78	0,83
Konya	0,79	1,34	0,75	0,89	1,21	1,37	1,76	1,41	0,95	1,03
Kütahya	0,35	1,18	2,18	1,79	1,65	1,68	1,48	1,65	1,58	1,50
Malatya	0,72	1,64	1,29	1,08	0,95	0,95	1,82	1,40	1,57	1,43
Manisa	0,21	0,61	0,92	0,96	0,97	1,02	1,08	1,05	1,05	0,99
Kahramanmaraş	1,25	1,05	0,46	0,54	0,78	0,89	0,82	0,93	0,92	0,99
Mardin	2,15	1,92	1,42	1,25	1,93	1,91	1,65	1,37	1,75	1,61
Muğla	2,01	1,10	0,99	0,85	1,11	1,00	0,92	0,95	0,96	0,97
Muş	0,97	2,72	2,28	2,45	1,96	2,01	2,39	2,31	2,71	5,91

(continued on next page)

Tab. 4: (continued)

Provinces	2008	2009	2010	2011	2012	2013	2014	2015	2016	2017
Nevşehir	1,39	4,17	1,59	1,84	1,77	1,41	1,48	1,54	1,70	1,49
Niğde	1,15	0,98	2,16	1,81	1,47	1,75	1,36	1,33	1,36	1,40
Ordu	0,92	0,78	1,19	1,45	1,72	1,76	1,72	1,69	1,76	1,62
Rize	0,43	0,42	1,15	1,49	1,44	1,52	1,25	1,20	1,37	1,48
Sakarya	0,84	0,67	0,76	0,84	1,16	1,09	1,15	1,21	1,02	0,95
Samsun	0,39	1,33	1,89	2,03	1,93	1,85	1,72	2,07	1,53	1,49
Siirt	0,00	0,78	2,98	3,19	3,65	3,70	3,07	3,38	4,13	3,17
Sinop	1,58	0,82	2,41	2,70	2,39	2,16	2,86	2,03	1,82	1,58
Sivas	0,32	2,52	1,66	1,92	2,13	2,13	1,73	1,62	1,70	1,37
Tekirdağ	0,24	0,73	0,42	0,38	0,62	0,63	0,56	0,51	0,54	0,56
Tokat	0,18	1,53	0,95	0,97	0,87	0,86	1,35	1,35	1,62	1,66
Trabzon	0,67	1,91	0,50	0,85	0,83	0,94	0,96	0,91	0,94	1,00
Tunceli	3,18	1,18	2,04	1,94	3,49	3,49	3,31	2,91	2,19	1,78
Şanlıurfa	2,24	5,32	4,61	4,03	4,88	3,04	3,01	3,13	3,36	3,11
Uşak	1,53	1,31	1,08	1,78	1,70	1,12	1,00	0,97	0,93	0,99
Van	0,66	0,51	1,15	0,81	1,09	1,35	1,96	1,53	1,65	1,69
Yozgat	0,87	1,06	1,58	2,00	2,38	2,24	2,11	2,97	3,02	2,90
Zonguldak	1,06	0,82	0,55	0,50	0,93	1,06	1,11	1,15	1,31	1,41
Aksaray	1,75	0,74	0,53	0,72	1,14	1,21	1,24	1,39	1,38	1,17
Bayburt	1,63	1,43	4,88	4,24	3,08	3,70	2,73	1,95	2,37	1,60
Karaman	0,09	0,37	2,75	1,98	1,68	1,88	1,81	3,04	3,16	2,66
Kırıkkale	1,60	1,86	0,86	0,95	1,41	1,20	0,71	1,37	1,23	1,35
Batman	0,42	0,30	0,58	0,45	1,01	1,28	0,72	0,80	0,90	1,05
Şırnak	1,20	0,42	0,02	0,00	0,00	0,27	0,26	0,15	1,30	1,09

Bartın	1,06	2,19	0,80	0,72	0,60	0,55	0,48	0,63	0,49	0,58
Ardahan	1,28	0,48	3,43	3,86	3,86	4,07	4,95	3,10	3,47	2,18
Iğdır	0,00	1,68	1,97	0,72	0,96	1,20	1,24	0,99	0,72	0,75
Yalova	1,50	0,51	0,59	0,51	0,48	0,48	0,57	0,71	0,75	1,04
Karabük	0,39	0,53	1,61	1,90	1,45	1,78	1,53	1,81	1,34	1,29
Kilis	0,00	1,14	3,17	2,46	2,77	11,53	8,15	2,53	3,92	4,41
Osmaniye	1,69	1,46	0,75	0,89	1,47	1,05	1,28	1,99	1,41	1,14
Düzce	0,13	0,06	1,78	1,31	1,28	1,34	1,19	1,49	1,56	1,33

Tab. 5: Value of Focus (2008–2017)

Provinces	2008	2009	2010	2011	2012	2013	2014	2015	2016	2017
Adana	0,000	0,001	0,002	0,002	0,002	0,002	0,003	0,003	0,004	0,004
Adıyaman	0,000	0,000	0,002	0,003	0,002	0,002	0,004	0,004	0,005	0,006
Afyon	0,000	0,000	0,001	0,003	0,002	0,002	0,003	0,002	0,003	0,003
Ağrı	0,002	0,004	0,006	0,006	0,005	0,004	0,004	0,005	0,006	0,006
Amasya	0,000	0,002	0,002	0,003	0,003	0,003	0,005	0,004	0,005	0,006
Ankara	0,001	0,002	0,003	0,004	0,004	0,004	0,004	0,004	0,004	0,005
Antalya	0,001	0,001	0,002	0,002	0,002	0,003	0,003	0,003	0,004	0,005
Artvin	0,000	0,001	0,002	0,002	0,003	0,003	0,003	0,004	0,004	0,004
Aydın	0,001	0,001	0,003	0,002	0,003	0,004	0,004	0,006	0,004	0,004
Balıkesir	0,000	0,001	0,001	0,001	0,002	0,002	0,002	0,003	0,003	0,003
Bilecik	0,001	0,001	0,001	0,002	0,002	0,002	0,002	0,002	0,003	0,003
Bingöl	0,001	0,001	0,005	0,003	0,005	0,004	0,008	0,005	0,006	0,006
Bitlis	0,000	0,004	0,008	0,008	0,007	0,008	0,008	0,006	0,007	0,005
Bolu	0,000	0,000	0,001	0,002	0,002	0,002	0,002	0,002	0,002	0,002
Burdur	0,001	0,003	0,003	0,003	0,004	0,004	0,005	0,004	0,004	0,004
Bursa	0,000	0,001	0,001	0,001	0,001	0,001	0,002	0,002	0,002	0,002
Çanakkale	0,001	0,002	0,002	0,002	0,002	0,002	0,003	0,003	0,004	0,004
Çankırı	0,000	0,001	0,002	0,002	0,002	0,002	0,002	0,002	0,002	0,002
Çorum	0,000	0,001	0,002	0,002	0,004	0,002	0,002	0,002	0,002	0,002
Denizli	0,000	0,001	0,002	0,002	0,002	0,003	0,004	0,002	0,003	0,003
Diyarbakır	0,000	0,000	0,001	0,001	0,002	0,003	0,003	0,003	0,005	0,006
Edirne	0,000	0,001	0,001	0,001	0,001	0,002	0,003	0,002	0,002	0,002
Elazığ	0,000	0,000	0,002	0,002	0,003	0,006	0,003	0,004	0,005	0,005
Erzincan	0,000	0,000	0,001	0,001	0,001	0,001	0,001	0,003	0,004	0,004

Erzurum	0,001	0,003	0,003	0,003	0,003	0,004	0,005	0,005	0,005	
Eskişehir	0,000	0,001	0,003	0,002	0,003	0,003	0,003	0,002	0,003	
Gaziantep	0,000	0,002	0,003	0,003	0,003	0,003	0,004	0,004	0,004	
Giresun	0,000	0,001	0,001	0,001	0,003	0,004	0,005	0,005	0,005	
Gümüşhane	0,001	0,003	0,004	0,004	0,005	0,005	0,004	0,005	0,004	
Hakkari	0,000	0,000	0,000	0,000	0,001	0,000	0,000	0,000	0,000	
Hatay	0,000	0,000	0,002	0,002	0,003	0,004	0,004	0,006	0,006	
Isparta	0,000	0,002	0,002	0,001	0,003	0,003	0,003	0,004	0,004	
Mersin	0,000	0,002	0,006	0,004	0,004	0,002	0,003	0,003	0,003	
İstanbul	0,000	0,001	0,002	0,002	0,002	0,002	0,002	0,002	0,002	
İzmir	0,000	0,001	0,001	0,002	0,002	0,003	0,003	0,003	0,003	
Kars	0,001	0,004	0,005	0,006	0,005	0,006	0,008	0,008	0,008	
Kastamonu	0,001	0,001	0,005	0,008	0,007	0,006	0,005	0,006	0,006	
Kayseri	0,000	0,000	0,001	0,002	0,002	0,003	0,003	0,004	0,004	
Kırklareli	0,000	0,001	0,001	0,001	0,001	0,001	0,001	0,002	0,001	
Kırşehir	0,001	0,003	0,004	0,006	0,005	0,006	0,006	0,006	0,006	
Kocaeli	0,000	0,000	0,002	0,001	0,002	0,003	0,002	0,003	0,003	
Konya	0,000	0,001	0,002	0,002	0,003	0,005	0,004	0,003	0,004	
Kütahya	0,000	0,001	0,005	0,004	0,004	0,004	0,005	0,005	0,005	
Malatya	0,000	0,002	0,003	0,002	0,002	0,005	0,004	0,005	0,005	
Manisa	0,000	0,001	0,002	0,002	0,003	0,003	0,003	0,003	0,003	
K.maraş	0,001	0,001	0,001	0,001	0,002	0,002	0,003	0,003	0,003	
Mardin	0,001	0,002	0,003	0,003	0,005	0,005	0,004	0,006	0,004	
Muğla	0,001	0,001	0,002	0,002	0,003	0,003	0,003	0,003	0,006	
Muş	0,000	0,003	0,005	0,006	0,005	0,007	0,007	0,009	**0,021**	

(continued on next page)

Tab. 5: (continued)

Provinces	2008	2009	2010	2011	2012	2013	2014	2015	2016	2017
Nevşehir	0,001	0,004	0,004	0,004	0,004	0,004	0,004	0,005	0,006	0,005
Niğde	0,001	0,001	0,005	0,004	0,004	0,005	0,004	0,004	0,004	0,005
Ordu	0,000	0,001	0,003	0,003	0,004	0,005	0,005	0,005	0,006	0,006
Rize	0,000	0,000	0,003	0,003	0,004	0,004	0,004	0,004	0,004	0,005
Sakarya	0,000	0,001	0,002	0,002	0,003	0,003	0,003	0,004	0,003	0,003
Samsun	0,000	0,001	0,004	0,005	0,005	0,005	0,005	0,006	0,005	0,005
Siirt	0,000	0,001	0,007	0,007	0,009	0,010	0,009	0,010	**0,014**	**0,011**
Sinop	0,001	0,001	0,005	0,006	0,006	0,006	0,008	0,006	0,006	0,006
Sivas	0,000	0,003	0,004	0,004	0,005	0,006	0,005	0,005	0,006	0,005
Tekirdağ	0,000	0,001	0,001	0,001	0,002	0,002	0,002	0,002	0,002	0,002
Tokat	0,000	0,002	0,002	0,002	0,002	0,002	0,004	0,004	0,005	0,006
Trabzon	0,000	0,002	0,001	0,002	0,002	0,002	0,003	0,003	0,003	0,004
Tunceli	0,001	0,001	0,005	0,004	0,009	0,009	0,010	0,009	0,007	0,006
Şanlıurfa	0,001	0,005	0,010	0,009	**0,012**	0,008	0,009	0,009	0,011	0,011
Uşak	0,001	0,001	0,002	0,004	0,004	0,003	0,003	0,003	0,003	0,004
Van	0,000	0,001	0,003	0,002	0,003	0,004	0,006	0,005	0,005	0,006
Yozgat	0,000	0,001	0,004	0,005	0,006	0,006	0,006	0,009	0,010	0,010
Zonguldak	0,000	0,001	0,001	0,001	0,002	0,003	0,003	0,003	0,004	0,005
Aksaray	0,001	0,001	0,001	0,002	0,003	0,003	0,004	0,004	0,005	0,004
Bayburt	0,001	0,001	0,011	0,010	0,008	0,010	0,008	0,006	0,008	0,006
Karaman	0,000	0,000	0,006	0,005	0,004	0,005	0,005	0,009	0,010	0,010
Kırıkkale	0,001	0,002	0,002	0,002	0,004	0,003	0,002	0,004	0,004	0,005
Batman	0,000	0,000	0,001	0,001	0,003	0,003	0,002	0,002	0,003	0,004
Şırnak	0,001	0,000	0,000	0,000	0,000	0,001	0,001	0,000	0,004	0,004

Bartın	0,000	0,002	0,002	0,002	0,002	0,001	0,001	0,002	0,002	0,002
Ardahan	0,001	0,000	0,008	0,009	0,010	0,011	0,014	0,009	0,011	0,008
Iğdır	0,000	0,002	0,004	0,002	0,002	0,003	0,004	0,003	0,002	0,003
Yalova	0,001	0,001	0,001	0,001	0,001	0,001	0,002	0,002	0,002	0,004
Karabük	0,000	0,001	0,004	0,004	0,004	0,005	0,004	0,005	0,004	0,005
Kilis	0,000	0,001	0,007	0,006	0,007	0,030	0,024	0,008	0,013	0,016
Osmaniye	0,001	0,001	0,002	0,002	0,004	0,003	0,004	0,006	0,005	0,004
Düzce	0,000	0,000	0,004	0,003	0,003	0,003	0,003	0,004	0,005	0,005

www.ingramcontent.com/pod-product-compliance
Lightning Source LLC
LaVergne TN
LVHW010322070526
838199LV00065B/5637